MW00612709

VOICES FROM
MEADOWBROOK
·P·A·R·K·

For Chinh—

Kit

VOICES FROM

MEADOWBROOK

· P · A · R · K ·

MEMORIES OF GREENVILLE, SOUTH CAROLINA'S
HISTORIC BASEBALL PARK
(1938 - 1972)

———————————————

MIKE CHIBBARO

P.O. Box 3714
Greenville, SC 29608

www.thirtysevenpublishing.com

For information about special discounts for bulk purchases,
please contact Thirty-Seven Publishing.

Cover design: J.J. Puryear
Copyediting: Amanda Capps
Page Layout: Michael Seymour

ISBN - 978-0-578-34814-8

Library of Congress Control Number: 2022903090

Dedication

This book is dedicated in memory of Coach William B. Phillips who shared his life, his love of baseball and his faith with so many of us. We can still hear your voice.

Author's Note

In telling the story of Meadowbrook Park, I have written about selected individuals who played a role in the park's history. I focused primarily on professional baseball at Meadowbrook. In doing so, I recognize that I have not done justice to the rich heritage of Greenville's textile baseball leagues. For a comprehensive discussion of textile baseball in Greenville, I recommend Thomas K. Perry's *Textile League Baseball* (McFarland & Company, Inc., 1993).

It is my hope that this book, despite its many omissions, will stir memories and stimulate discussion about Meadowbrook Park, its cast of characters and the game of baseball.

Contents

Preface

1   Beginnings 1

2   Papa Joe 13

3   90 Days 35

4   Yankee Clipper..57

5   Mike and Reggie..71

6   War Years 89

7   Jimmy..113

8   Coach 133

9   Ted and Mickey...153

10 Big Chief...179

11 Greasy Corner 193

12 Super Scout...223

13 Kooz and Ryan...237

14 Kat..261

15 Verner..279

16 The Alamo..297

Afterward 319

Author's Reflections 324

Appendix 1 —

    Professional Teams at Meadowbrook 327

Appendix 2 —

    From Meadowbrook to the Hall of Fame 328

Acknowledgements...330

Bibliography 334

Notes 338

Preface

It's hard not to be romantic about baseball.

—Billy Beane, *Moneyball*

No sport connects us more to our youth than baseball. As adults, we can recall with certainty the name of the big leaguer whose signature was etched across our first baseball glove, a prized possession that sometimes found its way underneath our pillow at bedtime. We remember fondly opening a pack of Topps trading cards and chomping on a brittle piece of bubblegum while praying that would be the pack that contained our favorite baseball hero.

Perhaps the most vivid of all childhood baseball memories is that first trip to a ballpark inhabited by professional players. Remembering the hurried walk through a grandstand portal and catching an initial glimpse of a well-manicured infield transports us to a simpler and more romantic time in our lives . . . a time when we lived and loved baseball.

For those who didn't live near a major league city, that initial trip was likely to a minor league park. These smaller ballparks dot the landscape of America in towns like Toledo, Salisbury, Chattanooga, Sioux City and Greenville. Stories of the players and the games they played in these parks are a part of the local folklore.

From 1938 to 1972, professional baseball was played in Greenville, South Carolina, in Meadowbrook Park. By today's standards, it wasn't much of a structure—a horseshoe-shaped wooden grandstand, a cinder block outfield wall, cramped locker rooms with showers that rarely worked, a rooftop press box and a single concession stand. It was located in what grew to be a seedy area of town, with a prison and a junkyard as its closest neighbors. Meadowbrook was susceptible to frequent flooding from the nearby Reedy River, and it generally stayed in a worn-out state of repair. It was damaged by two fires, the last one leading to its merciful end—but the grass was green, the hot dogs were tasty and the baseball was storied.

Despite its inadequacies, Meadowbrook Park has a very proud history. In addition to being the home field for over three decades of minor league baseball, it also was the site of high school, college, American Legion and Negro League games. It became a multipurpose venue, hosting a traveling circus, stock car racing, professional boxing and wrestling, religious events and annual dog and horse shows.

Greenville's textile baseball leagues had their own set of ballparks, but occasionally Meadowbrook hosted a textile league event. Also, several of Greenville's textile stars played on one of Greenville's professional teams over the course of the park's history. Although his playing days had ended by the time Meadowbrook was built, Greenville's most famous baseball player, Shoeless Joe Jackson, was given a lifetime complimentary pass to all of Meadowbrook's games. He and his wife, Kate, were frequent patrons.

Many of the minor leaguers who played in Greenville attained success in the big leagues, none more notable than Nolan Ryan. The Hall of Fame pitcher has referred to his 1966 season with the Greenville Mets as "one of my most pleasant and successful seasons in baseball."

Meadowbrook was also a popular stopover for major league teams barnstorming their way north at the end of spring training. Preseason exhibition games featured baseball immortals such as Lou Gehrig, Joe DiMaggio, Mickey Mantle and Ted Williams. More than 40

Hall of Famers walked across the grass at the historic Greenville ballpark. This is why when old-timers speak of Meadowbrook, a hint of reverence can be detected in their voices.

Meadowbrook was in the heart of one of Greenville's most densely populated Black communities, but Blacks were not openly welcomed in the park. For most of Meadowbrook's existence, Jim Crow ruled the day, forcing Black spectators to sit in a segregated bleacher section near the outfield. Neighborhood kids stood on a small hill beyond the left field wall straining to get a glimpse of the action. Negro League teams were allowed to play at Meadowbrook only on certain odd days and times.

Currently, the city of Greenville plans to spend $60 million to build a 40-acre park on land that includes the site of the former Meadowbrook Park. It will be called Unity Park and has been acknowledged as an attempt to right some of the past wrongs that occurred in this section of town.

Meadowbrook has its own story of diversity to tell. Within the pages of this book, you will read about how the following things came to be: the park was built by a first generation Sicilian immigrant; a Cuban immigrant on the 1939 Greenville Spinners became a local fan favorite; The Negro League's most famous pitcher Satchel Paige hurled three scoreless innings at Meadowbrook in 1962; the first Black man to manage a team to a World Series championship played for the 1964 Greenville Braves; and a star player for the 1967 Greenville Red Sox began his life in a Japanese internment camp during World War II. You can also read about the way students from Sterling High School, Greenville's oldest Black high school, remember Meadowbrook as their "home field" and how one of their star players ended up with a role in Universal Pictures' 1976 sports/comedy film *The Bingo Long Traveling All-Stars & Motor Kings*.

In the pages that follow, you will walk through the history of Meadowbrook Park, from its initial funding and construction all the way to the charred remains of its final professional season in 1972. Helping tell the story are the voices of many who played, worked or simply watched baseball at Meadowbrook. As thousands of visitors will begin to enjoy the many activities of the new Unity Park, all lovers of the game of baseball can only hope that the Voices From Meadowbrook Park will not grow faint.

1
Beginnings

*Good professional baseball is a big asset to Greenville . . . It helps to give
Greenville a good name as a splendid place to visit for amusement, for
entertainment, for shopping and for business reasons.*
—The Greenville News, April 1925

The earliest documented mention of the game of baseball in
America was shortly after the country's birth. John Rhea Smith, a
Princeton student, wrote in his diary on March 22, 1786: "A fine day,
play baste ball [sic] in the campus, but am beaten for I miss both
catching and striking the ball."[1]

Smith's diary entry, along with the belief that the roots of baseball
are traceable to various folk games played throughout early Continental Europe, discredits the common American thinking that the
game was invented by Abner Doubleday in 1839. Historians have
refused to agree on baseball's exact origins, but one thing is certain:
once baseball found its way to America, it spread through the fabric
of the country like no other sport. It became *The American Pastime.*

Legend has it that baseball was introduced in the state of South
Carolina by federal troops stationed there for the purpose of overseeing post-Civil War reconstruction efforts. The Union soldiers
engaged in competitive games of baseball with their Confederate
detainees, who were reportedly willing and capable students of the
game.

Along with baseball, the textile industry of the Northern states found its way to the post-Civil War South. The availability of land and flowing rivers for power, combined with a cheap labor pool, made the Southern states ripe for the emergence of cotton mills. Southern mill owners followed the example of their Northern counterparts and typically employed a "village" system for their factories. Mill villages were self-contained communities designed to meet nearly every household and personal need of the mill's employees. They included housing, churches, schools and company stores. Most also provided structured recreation and entertainment activities, including outdoor swimming pools, skating rinks, dance pavilions, gymnasiums and well-maintained baseball fields.[2]

Author Thomas Perry describes the environment of textile league baseball within the mill villages in his book *Textile League Baseball*:

> *Baseball quickly became an integral part of the village life, with the ball clubs getting started almost as soon as the big machines in the mills started humming . . . The game provided recreation, competition and community pride for players and spectators alike. Nowhere was the level of skill and intensity to win greater than in inland and upstate South Carolina . . . Winning programs provide tremendous boosts to employee morale, a major productivity tool deftly used by the new mill owners.*

Production in most textile plants ceased on Saturday afternoons in time to allow the workforce to attend the popular baseball contests. Some of the games drew crowds in excess of 5,000 people. During wintertime, highly competitive textile basketball leagues filled the void left by the summer baseball.

2

The quality of play within the textile baseball leagues attracted the attention of major league scouts and, according to Perry's exhaustive research, nearly 80 textile league players also played in the major leagues, none more famous than Joe Jackson. At the age of 6, Jackson began sweeping floors in the Pelzer Mill, and later, as a young boy, he performed menial tasks at Brandon Mill. By age 13, his prowess as a baseball player earned him a spot on the Brandon team, marking the beginning of a baseball legend. In *Growing Up With Shoeless Joe*, Joe Thompson writes:

> *[Jackson's] home run fame had spread throughout the Textile Leagues of upper South Carolina and he became known as "The pride of Brandon." Sports reporters covering games that Joe played in began to describe his line drives as "blue darters" because of the way they buzzed so low and far, mythically leaving a blue trail of smoke in the air."*

During his early playing days, Joe acquired arguably the most recognized nickname in the history of modern baseball. Prior to a game against the Anderson Electricians, Joe's manager gifted him a new pair of baseball cleats. Joe's feet became so blistered and painful by the second game, he removed his new shoes and played in his stocking feet. Jackson hit a long home run in the contest, and as he rounded third base, an opposing fan heckled him, calling him a "shoeless son-of-a-gun." A young sports writer overheard the fan's taunts, and with the swipe of his pen, Jackson forever became "Shoeless Joe." He said later that was the only day he ever played a baseball game in his stocking feet.

At least in theory, textile leaguers were considered amateurs as they were not paid to play baseball; instead, they were given salaried jobs by the mills they represented. No doubt, many of the best ball players were assigned the factory's least taxing jobs.

The growing national popularity of baseball, along with Greenville's reputation as a city that loved the game, fueled the arrival of professional baseball in 1907. Greenville's first professional team was an entry in the Class D Carolina Association, and they were known as the Moutaineers. In reference to the textile heritage of the Greenville community, the following year, the team adopted the mascot "Spinners."

Twenty-year-old "Shoeless Joe Jackson" signed a contract with the 1908 Spinners for a monthly salary of $75, roughly equivalent to $2,000 in today's money. With a league-leading batting average of .346, Jackson caught the attention of Philadelphia Athletics manager Connie Mack, who purchased Jackson's contract before the end of the Spinners' season.

Jackson joined the Athletics late in the summer of 1908 and began a legendary 13-year major league career, playing for the Athletics, Cleveland Naps (who became the Indians in 1915) and Chicago White Sox. Despite a .356 lifetime batting average and being called by many baseball experts "the greatest natural hitter to play the game," Joe's image as a baseball player was forever tarnished by the Black Sox scandal of 1919.[3]

Jackson, along with seven of his White Sox teammates, was accused of taking money from a gambling syndicate as part of a conspiracy to throw the 1919 World Series. Jackson fervently proclaimed his innocence, and a grand jury trial found all eight of the players not guilty; however, the day after the acquittal, Baseball Commissioner Kenesaw "Mountain" Landis ruled that the accused players were banned from the game of baseball for life.

Jackson had 12 hits in the 1919 World Series and claimed his performance proved his lack of complicity in the scheme. "If I had been out there booting balls and looking foolish at bat, there might have been some grounds for suspicion," he told *The Greenville News* in 1942. Jackson avowed his innocence in the scandal until the day he died, proclaiming to his brother moments before passing, "I'm going to meet the greatest umpire of all. He knows I'm not guilty."

Despite the passionate efforts of many, Jackson remains excluded from the Baseball Hall of Fame at Cooperstown. The Shoeless Joe Jackson Museum and Baseball Library is located adjacent to Fluor Field, Greenville's current minor league park. The museum is housed in Jackson's restored Greenville home and serves as a tribute to the life and legacy of Greenville's most famous baseball player.

Greenville's early professional teams played in a series of makeshift ballparks that typically consisted of a converted open field with some modest bleacher seating. From 1907 to 1912, the Spinners played on a diamond located on Memminger Street. After a seven-year absence from professional baseball, Greenville joined the South Atlantic League and moved to a slightly improved field on Augusta Street near Mills Avenue, where they played for only a couple years.

In 1921, a group of investors leased an open field on Perry Avenue that had been used primarily in the past for the circus and other traveling shows. The new owners funded construction of a larger stadium that became known as Spinners Park. Even with the expansion and improvements, the park was generally not considered up to "professional baseball" standards. Outfielders complained about the uneven terrain and potholes. The home team's single shower consisted of a garden hose that drained into a suspended metal washtub with holes in the bottom.

Despite the inadequacies of their ballparks, the early Spinners teams were competitive. The 1908 team finished 48-36 and second in the league. Locals believed that if Joe Jackson had not been sold to Philadelphia before the end of the season, they would have captured the league championship.

The Spinners were managed by Tom Stouch, a 38-year-old Ohio native who had spent his playing days as a 20-year minor league journeyman. He left his job as head baseball coach at the University of Georgia to become the field general for the Spinners. In their third season, Stouch's Spinners brought Greenville its first professional championship in 1911 when his squad finished 63-40 and atop the Carolina Association.

The Spinners drew modest crowds, always in competition with the ever-popular textile league games. Also, the salaries demanded by professional ballplayers strained the cash flows of the club's owners, which led to the Spinners eventually folding by the end of the 1912 season. This would be the beginning of a 100-year on-again, off-again affair for the city of Greenville and professional baseball.

After the conclusion of World War I, Billy Laval, a legendary local athlete and coach, led a group that returned professional baseball to the textile city. Laval and his partners established a ball club in the Class C South Atlantic ("Sally") League in 1919. The team retained the Spinners mascot, and with Laval as its player-manager quickly became a respectable Sally League franchise.

In 1925, Alan Graham, chief executive of the Camperdown Mill and President of the Spinners, organized a cooperative effort between the chamber of commerce and Furman University to construct a legitimate baseball park. Named in honor of Graham, the ballpark was located at the intersection of Augusta and Dunbar streets near the original campus of Furman University. It was built at an estimated cost of $10,000 and featured a large, covered wooden grandstand as well as a bleacher area that brought the park's seating capacity to approximately 3,000.

To pay for the park, tickets for the first game were sold at the unheard of price of $5 for a box seat and $2 for a bleacher seat. An editorial appearing in The Greenville News a few days before the 1925 season opener appealed to Greenville's citizens to support the Spinners and emphasized the benefits that professional baseball accrued to the community:

> *Good professional baseball is a big asset to Greenville. It brings to this city during the course of the season thousands of people from all parts of this section and from distant parts of the state. It helps to give Greenville a good name as a splendid place to visit for amusement, for entertainment, for shopping and for business reasons. That is something that will make innumerable friends for us throughout this section and help us to become a greater and more prosperous community.*

On the day of the first game at Graham Park, local businesses closed shop at 3:45 in deference to the 4 p.m. first pitch. Trolley cars ran a steady stream of fans from downtown Greenville to the new ballpark. City and state dignitaries filled the prime box seats, and a full brass band played patriotic music between innings. Nearly 2,000 fans, who had paid the hefty admission prices, braved cooler weather and a threat of thunderstorms to watch their hometown Spinners lose 8-3 to the Augusta Champions.

In 1926 and 1927, the Spinners won the Sally League championship. By this time, the Sally League had risen to a Class B league, roughly equivalent to the AA classification used today in the minor leagues. Eight players from the 1926 championship team eventually made it to the major leagues.

The 1927 Spinners finished with an impressive 92-56 record, 13 games ahead of its nearest competitor. They had a team batting average near .300 and were led by power-hitting first baseman Mule Shirley, who belted 32 home runs. Lefthander Bill Bayne was the Spinners' top pitcher, leading the Sally League in both wins (26) and earned run average (2.67).

The Spinners had their best attendance year to date in 1927, drawing 71,380 fans in 63 home contests at Graham Field. The city of Greenville took great pride in the success of its pennant-winning team. The 1927 season at Graham Field, however, nearly ended on a cold January day.

1927 Greenville Spinners: South Atlantic Association Champions
(Courtesy of The Greenville County Historical Society—William B. Coxe Collection)

Around noontime on January 4, 1927, a local man happened to be walking by Graham Field and noticed a billow of smoke coming from the grandstand section. Within minutes, the wooden structure was in flames, and fire trucks rushed to the scene. The first truck to arrive attempted to drive across the field and got stuck in the mud, unable to reach the flaming grandstand. Eventually, other trucks arrived and contained a large blaze—but not before most of the grandstand had been destroyed.

Later that day, authorities arrested two 16-year-old boys who confessed to setting the fire. They explained that their motivation for the arson was they "just wanted to hear the big fire trucks roar." The two boys had also been responsible for setting fire to a home in a nearby neighborhood.

City leaders quickly rallied around the damaged stadium and raised $8,000 in a 24-hour period to help fund reconstruction efforts. The grandstand was rebuilt in time for opening day in April. The 1927 fire was an ominous foreshadowing, as it was the first of three ballpark fires that had an impact on professional baseball in Greenville over the next four decades.

Graham Field became a multiuse facility for the city, hosting high school, college and textile baseball games, Negro league games, school graduations and other community affairs.

In 1925, the first high school rivalry football game between Greenville High and Parker High was played at Graham Field. Two thousand fans showed up on Armistice Day (November 11) to watch a football game in a stadium designed for baseball. The Parker-Greenville matchup eventually moved to Thanksgiving Day and was known as the "The Turkey Bowl." In 1936, Greenville added a true football stadium to its landscape, and the 15,000-seat Sirrine Stadium became the permanent home for the game between the two rival high schools.

Graham Field also became a stopover for major league teams traveling north from Florida at the end of spring training. On April 4, 1928, the New York Giants and the Washington Senators played an exhibition at Graham Field. The rosters of the two teams featured 11 future Hall of Famers, including the Giants' manager John McGraw, pitcher Carl Hubbell, outfielder Mel Ott and first baseman Bill Terry. More than 3,000 fans crammed into Graham Field to get a glimpse of the big league players. Other famous major leaguers who participated in exhibitions at Graham Field included Hall of Famers Ty Cobb and Jimmie Foxx.

Owners of the Spinners franchise continued to battle competition from the textile leagues and feel the impact of the Great Depression on Greenvillians' discretionary spending. As the 1931 season began, the Spinners were struggling to survive. The Depression had caused a shutdown of the Sally League in 1930, but Greenville secured a spot in the Class D Palmetto League for the 1931 season. With a weak roster and waning attendance, the Spinners ran out of cash and folded by midseason.

A local group organized a semi-pro team in 1932 and used the Spinners' name. They played their home games at Graham Field. Around the same time, Shoeless Joe Jackson's mother became ill, and the former major league star and his wife Kate, who were living in Savannah at the time, returned to their hometown to help care for her.

The organizers of the Spinners heard of the 45-year-old Jackson's return to Greenville and convinced him to play center field for the

Spinners. One of Joe's teammates told Jim Anderson of The Greenville News in 1964 that Joe "averaged at least one home run a game" with the '32 Spinners. Jackson remained in Greenville for the rest of his life; initially, he operated a barbecue restaurant on Augusta Street and later owned a liquor store on Pendleton Street, not far from the Brandon Mill where he first began playing organized baseball.

Alan Graham had transferred ownership of the park to his alma mater Furman University, which in turn leased it back to the Spinners. With no professional team, Graham Field fell into what The Greenville News described as "a state of disuse and dilapidation." It became more of a liability than an asset for its owners. By spring of 1936, Furman made the decision to demolish the 10-year-old facility.

For Greenville fans, the only connection to professional baseball for the next seven years was listening to radio broadcasts or combing the daily box scores of their favorite major league teams. The Greenville News sports columnist Scoop Latimer reminisced of the "glory days" at the old Spinners Park or Graham Field. Parents were relegated to telling their children stories about their favorite Spinners players from the past, with little or no hope that a professional team would ever return to their hometown.

Finally, in December of 1937, Greenville's baseball fans received an unexpected Christmas gift. The Greenville News' Latimer reported the role of Santa Claus was played by 47-year-old Joseph Cambria.

Santa Claus came to Greenville a week ahead of time and presented the fans a baseball franchise in the South Atlantic League. Santa Claus is personified by Joe Cambria, Baltimore baseball magnate and sportsman. Mr. Cambria advised local sports writers by telegraph Saturday afternoon he accepted the franchise offered by President Eugene M. Wilder of the Sally League.

After a nearly seven-year hiatus, it appeared Greenville would once again be home to professional baseball. One "minor" detail had to be worked out for Cambria's new franchise: His team needed a ballpark.

2
Papa Joe

He [Joe Cambria] did everything in the world for the Cubans. He literally was their Papa.

—Clark Griffith

It was opening day 1938. Professional baseball had returned to Greenville, South Carolina. The big league Washington Senators were in town for an exhibition game against the Sally League's Greenville Spinners in the city's newly constructed ballpark. With the first pitch only moments away, Spinners' owner Joe Cambria sat in a reserved box seat behind home plate. It was the first time all day that Cambria had sat still as he anxiously tried to ensure every detail for the opening game had been properly addressed.

Seated on one side of the 47-year-old Baltimore businessman was Greenville's mayor, Fred McCollough. On the other was Calvin Griffith, Cambria's close friend, business associate and owner of the Senators.

Cambria leaned back in his chair and surveyed the large crowd that filled the wooden grandstand in the ballpark he had financed. In less than four months, Cambria had won the confidence of Greenville's local leaders, convincing them he would single-handedly return professional baseball to their community. He gave them good reason to put their trust in him. He had previously bought and sold multiple minor league teams and had spearheaded the construction of four different ballparks.

Cambria was intriguing. One minute, he could be as jovial as a vaudeville comedian and the next as cunning as a New York mobster. He packed a mountain of ambition into his sturdy 5'7" frame and combined strong business acumen with an insatiable love for baseball. He had converted profits from a successful laundry business into a growing baseball empire.

Cambria and his associates made several visits to Greenville to hammer out an agreement with city officials. Southern hospitality and especially Southern cooking brought out the best of his winsome personality. Over large platters of fried chicken, mashed potatoes and homemade biscuits, Cambria regaled his newfound friends with tales of his past baseball successes and stories about the gold mine of baseball talent he had discovered in the sugarcane fields of Cuba. He was passionate and convincing, and Greenville willingly entrusted its baseball future to the loquacious Italian laundryman turned baseball tycoon.

Shortly before the home plate umpire yelled, "Play ball," Cambria reached into his coat pocket and pulled out an expensive Cuban cigar, one he had purchased on a recent trip to Havana. He drew a deep breath from the freshly lit stogie, cocked his head back and blew smoke through the mesh screen in front of him. As he surveyed the newest addition to his baseball enterprise, a broad smile flashed across Cambria's round Italian face. Only in America could a dream like this come true.

———

Joseph Carl Cambria was born in the port city of Messina on the island of Sicily on July 5, 1890. His father, Giovanni, worked as a shoemaker. His mother died from unknown causes shortly after Joe's birth.[1]

During the summer of 1893, Giovanni reached a breaking point with his impoverished Sicilian life. He had heard many stories of friends and relatives who had gone to America and were now sending surplus cash back home to their families in Italy. Inspired by the hope of a better life, Giovanni booked steerage on a steamship for himself and his three young sons.

Giovanni, Charles (10), John (9) and Joe (3) boarded their vessel of hope at the port of Naples and began their two-week transatlantic journey to *La Merica*, the land of opportunity. They arrived on Ellis Island on August 2, 1893, with not much more than the clothes on their backs.

The Cambrias were among the over four million Italians who immigrated to the United States between 1880 and 1920. Most left bleak conditions in a homeland that was plagued by natural disasters and disease. Many families in Sicily were peasant sharecroppers or worse yet, subject to working in sulfur mines. The stench of a smell similar to rotten eggs billowed from the mines and rolled across the Italian countryside as a constant reminder of the depressing plight of the mine's workers.

Sicily's sulfur mines had a reputation for abusive child labor. Parents sold their children to mine owners who put the underage workers in the direst working conditions imaginable. American educator and author Booker T. Washington traveled to Sicily in 1910 to see for himself the horror of the working conditions in Sicily's sulfur mines. In *The Man Farthest Down*, Washington wrote, "Sulfur mines in Sicily are the nearest thing to hell that I expect to see in this life."

Transatlantic transportation had become more affordable in the late 1800s, and for a mere $16, an Italian immigrant could book a one-way passage to America. Their ticket guaranteed them nothing more than a place on an overcrowded steam ship as every inch of the boat's floor space was jammed with human cargo. For Giovanni Cambria and his three sons, this likely meant exposure to cold, damp and unsanitary conditions. Food and water were scarce and typically limited to a few scraps of raw vegetables or some rice and oats.[2]

Miriam Medina on *thehistorybox.com* described the difficult conditions of a typical ship filled with immigrants on its way to America around the turn of the century:

> *Everywhere there was confusion and disorder. Mothers saw their children starving before their eyes. The filth and stench of unbathed bodies were overpowering. Diarrhea was prominent among the passengers. Their few personal belongings were often stolen. Starvation, dampness and filth became the breeding ground for Cholera and death. The bodies were weighed down and tossed into the sea like animals. If they wanted to survive, the immigrants had to stay focused on one thing: "The American Dream."*

Upon arrival, the immigrants were tired, malnourished and covered in filth. They were placed in large public baths and scrubbed from head to toe. This was followed by a physical and mental examination, which led many of the immigrants to be put back on boats and returned to Italy. The more fortunate immigrants were met by relatives who had already made their way to America. Others ended up in places like Canal Street in New York City, which was lined with overcrowded tenement houses offering living conditions not much better than the boat that had brought them to America. Immigrants accepted work wherever they could find it, usually the dirty, menial jobs others did not want to perform.

The path for Italian immigrants, particularity Sicilians, was typical of America's newest class of foreigners. They faced prejudice and mistreatment at every turn. A little over a year before Cambria's arrival in New York, the largest mass lynching in the United States occurred in New Orleans. The victims were Sicilian immigrants.

On the evening of October 15, 1890, 32-year-old New Orleans Police Chief David Hennessy was shot multiple times by an armed gunman while walking home from work. Hennessy was rushed to the hospital where he remained alive for 10 hours. Shortly before his passing, he reportedly confided in a fellow police captain and identified his assailants. His alleged last words were "the *dagoes* did it." *Dagoes* was a slang term used commonly for Italian immigrants. Hennessy had a track record of arresting suspicious Italians along the New Orleans waterfront.[3]

Beginning in 1894, Sicilians began to populate an area of the French Quarter known as "Little Palermo." Historian Manfred Berg described the way many locals viewed the Sicilian immigrants in New Orleans: "Sicilians were viewed as culturally backward and racially suspect. Because of their dark skin, they were often treated with the same contempt as Black people. They were also suspected of Mafia connections, and their family networks were closely watched by New Orleans police."

Following Hennessy's murder, a manhunt unfolded in the streets of New Orleans, and 250 Italians were rounded up, nearly all without probable cause. Eventually, 19 Italians were indicted on murder charges. In February of 1891, a trial was held for nine of the accused. The jury was unable to reach a consensus verdict, and all nine of the accused were released.[4]

New Orleans citizens were convinced the jury had been bribed, and a vigilante mob sought their own justice for Hennessy's murder. The angry justice seekers captured and killed 11 of the 19 who were originally indicted. Among the murdered was a mentally ill immigrant, Emmanuelle Polizzi, who was hanged from a light post and shot. Another, Antonio Bagnetto, a fruit peddler, was hanged from a tree before his body was filled with bullets. The rest of the victims were brutally beaten to death.

The following morning, newspaper accounts across the country defended the New Orleans justice seekers. A New York Times editorial justified the vigilante killings of the 11 Italians and summarized current sentiments regarding Sicilian immigrants:

> . . . these sneaking cowardly Sicilians, the descendants of bandits and assassins, who have transported to this country the lawless passions, the cut-throat practices, and the oath-bound societies of their native country, are to us a pest without mitigation. Our own rattlesnakes are as good as citizens as they . . . Lynch law was the only course open to the people of New Orleans.

The lynchings created significant tension between America and Italy. President Henry Harrison agreed to pay $25,000 in reparations to the victims' families, but Congress attempted to stop these payments. Ultimately, the United States paid $2,211.90 to each of the families affected by the lynchings. The chasm between the way Americans and Italians viewed the lynchings was best summarized by a comment made by future U.S. President Teddy Roosevelt in a letter to his sister Anna. At the time, Roosevelt was serving as an appointee to the U.S. Civil Service Commission. He wrote the following words on March 21, 1891:

> *Monday we dined at the Camerons; various dago diplomats were present, all much wrought up by the lynching of the Italians in New Orleans. Personally I think it rather a good thing, and said so.*[5]

The story of the events surrounding the lynching illustrates the disdain most had for Sicilians around the time in which the Cambria family arrived in America.

The Cambrias eventually settled in the Boston area. When Joe was 10, his family was living in Ward 6 of the city's battery district. Census records indicate that Joe's father found work as a shoemaker while his older brother Charles (18) was a barber. Joe and his other brother John were listed as students.

Perhaps it was during this time that Joe became captivated by baseball. Maybe his love of the game was ignited in the schoolyard or in the neighborhood—or perhaps it was sparked by tales of the hometown Boston Red Sox or Boston Braves. No matter how it started, baseball had thoroughly mixed with Cambria's Sicilian blood, and by the time he reached age 21, census data listed him as a "professional baseball player."

Cambria played semi-professional baseball in Boston, Roxbury, Lowell and other nearby towns. He was an undersized outfielder, known more for his fielding than hitting. He joined his first professional team in Newport, R.I., in 1909. Brian McKenna, writing for the Society for American Baseball Research, provided details of Cambria's time with the Newport team:

. . . He [Cambria] joined his first professional club, New-port of the independent Rhode Island Interstate League, in July 1909, replacing a center fielder named Martin who had broken his leg. Cambria a short right-hander, made his pro debut on the 11th. The Newport Daily News commented, "Cambria, a dark, pleasant-looking player from Medford way, was secured for the outfield." In a game on August 1, the Daily News reported, "There was a two or three-bagger of [Louis] Lepine's which Cambria caught with his bare hand in the eighth, shutting off a run and bringing the spectators to their feet." Cambria received praise by the paper throughout the season for his splendid fielding in center.

Cambria played at Newport for the entire 1910 season before joining the Berlin, Ontario Green Sox in the Class D Canadian League the next year. As a regular for the Green Sox, Cambria played center field and batted .245 on a team that eventually won the league championship. While playing the following year for the Green Sox, Cambria suffered a broken leg that ended his professional baseball career. At the time of his injury, the 21-year-old Cambria was batting .231.

Cambria came back to the Boston area and found work in a variety of odd jobs before serving in the military during World War I. After the war, he married a Boston girl, Charlotte Kane. Together the couple purchased the Bugle Coat and Apron Company, which provided linen jackets and towels to various Baltimore area businesses. By 1928, it had become the biggest commercial laundry service in Baltimore and was one of the city's largest employers. Charlotte worked alongside her husband in the business until 1935 when she was stricken with a disease that left her an invalid for the remainder of her life. She passed away in 1958 in Baltimore at the age of 74. The couple never had children.

Flush with cash from his successful laundry business, Cambria returned to his first love: baseball. His foray into organized baseball began in 1928 as he sponsored the Baltimore Bugles, an amateur league team named after his laundry business. He advanced their play into the semi-pro ranks, and the team lasted through the 1932 season.

In 1929, Cambria assumed the debts of the Hagerstown (Md.) Hubs of the Class D Blue Ridge League, giving him ownership of his first professional team. Cambria did not let his love of baseball cloud his entrepreneurial spirit, and he quickly began to sell off the team's more expensive players and rebuild a low-cost roster in order to turn a profit. He established a pattern of operation: buy a team on the cheap, trim the fat as quickly as possible, build up gate receipts and then sell his interest at a substantial gain.

Cambria ran into problems in Hagerstown as local blue laws did not allow Sunday baseball, which he believed was essential to raise attendance and achieve profitability. He launched a personal crusade to petition the Maryland State Legislature to strike down the blue laws. Unsuccessful in his attempt, Cambria relocated the Hagerstown team to Parkersburg, W.Va., and later Youngstown, Ohio. While in the Blue Ridge League, Cambria became known as "Jabbering Joe" because of his verbose manner and tendency to always voice his opinion on just about any topic of interest.

Seeking to capitalize on a growing Black population in Baltimore, Cambria purchased the Baltimore Black Sox, a Negro League baseball team. Cambria established a unique payment plan for his Black

Sox players, agreeing to guarantee them only travel expenses and a share of gate receipts. Ultimately, his financial model failed, and his ownership of the Black Sox lasted only a couple of years.

Cambria also acquired Bugle Field, a ballpark in downtown Baltimore, and invested heavily in the 6,000-seat stadium, installing lights, along with a press box and showers, and renovating the grandstand. Located at the corner of Federal and Edison streets, Bugle Field became headquarters for all of Cambria's baseball operations.

As a former player, Cambria knew the importance of having an excellent playing surface, and he hired Matthew Reinholdt as the full-time groundskeeper and stadium overseer. Reinholdt, who lived adjacent to the park, manicured Bugle Field to perfection, which enhanced the popularity of the stadium to players and fans. When the St. Louis Browns moved to Baltimore in 1954 and became the Baltimore Orioles, Reinholdt was hired as their head groundskeeper at the newly built Memorial Stadium. Reinholdt died suddenly at 58 at the end of that first Orioles season and was unable to enjoy the spoils of his dream job beyond that initial season.

In February of 1933, Cambria purchased the Albany (N.Y.) minor league franchise from the Chicago Cubs for $7,500. He followed his normal operating model, replacing expensive player contracts with more affordable ones and promoting his team to improve attendance. After four years, Cambria unloaded the Albany franchise for a profit estimated to have been between $40,000 and $60,000 ($750,000-$1,200,000 in today's dollars). Around this time, he became known as "Salesman Joe," as he continued to "wheel and deal" amidst his many baseball ventures. Cambria made additional baseball investments in franchises located in Harrisburg (Pa.), Salisbury (Md.) and St. Augustine (Fla.).[6]

Along the path of his baseball travels, Cambria's life intersected with the Griffith family, forming a relationship that would forever solidify his influence on the game. Calvin G. Griffith, whose Uncle Clark owned the major league's Washington Senators, was a part-time outfielder for the Cambria's Baltimore Bugles. Clark Griffith and Cambria likely crossed paths as they both scoured for talent in amateur ballparks across the Maryland and Eastern Pennsylvania.

The Washington Senators were founded in 1901 as one of the American League's original eight teams. Owner Clark Griffith developed a reputation as a penny-pincher who cobbled together a low-budget team that was the league's perennial cellar dweller. The Senators' ineptness on the field inspired San Francisco columnist, Charley Dryden to famously write, "Washington: First in war, first in peace, and last in the American League."

Clark and Cambria were kindred spirits in that they were both frugal baseball men who sought to find the best, but cheapest talent possible for their teams. In 1934, Griffith put Cambria on his payroll as a "scout," formally beginning a long-term business relationship between Cambria, the Griffiths and the Senators. The relationship continued when Griffith relocated the Senators in 1961 to Minnesota. Over the course of the next 30 years, Cambria funneled hundreds of prospects to the Senators and Twins organizations.[7]

Typically, professional scouts attempted to sign players and sell them for top dollar based on their expected potential. Cambria took an alternative approach that endeared him to Griffith. He offered the Senators' owner players at a deep discount with the understanding that if "they made good," Griffith would make up the difference. Cambria was fiercely loyal to Griffith, turning down significantly higher offers for many talented players and allowing Griffith to secure them on a contingency basis.

In return for his loyalty, Griffith helped Cambria run his minor league teams, handled contractual paperwork and acted as a buffer between Cambria and Baseball Commissioner Kenesaw "Mountain" Landis. Cambria's questionable approach to player contracts, along with his minor league dealings, placed him squarely on Commissioner Landis' "Most Wanted" list.

Joseph Carl Cambria funded the construction of Meadowbrook Park in 1938.
(Courtesy of the National Baseball Hall of Fame Library)

In the early '30s, Cambria expanded his talent-searching efforts to the island of Cuba. He had seen firsthand the skill level of the Cuban players when his Baltimore Bugle team hosted the Havana Red Sox in 1929 and 1930. Cambria began spending extended periods of time in Cuba as he set up a network of birddog scouts to scour the most rural areas of the country. Quickly, he began to fill the Senators' roster and its minor league affiliates with a steady stream of *Cubanolas*. Thanks to Cambria's affordable Cuban pipeline, Griffith's financially strapped Senators remained solvent through the post-Depression and war years of the '30s and '40s.

Cambria's gregarious personality and generous spirit endeared him to the Cuban people. He was a purveyor of hope, his methods described by one writer in the following way, "He would wrap his arm around the shoulder of a young ballplayer and sell him a dream. He did this thousands of times across the entire island of Cuba."

Cambria drove around Cuba in a Lincoln Continental chauffeured by retired U.S. highway patrolmen. He had an affection for linen suits, white shirts and Panama hats, but could also be seen wearing a Washington Senators cap with his street clothes. He shuttled back and forth to Baltimore to check on his invalid wife, and typically while in the United States made stops in cities where he owned minor league clubs. Eventually, he established a permanent headquarters in Havana where his entrepreneurial spirit led him to purchase a restaurant, a minor league team and an apartment building.[8]

In his nearly 30 years of working as a scout in Cuba, Cambria signed more than 400 Cuban players to contracts. While the majority never made it out of the minor leagues, he was not without his successes, which did nothing but fuel the dreams of Cuba's youth.

One of Cambria's more notable Cuban success stories was a future two-time American League batting champion. The remarkable story of Tony Pedro Oliva demonstrates the fortuitous path often followed by Cubans on their way to the major leagues.

Cambria used his network to discover the young Oliva, who came from the rural farming district of Piñan del Rio. Cambria's policy was that he would not sign a player to an American contract unless his parents were agreeable. Oliva's father was a baseball fanatic, and he gave his blessing for his oldest son's chance at American baseball.

In 1961, Oliva left behind his parents and nine siblings to chase the dream of becoming a major league player. Getting young Cuban players into the country was a bureaucratic and sometimes perilous process. An essential document for entry was a birth certificate, which Oliva did not have. His younger brother Antonio did have one, and the family agreed that Pedro should make use of his brother's birth certificate to enter the United States. With Antonio's birth certificate in hand, Pedro quickly became "Tony" as he crossed the border onto U.S. soil.[9]

Oliva was 22 years old and spoke little or no English when Cambria had him sent, along with 21 other Cubans, to Fernandina Beach (Fla.) for a three-day tryout with the Minnesota Twins. Oliva and the other "dark skinned" Cubans were not allowed to stay at the team hotel and were housed in a home of a local Black woman. At the end of the tryout, Oliva was released and told that he was not capable of hitting big league pitching. With rising tensions between the United States and Cuba, Oliva knew that if he returned to Cuba, he would likely never be able to become a big leaguer; his dream appeared to be dead.[10]

With Oliva on the verge of heading back home, Cambria connected him with his friend Fred Howser, general manager of the Charlotte Hornets in the Class A Sally League. Howser offered Oliva a place to stay and $3 a day for meals. Howser was honest with the young Cuban telling him that he did not have a roster spot open on the Hornets, but he was welcome to practice with the team and make full use of their facilities at Charlotte's Griffith Park.

Oliva's work ethic and hitting skills caught the attention of Howser who ultimately helped him advance through the Twins minor league organization. In his first full season of minor league ball, Oliva batted .410 for the 1961 Wytheville Twins of the Appalachian League. The Hillerich & Bradsby Company awarded its annual Silver Louisville Slugger Award to the player with the highest batting average in the professional ranks. Oliva was presented this award by Cambria, as the 71-year-old was recuperating in a Charlotte hospital. Cambria passed away a few months after presenting the award to Oliva, his last significant baseball discovery.

By 1964, Oliva was a full-time major leaguer, earning Rookie of the Year honors in the American League with a league-leading .323 batting average. Oliva led the American League in hitting again in 1965 and finished a 15-year professional career with a lifetime average of .304. He was named an American League All-Star for eight consecutive years (1964-71) and is one of the most popular players in the history of the Twins franchise. In 2021, Oliva was voted into the Baseball Hall of Fame.

Another success story from Cambria's Cuban pipeline was pitcher Camilo Pascual, who in an 18-year major league career with the Senators, Twins and Indians, won 174 games and had a lifetime ERA of 3.63. Pascual, a five-time All-Star had his best year in 1962 when he finished 20-11 and led the league in shutouts, strikeouts and complete games. The following season, Pascual went 21-9 and once again led the American League in strikeouts and shutouts.

Pascual was asked about Cambria by author Paul Scimonelli as part of the research for his upcoming book on Cambria's life. Pascual spoke fondly of his relationship with Cambria. "O my God . . . he was in my wedding; I was at his funeral . . . He was a beautiful man, beautiful guy," Pascual told Scimonelli. "He was the guy that give me the opportunity, he gave me two opportunities!"

Pascual went on to say, "In those days, those leagues were full of veteran players. I was real young and I was not strong enough. My fastball was weak. He [Cambria] give me the opportunity, but they release me. So I went back to Cuba in 1951 and he signed me again in 1952 and he give me the opportunity to pitch in a league which at that time was a very strong league, the Havana Cubans . . . I play two years for Havana . . . then the Senators invited me to spring training in 1954 and I was very lucky, I made the team."

Cambria also signed Cuban shortstop Zoilo Versalles, who was the American League MVP in 1965, a year in which he helped the Twins capture their first AL Pennant.

According to a questionable but legendary story, Cambria may be best known for the prospect that he didn't sign. As the story goes, Cambria first saw Fidel Castro as a young teenage left-handed side-arm pitcher in Havana. Reportedly, the scout was impressed with Castro's athletic ability but told the future prime minister of Cuba that his fastball wasn't fast enough. Castro enrolled in the University of Havana where baseball took a back seat to politics. Respected Cuban baseball historian Roberto González Echevarria convincingly claims, however, that Castro was never scouted by any professional team and had an undistinguished amateur baseball career.

Life was not easy for the Cuban players trying to make it into the big leagues. They were met with hostility and prejudice. Dark-skinned Cubans were especially subject to extreme racism and treated in the South in a manner similar to Blacks. Bob Considine, writing for *Collier's* magazine in August of 1940, described the plight of the Cuban ballplayer in the United States:

They get bean balls thrown at their heads by rivals. They face pitchers who willingly will throw away their arms bearing down on them in an effort to escape the "ignominy" of yielding a hit to them. They get a measure of abuse from the "jockeys" on the enemy bench. From their own team they get rock-bottom pay, and from many of their own teammates they get a wintry ostracism. Those who want to befriend them are halted by the differences in language.

Cambria's methods of signing Cubans were criticized by some as he began to rob the local Cuban amateur leagues of talent. He was accused of being an "ivory hunter," pillaging the Cuban countryside for his own profit. Critics claimed he signed players to blank contracts that he would then sell to the Senators (and later the Twins) without much concern about the prospect's ultimate likelihood of making it to the majors. One Cuban writer taunted Cambria's Italian heritage, calling him the "Christopher Columbus of Baseball."[11]

Despite his critics, he was beloved within the Cuban baseball community. His paternal nature earned him the nickname of "Papacito," or "Papa Joe." The Cubans even named a cigar after the likeable Italian. On January 7, 1945, Cambria was given a gold watch by Cuban players who had made it to the big leagues. The watch was presented to him between games of a doubleheader at La Tropical Stadium in Havana. More than 15,000 fans were on hand and cheered for "Papa Joe."

Descriptions of Cambria by those who knew him range from cagey and cunning to jovial and generous. He was loved by many and despised by some. Perhaps a story about one of his Cuban signees reveals the very best of Joe Cambria.

In 1951, Cambria signed Julio Bécquer to a contract and brought him to America for a tryout with the Senators. By 1955, Bécquer had made it to the big leagues as a part-time first baseman and pinch hitter. In 1961, Bécquer was selected by the Los Angeles Angels in the expansion draft.

As the 1961 baseball season got under way, the failed Bay of Pigs invasion heightened tensions between Fidel Castro's Cuba and the United States. Bécquer's wife was stranded in Cuba at the time. Even though Bécquer was no longer playing for a team owned by Calvin Griffith, he reached out to his former boss in hopes of finding help to get his wife out of Cuba.

According to Thom Henninger's *Tony Oliva: The Life and Times of a Minnesota Twins Legend*, Griffith and Cambria took responsibility for the Cuban ballplayer's situation:

> *Griffith contacted Cambria, who completed all of Edith's paperwork and helped clear hurdles in Cuba. "I have a soft spot in my heart for that man," Bécquer says of his longtime scout. "He helped me a lot. While I was over here, Cambria spent one month (helping out), every day taking my wife to the American Embassy and then putting her on the plane for the United States." The Twins Owner (Griffith), who had been based in Washington for decades, worked his diplomatic contacts to facilitate the process. It took several weeks of wrangling before the newlyweds were reunited in the United States.*

"You don't get called 'Papa Joe' unless you are a good citizen,"

Calvin Griffith said of Cambria in an interview in 1991. "He did everything in the world for the Cubans. He literally was their Papa. He gave them things they never had before. Whatever he had in his pocket."

In 1937, Cambria owned three minor league teams: the Trenton Senators, Salisbury (Md.) Indians and the St. Augustine (Fla.) Saints. He was looking to expand. It's unclear exactly how Cambria heard about the opportunity to return professional baseball to Greenville, but encouragement most likely came via Zinn Beck, a well-known baseball influencer. Beck was a player manager in Greenville with the 1924 and '25 Spinners and worked as a professional baseball scout in the Southern states. As Beck and Cambria crossed paths on the scouting trail, Beck reportedly pitched Greenville as the ideal spot for a Class B minor league club, which piqued the interest of the always-opportunistic Cambria.

In September of 1937, Cambria dispatched his associate John "Poke" Whalen to Greenville for an exploratory visit. Whalen, another well-connected and seasoned baseball man, had previously been a manager for one of Cambria's minor league teams. The fellow Baltimore native knew the inner workings of a minor league club and became Cambria's trusted advance man for scouting locations for expansion.

Whalen delivered Cambria a glowing report on Greenville, telling his boss about a city that was hungry for the return of professional baseball. Within days, the Cambria enterprise was fast at work chasing all the details needed to create a new minor league franchise. Cambria received an initial verbal commitment from Dr. Eugene

Wilder, president of the Class B Sally League, for a team in Greenville.

During the week of December 13, Cambria dispatched Whalen and Fred "Red" Hering to Greenville with specific instructions to bring back to Baltimore the terms for a final deal. Hering was currently serving as the general manager of Cambria's St. Augustine team.

Whalen and Hering spent the week in Greenville meeting with Mayor Fred McCullough, Alderman Kenneth Cass and Parks Commissioner John McPherson. *The Greenville News* Sports Editor Scoop Latimer trailed alongside the contingent and leaked details of their discussions to the community through his daily column. Cambria sent word through his associates that if Greenville would provide the land, he would fund the construction of a suitable ballpark.

The Greenville delegation showed Cambria's associates a number of possible ballpark sites. The group finally reached consensus on an open low-lying meadowland along the banks of the Reedy River near the intersection of Mayberry and Hudson streets. The land had been cleared several years earlier and established as a public park and playground for the city's Black residents.

The location of the future park appeared, on the surface, to be ideal as it was less than a mile from downtown and a short distance from several of Greenville's largest mill villages. City officials assured Cambria's men that the land would be leased at no cost to Cambria for an initial term of five years, assuming he upheld his promise to construct the ballpark.

Whalen and Hering returned to Baltimore at the end of their week in Greenville with a strong recommendation to move forward with their plans for expansion to Greenville. Around 1 p.m. on Saturday,

December 18, 1937, Cambria sent a telegram to Greenville officials announcing his formal intention to field a professional baseball team in their city in the spring of 1938.

Separately, Cambria wrote the following letter to Scoop Latimer further detailing his plans:

Dear Mr. Latimer:

Mr. Whalen and Mr. Hering have just returned from your city and this is just to thank you for the courtesies extended them during their visit.

In addition to Trenton, we also operate Salisbury, Md., in the Eastern Shore League (Class D) and St. Augustine, Fla., in Florida State League (Class D). Trenton is Class A, and Greenville will be Class B. We work along with Mr. Clark Griffith, president of the Washington club, which owns the Charlotte, N.C. franchise in the Piedmont league. So you see we have quite a hook-up and we will do our best to give Greenville a fine ball club.

Right after the first of the year, we want to get started building the ballpark. Will send down a couple of local men to help supervise the job; these men have had considerable experience building ballparks, and know the set-up. Mr. John Milton will act as business manager for the time being.

With your support, we hope to have a fine club in the South Atlantic league, and want to thank you for your continued cooperation.

Yours very truly,

Joe Cambria, President

Trenton (N.J.) Baseball Club

With just a little over three months to build a ballpark and assemble a baseball team, the city of Greenville pinned its professional baseball future on a Baltimore businessman that they had yet to meet in person. President Whalen of the Sally League vouched for the credibility of Cambria and helped Greenvillians rest easy over the Christmas break.

"I know Mr. Cambria is good for any obligation he makes," Wilder said. "He's been highly successful in operating professional baseball clubs and has been prominently identified with the game. Besides, he's a man of big business connections and also a sportsman of varied interests."

3
90 Days

I'm wrapped up in this Greenville spot and am as happy over the new park as a kid with a big red apple.

—Joseph Cambria, March 1938

On the afternoon of Thursday January 6, 1938, Joe Cambria's front men traveled by automobile to Greenville. The Baltimore-based group of baseball executives included Poke Whalen, Fred Hering, groundskeeper Matt Reinholdt, business manager John Milton and construction engineer Henry Brock. They checked into the Poinsett Hotel and retired early in preparation for a busy next day in which they hoped to finalize plans for a new baseball park. A steady rain fell in downtown Greenville throughout the night.

Cambria's men enjoyed a hearty Southern breakfast at the hotel coffee shop and then drove the short distance to the planned ballpark site on Mayberry Street. There they were met by Kenneth Cass, city alderman for Ward Two, and John McPherson, chairman of the Park and Tree Commission. After exchanging pleasantries, they stood along the shoulder of Mayberry Street looking northeast toward the Reedy River and across a low-lying, rain-soaked meadow. The Reedy was cresting near the top of its banks.

Portions of the meadow resembled a shallow lake. The muddy soil made it impossible for the men to traverse the property. Whalen, Hering, Reinholdt, Milton and Brock whispered their concerns to one another. Speaking for the group, Whalen politely asked Cass and

McPherson if there were any other possible locations that should be considered for the new baseball field.

They spent the remainder of the day reviewing a handful of alternative sites. Each one had drawbacks, and the group returned to Mayberry Street, concluding that it was the best location the city could offer. Cass and McPherson assured their guests that the city would absorb the cost of additional piping for drainage and if needed would deepen the Reedy's riverbed.

The men shook hands and made it official. The new home for the Greenville Spinners was to be built on Mayberry Street, just beyond the intersection of Hudson Street adjacent to the city stockade. Opening day was 90 days away.

———————

The land for the proposed ballpark had a checkered past. How much of its unfavorable history was shared with Joe Cambria and his agents cannot be known, but with Greenville's strong desire to see the return of professional baseball, one can only suspect that officials may have sugarcoated some of the less favorable details about the history of the site.

The entire piece of property would be considered a flood zone by today's standards. The nearest neighborhood was a Black community whose residents were accustomed to evacuating to higher ground whenever heavy rains arrived.

Local historian Judith Bainbridge, writing for *The Greenville News* in 2021, described in detail the history of the surrounding area that encompassed the land identified for the new ballpark:

"The Medder," Greenvillians used to call the swampy land around the Reedy River west of Main Street . . . The Reedy River ran through it, surrounded by a jungle of canebrakes, cattails, and water plants. When it rained, its waters over-flowed, spreading out in every direction, forming lagoons and shallow pools where blue cranes, redwing blackbirds and occasionally wild ducks fed and lived.

Around the turn of the century, the Greenville Municipal League hired renowned botanist and landscape architect Harlan Kelsey to recommend improvements for the beautification of the city. Kelsey issued his findings in a 50-page booklet titled "Beautifying & Improving Greenville, South Carolina." He recommended that Greenville establish a series of parks along the banks of the Reedy River.

The first of these parks, Cleveland Park, was built 20 years after Kelsey issued his report. A second, Falls Park, was constructed nearly 100 years later. Kelsey also suggested that an area south of downtown along the Reedy be utilized for a collection of athletic fields, tennis courts, a swimming pool, a clubhouse and children's playgrounds. This area, which Kelsey named "Hudson Athletic Fields," covered approximately 355 acres and included the land where the Spinners' new baseball park was eventually constructed, as well as the 60 acres that today has been earmarked for Greenville's new Unity Park.[1]

Establishment of the "Hudson Athletic Fields" took a backseat to other projects, and the area became a dumping ground for unwanted activities. In the early 1920s, land was purchased near the intersection of Hudson and Mayberry streets to construct a city stockade to house a growing prison population. Around the same time, a large trash incinerator was built nearby.

In 1924, construction began on the 110-acre Cleveland Park, but in a fully segregated city where "Jim Crow" laws ruled, Blacks were not welcomed there. At the time, nearly one-third of the city's 30,000 residents were Black, with a significant portion of them living in rental homes that had been built by local developers near Mayberry Street around the turn of the century. In 1924, Greenville City Council allocated $15,000 to purchase 15 acres on Mayberry Street to establish a park for its Black citizens. Mayberry Park opened in 1925, and it became the lone outdoor gathering place available for Blacks and their families.

For its first 10 years, Mayberry Park consisted primarily of a multiuse athletic field with modest bleacher seating, tennis courts and some open grassy areas. Sterling High School, Greenville's first Black secondary school, used the athletic field at Mayberry Park as home for its athletic teams. Leaders in the Black community petitioned the city council to make needed improvements to the park. In 1934, nearly 10 years after the park opened, the first children's playground equipment was added.

By the late 1930s, the city began to strip away portions of the property it had originally purchased for the Black community. Approximately seven acres were allocated for the construction of the new baseball park in 1938. Around the same time, another parcel along the park's northern end was designated for a police shooting range.

With a growing Black population and reductions in the size of Mayberry Park, additional recreational space for Blacks was needed. The Reverend E.B. Holloway appeared before city council and pleaded for expanded facilities for Black children. Holloway, Greenville's first Black mail carrier and a minister at John Wesley United Methodist Church, asserted that much of Mayberry Park had been taken from Blacks with the construction of the new professional baseball field.

Mayor Fred McCullough dismissed Holloway's assertions and said that the baseball park had been built with the consent of the Park and Tree Commission on land owned by the City. He said that it was built "after arrangements had been made to allow Negroes to hold baseball games on the field." The reality of those "arrangements" was that the new ballpark would be available for Blacks only if and when it was not being used by the Greenville Spinners or by White citizens and their related organizations for other scheduled activities.

In 1938, the local newspaper was as influential as modern-day social media. Workers began their day by reading the headlines in the daily paper. It was passed around and discussed in barbershops, drugstores and restaurants. The paper was used like a textbook for current events in schools. In a small Southern town like Greenville, reading the Sunday edition from front to back was as sacred a tradition as attending Sunday school.

Nobody was more influential in the Greenville sports community than J. Carter "Scoop" Latimer, sports editor for *The Greenville News*. With a few keystrokes from his typewriter, Latimer could make things happen. Known as the "Dean of Southern Sports Reporters," he used his daily sports column "Scoopin' Em Up" to keep readers abreast of the important sports news and share his informed opinions.

Latimer was well connected and counted celebrities such as Babe Ruth, Ty Cobb, Jack Dempsey and Will Rogers as friends. He was a member of the Downtown Athletic Club, which selected college football's annual Heisman Trophy winner. Latimer was a close friend of Shoeless Joe Jackson and spent his professional lifetime leading a personal crusade to get Jackson reinstated in Major League Baseball.

Born in 1894 in Donalds, South Carolina, Latimer moved to Greenville at the age of 4, and at age 18, he began his 40-year journalism career as a proofreader for *The Greenville News*. Working as a young reporter for the *Greenville Piedmont* (afternoon paper), he earned his nickname, reference to a popular cartoon of the day called Scoop the Cub Reporter. He left Greenville in 1929 to work as the sports editor for a chain of local papers but returned in 1933 as sports editor of *The Greenville News*, a position he held until his sudden death in 1953.

Baseball was Scoop's first love, and his knowledge of the game made him a sought-after resource by professional scouts looking for an initial take on a local prospect. He helped with the rebirth of the South Atlantic League in 1919 and boasted that he had attended 28 consecutive World Series from 1924 through 1952.

Latimer's colleagues in the newsroom called him "the Colonel." He named his office in the News-Piedmont building the "green and gold room." It was known around the South as a nerve center for the latest sports news. He typed his stories on an ancient manual typewriter that had been with him since his early reporting days.

From the day Joe Cambria showed an interest in Greenville, Latimer was glued to his every move. Cambria recognized that Latimer was vital to his efforts to promote his new baseball franchise and sent Latimer personal letters updating him on the latest news about the Spinners. Whenever Cambria came to Greenville, he always made a respectful visit to Scoop's green and gold room.

Latimer used his platform to establish names and/or nicknames for teams, players and venues. He gave Erskine College its mascot, "the Flying Fleet," and he claimed he was the first to call Furman "the Paladins." When Camperdown Mill President Alan Graham sponsored the construction of a new baseball park in 1925, Latimer officially tagged it Graham Field.

As construction progressed on the Spinners' new park, Latimer took it upon himself to recommend a name. He wrote on January 4, 1938:

> *A name that occurred to us last night was MEADOW-BROOK. Meadowbrook is both significant and high-sounding. Meadowbrook, y'know is the famous spot near New York City where the celebrities in polo, tennis and other sports perform.*
>
> *And the site of the proposed new Greenville baseball park is in what was once called the "meadow" along the banks of the meandering Reedy River. . . In combining form, MEAD-OWBROOK, we have both the lea and the river represented. Joe Cambria, Greenville club owner may have another name for his muscle ranch here. Or he might be induced to offer a prize—a season or half season ticket or something like that—for the most appropriate appellation.*
>
> *But until a change is officially made, if any, don't be alarmed if our park is called MEADOWBROOK.*

Latimer's suggestion stuck, and a week later City Council ratified "Meadowbrook" as the official name for the new ballpark. However, by early April, a movement began to show appreciation to Cambria for his financial investment in Greenville. A petition was put forth to city council to rename the new park "Cambria Park," but no record exists indicating the council approved the change. For most of the early years of the park's existence, Greenvillians referred to it as either Meadowbrook or Cambria Park.

Latimer also used his influence to help a local civic leader gain a spot on Cambria's management team. Writing in his column on January 7, 1938, he pitched the idea that Alderman Kenneth Cass be added to Cambria's team of Baltimore-based executives responsible for running the Spinners' affairs.

Cass was a former outstanding athlete at Greenville High and Furman University, and Latimer touted him as a "prominent, capable and energetic young man" and as someone who was instrumental in bringing professional baseball back to Greenville. Cass operated a full-service automotive shop on West Court Street while also serving as alderman for Ward 2 on city council. He had chaired the committee responsible for the return of baseball to Greenville in 1938. Cass, a lifelong public servant, was elected mayor of Greenville in 1947, a position he held for the next 14 years. Ten days after Latimer puffed Cass for the job, Cambria named Cass as business manager for the 1938 Greenville Spinners.

Cambria's skilled groundskeeper Matt Reinholdt supervised the grading of the property on Mayberry Street and staked the field's boundaries. Greenvillians told Reinholdt they desired to have a spacious ballpark with dimensions like that of a major league facility. Previous baseball parks in Greenville had been squeezed tightly into available land spaces, with short outfield measurements. These earlier fields were a source of embarrassment for Greenville's baseball purists.

Reinholdt quickly realized that an inadequate amount of land had been allocated for a park of that size, and so, without hesitation, city leaders clipped another 200 feet off of Mayberry Park to accommodate the expanded layout. Reinholdt mapped out "big league" dimensions that were 310 down each foul line and jutted out sharply to a deep straightaway center field of 435 feet. The power alleys in left and right field were approximately 390 feet from home plate. With these roomy dimensions, Meadowbrook would forever be known as a "pitcher's park." Home plate was set facing north toward the Reedy River, and the right field fence ran parallel to the river.

Cambria's men brought with them a rough architectural sketch of a ballpark that had been patterned after Gordy Park in Salisbury, Md., home of another of Cambria's minor league teams. Local architect L.D. Allison was hired to take Cambria's initial drawings for Meadowbrook and prepare a final rendering. Allison expanded the size and seating capacity which reached deeper into Cambria's wallet. Initial estimates of construction costs were $15,000. Revised estimates were closer to $25,000.

Seating capacity was planned for 5,560, with the horseshoe-shaped covered grandstand seating 3,100 and the bleachers another 2,460. A primarily wooden structure with steel beams would sit on a concrete foundation. The first row of seating was set approximately seven feet above the playing surface to facilitate viewing of the field. The outfield wall was made of wooden planks with several sections serving as billboard advertising for local businesses. A large hand-operated scoreboard detailing the score by inning was placed above the outfield fence in right center field. A press box sat atop the roof of the main grandstand. Nine 60-foot light poles hosting 136 lamps were planned to illuminate the field for night contests. A central concession stand, home and visiting locker rooms and a dressing room for the umpires were located underneath the main grandstand.

A request made of the city of Greenville for any permits, blueprints or other archived documents related to the construction of Meadowbrook yielded nothing, implying that perhaps Greenville municipal officials may have likely allowed Cambria to fast-track construction of the park.

In keeping with segregated protocols of the Southern community, Cambria agreed to include a designated seating area and restroom facilities for Black spectators. This seating area was located down the third base line, outside of the large covered grandstand. Other areas of the ballpark, including the main concession stand, were off-limits to Black patrons. In the 1896 *Plessy v. Ferguson* ruling, the U.S. Supreme Court stated that racially separate facilities, if equal, did not violate the Constitution. The facilities for Blacks at Greenville's new ballpark were separate but certainly not equal to those afforded White spectators.

By January 13, a temporary engineering workshop had been constructed on the property, and the sound of buzzing saws and cracking hammers could be heard at the site from sunrise to sundown. An optimistic completion date of March 15 was promised. Greenville citizens drove or walked along Mayberry Street daily, watching as their new professional ballpark rose out of the dirt.

During construction, Cambria's management team lodged at the Poinsett Hotel. They received the finest Southern hospitality that Greenville could offer. Matt Reinholdt had traveled much of the eastern United States building and improving ball fields at the behest of his boss. Writing to Scoop Latimer a couple of years after his time in Greenville, Reinholdt recalled with fondness the treatment he received while building Meadowbrook Park:

> *Boy, you can believe me or not. I have been to many places but Greenville is really the only place I felt like I was at home. I really want you to believe me because I am not the type who would make you think he was at home and at the same time his head was thumping for some place else. I enjoyed every hour spent with you folk down in Greenville and surely hope something will spring up for me to return to your city.*

Joe Cambria hinted at trying to visit Greenville in early January, but business conflicts and tending to his ailing wife pushed his first trip to Greenville to Friday, January 13. He arrived by train from Baltimore at 5:30 a.m. and held an early meeting with Mayor McCullough and other city officials. The remainder of his day was spent structuring a plan for ticket sales and inspecting the work at the ballpark.

Saturday evening, the Retail Merchants Bureau sponsored an informal dinner for Cambria and his associates in the main ballroom of the Poinsett Hotel. E.M. Wilder, president of the South Atlantic League, was on hand to welcome Cambria, along with officials from the Spartanburg minor league team. Spartanburg had been without professional baseball for the past 10 years, and like Greenville was readmitted to the Sally League in 1938.

Cambria delivered a short speech filled with promises for his team and appreciation for the support of the Greenville community. He stated that the park would be made available to local high school, college and American Legion teams. He also committed to conducting junior baseball schools designed to introduce and teach the game to children in the area.

The Spinners' chief promised to name the manager of the team as soon as possible. Speculators, primarily Scoop Latimer, predicted that the field leader for the Spinners would be Jake Flowers, who had guided Cambria's Salisbury Indians to an Eastern League championship in 1937.

The Spinners' owner closed his remarks by saying, "I want the people of Greenville to feel that this is their team. In this day of such keen competition, it's mighty hard to produce winners, but we are going to try awfully hard to do our best."

Cambria departed Greenville on Sunday on the 2:35 p.m. Crescent Limited train to Baltimore. Back home, he went to work trying to hire a manager and assemble a potential roster of players to fulfill the promises he had made.

The South Atlantic League released a 140-game schedule for the 1938 season. The Spinners were to open a 70-game home schedule against rival Spartanburg on April 21. Joining Greenville and Spartanburg in the league were teams from Columbia, Columbus, Macon, Jacksonville, Augusta and Savannah. To handle transportation for the Spinners, Cambria purchased a new 19-passenger bus.

Ticket prices for the inaugural season at Meadowbrook were set as follows:

45¢ — general admission

65¢ — unreserved grandstand

75¢ — reserved grandstand

Ordained ministers would be given complimentary tickets, and a knothole gang for boys and girls under age 12 was established to admit them free to the game, conditional on their compliance with certain regulations such as regular attendance in Sunday school. All the Spinners games were to be broadcast on WFBC radio made, thanks to sponsorship from the Kellogg cereal company. Local sports reporter Jimmy Thompson was set to handle the play-by-play.

At the end of January and to no one's surprise, Cambria announced an affiliation agreement between the Spinners and the Washington Senators. Cambria and Senators owner Clark Griffith also agreed that an exhibition game between the two teams would be the most fitting way to open the new ballpark in Greenville. Cambria extended an invitation to Griffith to attend the opening game, which was scheduled for Saturday, April 9, at Meadowbrook.

By mid-February, most of the outer structure of the grandstand had been erected. Matt Reinholdt began planting a combination of Italian rye and Bermuda grass across the expansive field. He prayed for rain to assist his efforts.

Cambria made it back to Greenville on February 25, arriving again on the 5:30 a.m. train from Baltimore. Scoop Latimer described his one-day visit as a "five ring circus of action," as the Spinners' owner attended to the many details of his new team and ballpark. While in town, Cambria dispelled the rumors that Jake Flowers would be the manager of the Spinners. He said Flowers had some business interests in Florida that would not allow him to relocate to Greenville.

While the claim is difficult to substantiate, Joe Thompson, in *Growing Up With Shoeless Joe*, stated that Cambria approached Joe Jackson about the possibility of becoming manager of the Spinners, but Baseball Commissioner Landis quickly put an end to any hopes Joe had of returning to professional baseball.[2]

On March 12, Cambria named Edward A. "Jiggs" Donahue as the skipper of the 1938 Spinners. Donahue was familiar to Greenvillians, having coached football, basketball, baseball and track at Clemson College from 1917 to 1921. He was a graduate of Washington and Lee where he played football and baseball and had played one season of minor league baseball.

Shortly after Donahue was named to the Spinners post, a college football teammate of Donahue's sent a letter to *The Greenville News* applauding the hire and praising the grit of his friend. The writer told how Donahue had broken his ankle in a scrimmage prior to Washington and Lee's rivalry game against Virginia Tech. Donahue stood on the sideline on crutches and watched his teammates fall behind in the first half. Sensing the need for improvement and inspiration, Donahue suited up to play. Early in the second half, he hopped onto the field, holding his casted broken ankle, and he somehow managed to play the remainder of the game. According to his old friend, Donahue's courage that day inspired Washington and Lee to a one-point win over Virginia Tech.

Donahue had eight years of experience as a minor league manager and won pennants with the 1923 and 1926 Dover Senators of the Class D Eastern Shore League. The Boston native arrived in Greenville with his wife and three sons on March 15 and took up temporary residence at The Hotel Greenville.

After getting his family settled, Donahue was instructed to report to St. Augustine, Fla., where Cambria's four minor league teams were gathering for spring training. Cambria signed approximately 100 ballplayers to be divvied up between the Trenton Senators, Salisbury Indians, Greenville Spinners and St. Augustine Saints.

Cambria made another trip through Greenville on his way back to

Baltimore from St. Augustine on March 18. Once again, he arrived early and spent a whirlwind day checking on the ballpark and ironing out details for his new franchise. Bad weather had slowed progress on the ballpark, but Cambria was confident it would be ready by opening day. Cambria hand delivered a signed five-year lease agreement to the city officials for the ballpark's land. Before catching a late afternoon train, the always-positive baseball executive affirmed his commitment to Greenville.

"I'm wrapped up in this Greenville spot and am as happy over the new park as a kid with a big red apple," Cambria said. "If it is humanly and financially possible, we don't intend to let Greenville down, or let our hearts sink in discouragement. From what I've seen of Greenville and the fans, I feel sure your city is a natural for professional baseball."

Cambria decided to bring a collection of 32 players to town and allocate them between his Greenville and Trenton squads. Rain fell during much of the week of the players' arrival, and to protect the recently planted grass at Meadowbrook, workouts were held at the nearby Judson Mill ballpark.

The Washington Senators broke camp in Orlando during the same week and made their way to Greenville by train, stopping first for a scheduled game with the Atlanta Crackers. Rain washed out the Atlanta contest, and the Senators caught an early morning train to Greenville landing at the Southern Railway station on West Washington Street at 7:30 a.m. on April 9. The team enjoyed a hearty breakfast at the Poinsett Hotel and lounged in the hotel lobby while waiting to see if the exhibition game would be played.

This photo was taken shortly before the opening of Meadowbrook Park in April of 1938. The outfield scoreboard and lights had not yet been installed. *(Courtesy of the Greenville County Historical Society—William B. Coxe Collection)*

All week, it rained off and on, and the playing surface at the park was saturated. Starting early in the morning on game day, Cambria and his staff made hourly trips to Meadowbrook to check on the field condition. A cold front followed the rains, and unseasonably cool temperatures were expected for the opening tilt.

Cambria told reporters that cold would not halt the opener; only another round of rain could do that. First pitch was set for 2:45 p.m. to allow the Senators to catch a late afternoon train to Charlotte where they were scheduled to play another exhibition game the following day. Around noon, Cambria made the decision that the game would be played. He was not about to let wet grass spoil his grand opening.

The Senators brought a respectable team to Greenville that included four future Hall of Famers: outfielders Leon Allen "Goose" Goslin and Al Simmons, catcher Rick Ferrell and manager Bucky Harris.

Goslin was no stranger to the area having played two years of minor league ball for the Columbia Reds in the Sally League in 1919 and 1920. He earned his nickname from the way he flapped his arms as he tracked down fly balls.

Simmons was in his 15th season in the majors and had been on two World Series championship teams for Connie Mack's Philadelphia Athletics. One of baseball's most prolific hitters, Simmons batted over .380 in four different seasons and ended his career with a .334 lifetime average, ranking him 23rd on the all-time list.

Ferrell was a strong-armed, durable catcher from Greensboro, N.C., who split an 18-year big league career with the St. Louis Browns, Boston Red Sox and the Senators. A lifetime .281 hitter, Ferrell had three brothers who also played professional baseball. Younger brother Wes, a pitcher, was a teammate of Rick's on the 1938 Senators.

Harris became manager of the Senators in 1924 when owner Griffith took a chance on the 27-year-old second baseman who had only five years of professional baseball experience. Serving as a player/manager, Harris led the 1924 Senators to their one and only World Series championship and earned the nickname "The Boy Wonder." He was one of the first managers in baseball to employ relief pitchers. Harris served three different stints as manager of the Senators from 1924 to 1928, 1935-1942 and finally, 1950-1954.

The Senators' opponent in the exhibition game was comprised of prospects who were vying for positions with either Greenville or Trenton, making it difficult for local fans to attach any loyalties to players. The night before the game, Greenville's manager Donahue and Trenton's boss, Spencer Abbott, along with Cambria, met to decide which players would suit up for the game.

Cambria and his staff had worked tirelessly to ensure that the

Greenville fans were impressed with the new ballpark. Scoop Latimer described Cambria on game day as buzzing around Meadowbrook "like a bee in a blooming honeysuckle vine."

Sixty-nine-year-old Clark Griffith, owner of the Senators, along with his wife, Addie, joined Cambria and Greenville Mayor McCullough in box seats behind home plate. Addie sat wrapped up in a couple of wool blankets as she braved a wind chill that hovered around the freezing mark. Cambria was proud and thankful to have his close friend and mentor on hand for the grand opening. Griffith was impressed with Cambria's new ballpark, saying it compared favorably with any minor league park in the country.

The Spinners were dressed in new white wool uniforms. They were trimmed in red and black with a red "G" stitched into the left sleeve of each jersey. Their caps were black with the letter "G" displayed in the center. Ushers wore fancy green coats and stiff-brimmed caps emblazoned with the Spinners logo. The Senators wore their gray traveling uniforms. Outfielders from both teams borrowed cleats from the Furman University football team because they were longer than standard baseball cleats and afforded the players better traction on the soggy playing surface.

Approximately 3,500 fans filled the stands at Meadowbrook on the cold, windy Saturday afternoon to witness the return of professional baseball to Greenville. Longtime Senators base coach and part-time baseball comedian Nick Altrock was hired to entertain the crowd with his antics throughout the game.

Pitching for the Greenville/Trenton team was one of Cambria's Cuban prospects, Rene Monteagudo. The stocky left-hander, who spoke no English, shut out the Senators for six consecutive innings. He struck out future Hall of Famer Goslin twice, which drew a loud roar of approval from the crowd. His stellar pitching performance all but guaranteed him a spot on the higher-level Trenton team where he ultimately won 19 games before finishing the 1938 season on the big league Senators roster.

The Spinners scored first on a solo home run in the second inning by Girard Corrado. They added a run in the fourth and led 2-0 until the eighth inning when the Senators tied the game. With the departure time for the Senators' train looming, the exhibition game was called after nine innings and ended in a 2-2 tie.

Cambria was pleased with the attendance, telling Scoop Latimer, "I figured we wouldn't have had more than 300 customers considering the weather . . . wasn't it a dandy crowd? It convinces me that Greenville is a corking good town, and you bet your life we are going to give this city a real ball club."

Cambria remained in Greenville for the next couple of weeks helping Donahue assess talent and allocate players between his Greenville and Trenton ball clubs. Practices were held at the Judson Mill Park while finishing touches were put on the construction of Meadowbrook.

The Spinners opened the season with a road win over rival Spartanburg, but things went downhill from there as they lost 15 of their next 20 games. A clubhouse fight after a loss at Jacksonville in early May highlighted a spirit of disunity on the team. A modest June winning streak provided a glimmer of hope, but by early July, they returned to their losing ways and fell deep into the cellar of the Sally League. The team had not lived up to Cambria's optimistic preseason promises.

Fans expressed their disappointment in letters to Scoop Latimer. They pleaded for more experienced and skilled players. Today the emphasis in the minor leagues is on player development. Winning games is secondary. In 1938, however, towns like Greenville took great pride in the success of their teams, and they had little patience with losing records.

A veteran scribe, Latimer did not hold back in his criticism of the Spinners, saying they "lacked spirit" and "didn't take the game seriously enough." A propensity for defensive miscues led Latimer to refer to the Spinners' play as "burlesque baseball." Cambria rotated 64 different players through Greenville in 1938, hoping to find a winning combination of talent. The Spinners finished the season with a 52-83 record and a last-place finish in the Sally League.

The Greenville "Black Spinners," a loosely organized semi-pro Negro baseball team had been playing in Greenville since the early 1920s. Prior to the construction of Meadowbrook, they had played games at Graham Field, but with the demolition of that park in 1936, they moved their home games to Mayberry Park. Just as Cambria had promised, the Black Spinners were allowed access to Meadowbrook, albeit only when the White Spinners were on the road. While the White Spinners garnered significant press for their inaugural season and a last-place finish, Greenville's "Black Spinners" were typically given only a small advertisement in *The Greenville News* providing notice of an upcoming game.

On September 18,1938, an advertisement touted a matchup between the Black Spinners and the Asheville Black Tourists. The winner of the contest was to be crowned champion of the Carolinas Colored League. This ad, along with all others promoting the Black Spinners' games, included the following statement: "A special section for white fans will be reserved at the game."

A bright spot from the Spinners' 1938 season was the play of first baseman John "Mickey" Vernon. The 20-year-old Vernon had dropped out of Villanova and was playing on the sandlots of Marcus Hook, Pa., when Cambria found him and offered him a contract with Greenville.

Vernon won local fans over with his skillful play at first base and his smooth left-handed batting stroke. He finished the year with a team leading .328 batting average. Scoop Latimer correctly predicted that Vernon was too good to return to Greenville next season, and by July of 1939, Vernon was a regular with the Senators on his way to a successful 20-year major league career. Vernon was named to the American League All-Star team seven times.

Mickey Vernon (left) stands alongside Greenville Spinners teammate Al Brancato in 1938 at Meadowbrook Park.
(Courtesy of the Greenville County Historical Society)

Despite the Spinners' poor performance, approximately 4,000 appreciative baseball fans showed up for the final game, a 5-3 loss to Spartanburg. Cambria was pleased with the fan support but sorely disappointed in the product he had put on the field. He had built a spacious first-rate ballpark but had fielded a second-rate team. He knew how important winning games was to the local fans, and he vowed next year would be different.

To get things started on the right foot in 1939, Cambria used every angle of his baseball connections to schedule an opening exhibition game featuring a team that many baseball pundits consider to be the greatest major league team of all time.

4
Yankee Clipper

I played my best every day. You never know when someone may be seeing you play for the first time.

—Joe DiMaggio

Joe DiMaggio sat comfortably on a couch in the lobby of Greenville's Poinsett Hotel. Several of his New York Yankee teammates, along with members of the Brooklyn Dodgers, were scattered throughout the lobby, awaiting the start of their scheduled exhibition game at Meadowbrook Park on the afternoon of April 11, 1939.

The 24-year-old Yankee center fielder sipped a cup of coffee and skimmed the headlines of the morning paper. As he folded his paper to turn the page, he looked up and saw one of the most beautiful women he had ever seen in his life. A striking brunette sat perched on a railing on the hotel's mezzanine floor. Her hair was tightly coiled behind her head, and she wore a sleek floral dress that highlighted the curvature of her body.

DiMaggio's line of sight gave him a perfect view of her finely toned legs that hung alluringly over the balcony railing. He stuck his newspaper in the couch's armrest. The beautiful mystery woman was far more interesting than reading about Adolph Hitler and the Nazi Party's advance across Europe. Who was this beautiful lady in the lobby of this small Southern town? The star was starstruck.

DiMaggio made an inquiry of a nearby bellhop and learned he wasn't the only celebrity in Greenville that day. The girl on the balcony was world-renowned dancer Lisa Parnova. The night before, Parnova had performed a recital of classic and modern ballet in front of a sold-out audience at the Women's College of Furman University.

Parnova earned global recognition as a premier ballerina, first for the Cologne (Germany) Opera and then at New York's Metropolitan Opera. A New York paper once described Parnova as a woman with "an exotic face, a beautiful body and the exquisite grace of a ballerina."

Her name was familiar to DiMaggio. In his first year with the Yankees (1936), the sordid story of Parnova's divorce from well-known artist Hollis B. Shaw was spilled across the New York tabloids. The media feasted on the risqué details of the couple's separation, which included Parnova's confession of an adulterous affair with her husband's cousin.

Most of the ballplayers simply gawked at Parnova, but DiMaggio had to meet her. He climbed the stairs to the mezzanine and waited for the right moment to introduce himself—not that an introduction was really needed. By 1939, there weren't many females in the country who didn't know "Joltin' Joe DiMaggio," America's most eligible bachelor.

The two struck up a friendly conversation as Brooklyn Dodger pitcher and South Carolina native, Van Lingle Mungo joined them. DiMaggio wished he would disappear. Parnova told them how she had mistakenly arrived in Greenville, N.C., instead of Greenville, S.C., on the day of her recital. Realizing her mistake, she and her traveling party had to race to make it to the correct Greenville in time for her concert. The Greenville News reported that Parnova's performance started an hour late, but despite the delay, the beautiful dancer won over the crowd with a sincere apology and an exhilarating performance.

The Yankees star was so smitten by Parnova's grace and style, he felt an urge to do something that he had rarely ever done—something that had been asked of him thousands of times—but not something he was comfortable asking of someone else. He reached down and picked up a notepad and pen from a coffee table and politely asked Parnova for her autograph.

DiMaggio, wearing a tailored pinstripe suit, stood on one side of Parnova. Mungo, holding a half-lit cigarette, was on the opposite side. Both ballplayers smiled broadly as they watched Parnova scribble her name on the paper. At that exact moment, photographer Frank Simpson flashed his camera. Simpson's photo appeared on the front page of the *Greenville Piedmont* that afternoon, and within hours, the paper sold out at newsstands. Nearly every man and woman in Greenville wanted a copy, albeit for different reasons.

Parnova and DiMaggio parted company, and DiMaggio expressed regret that he did not arrive in Greenville in time to see the dancer's show. He told her he hoped to see her perform in the future. There is no way to know if the two ever met again.

Sixteen days after his chance encounter with Parnova, DiMaggio announced his engagement to actress Dorothy Arnold. The celebrity couple were married at the end of the 1939 season and divorced in 1944. Ten years later, DiMaggio wed American sex symbol Marilyn Monroe. Their marriage lasted nine months. In 1943, Parnova got married again—this time, to a wealthy mining executive.

The Yankees exhibition in Greenville was part of a 14-game cross-country tour that began March 30, the day they broke training camp in St. Petersburg, Fla. The trip started with matchups against minor league opponents in Tallahassee, New Orleans, Houston, San Antonio and Fort Worth. A rainout in Dallas provided a welcome respite from their grueling travel schedule. After games in Oklahoma City and Little Rock, the team traveled to Atlanta where it met the Brooklyn Dodgers for exhibitions in Atlanta, Greenville, Charlotte and Norfolk before heading to Brooklyn for two final contests at Ebbets Field.

In 1939, only 10 cities in the United States had major league baseball teams. Television did not bring baseball into the living rooms of most U.S. homes until the 1950s. The nearest major league city to Greenville was 500 miles away in Washington, D.C. For fans in cities like Greenville, the only chance of seeing a major league player in person was at one of these preseason exhibition events.

The exhibitions were for the benefit of the fans and owners. The players were not fond of these small-town preseason games and for good reason. The exhausting travel schedule meant most nights were spent in a cramped railroad sleeper car. Players received no additional compensation for the games. Gate receipts were shared between the owners of the big league clubs and the local minor league clubs that hosted the games.

Rain was forecasted for Greenville on game day, and the Yankee and Dodger players secretly wished for a washout. Meanwhile, every baseball fan in Greenville prayed fervently for the game to be played.

Despite the threatening skies, an overflow crowd was expected at Meadowbrook. During the offseason, owner Joe Cambria added approximately 2,000 bleacher seats to bring the park's capacity to around 7,000. General admission seats were 75 cents while fans in the grandstand paid $1.10, and box seats were $1.50.

Manager Joe McCarthy's Yankees were coming off three consecutive World Series championships and were a clear favorite to win a fourth in '39. Their star-studded roster included eight future Hall of Famers. Joining DiMaggio and McCarthy on the road to Cooperstown were first baseman Lou Gehrig, second baseman Tom Gordon, shortstop Frankie Crosetti, catcher Bill Dickey and pitchers Red Ruffing and Lefty Gomez.

Gehrig was nearing the end of his legendary career. He mysteriously collapsed during a spring training game and his doctors were perplexed by his loss of strength and stamina. As the '39 season began, the man known as "Iron Horse" was a shadow of the player that had been a two-time American League MVP and had helped lead the Yankees to six World Series championships.

Joseph Paul DiMaggio was born on November 25, 1914, in Martinez, Calif., about 25 miles south of San Francisco. His family moved to the Fisherman's Wharf area of San Francisco when Joe was a year old. He was the eighth of nine children born to Sicilian immigrants. His father came from a long line of fishermen, and it was expected that all of his sons would follow him into the fishing business. Joe, however, hated fishing and complained that the smell of fish and the waves made him nauseous.

He sold newspapers in downtown San Francisco to avoid helping his father unload and fold fishing nets at Fishermen's Wharf. Baseball was the avenue that ultimately helped him escape a life at sea. DiMaggio said of his father and fishing, "I was always giving him excuses, principally that I had a weak stomach, but he insisted I was *lagnuso* [lazy] and to tell the truth, I don't know which he thought was the greater disgrace to the family, that a DiMaggio should be lazy or that a DiMaggio should have a weak stomach."[1]

In 1932, Joe's older brother Vince was playing for the San Francisco Seals of the Pacific Coast League, and near the end of the season, when he convinced his manager to give his younger brother a spot on the team. Joe was two months shy of his 18th birthday and had dropped out of high school. In his first full season with the Seals (1933), DiMaggio played in 187 games, hit .340 and smacked 28 home runs.

Joe's oldest brother, Tom, considered the brains of the family, helped Joe negotiate his first contract with the Seals which paid him $225 per month, nearly double what most PCL rookies earned. Joe's father, Giuseppe, seeing that real money could be made playing baseball, reluctantly gave his blessing to his son's pursuit of a baseball career.[2]

In his second season with the Seals, DiMaggio hit .341 and established a PCL record by hitting in 61 consecutive games. The publicity around the hitting streak had major league scouts flocking to the Bay Area. The 6'2" 190-pound DiMaggio was what today's scouts refer to as a five-tool player; he could hit for average, hit with power, run, throw and field.

Unfortunately, his 1934 season was cut short by a freak knee injury sustained while stepping off a bus. The Yankees used the uncertainty surrounding the injury to negotiate a bargain price of $25,000 for DiMaggio's contract. The Seals agreed to the price under the condition that DiMaggio be allowed to play one additional season with them. He had become a West Coast celebrity, and having him in the lineup guaranteed the Seals a successful year at the box office. DiMaggio hit .398 with 34 home runs in his final season with the Seals.[3]

Once he joined the Yankees, DiMaggio immediately established himself as a fixture in their outfield and became the heir apparent to the great Babe Ruth. He hit .323, with 29 home runs and 125 RBIs in his rookie season and led the '36 Yankees to the World Series championship.

Italian-Americans adopted DiMaggio as their hero. Hall of Fame manager Tommy Lasorda said of the second-generation Sicilian, "I knew every big leaguer when I was growing up, but Joe DiMaggio was my hero. He was our hero; he was everything we wanted to be." Basil Russo, President of the Italian Sons and Daughters of America, wrote in January 2020:

> *Joe conducted himself as a gentlemen and a role model not only on the field but off the field as well. Joe DiMaggio created a very positive image for Italian Americans with all other Americans. . . . The fact that some Italian American ballplayers could attain celebrity status gave Italian immigrants, and their children both a sense of pride and a feeling of hope. Pride that some of their own people could attain positions of respect in America and hope that they and their children would also be able to fulfill their dreams in America.*

He picked up many nicknames during his playing days including Joltin' Joe, the Wallopin' Wop and Joe D., but the most recognizable was given to him by the Yankees' radio announcer, Arch McDonald, during the 1939 season.

Joe DiMaggio and the New York Yankees appeared in an exhibition game at Meadowbrook Park in April 1939.
(From the author's collection)

Pan American Airways had recently released an impressive new airplane, the Boeing 314 Clipper. It had the capability of flying across the Atlantic and Pacific Oceans and was heralded for its first-class service that included a 14-seat dining room with linen tablecloths and sleeping quarters for all its passengers. Pan Am placed its initial Boeing 314 in service in March of 1939. It was christened by first lady Eleanor Roosevelt and named "The Yankee Clipper."

Early in the '39 season, McDonald introduced DiMaggio across the airways on the 50,000-watt WABC with these words, ". . . batting cleanup, Joe DiMaggio—The Yankee Clipper . . ." In doing so, McDonald drew a parallel between DiMaggio's ability to gracefully cover vast amounts of the outfield to the sleek long-range flying ability of Pan Am's newest flying machine.[4]

The gates at Meadowbrook Park opened at 1 p.m., two hours before the first pitch of the Yankees-Dodgers game. Both teams took batting practice with the Yankees getting first cracks. Fans *oohed* and *aahed* as DiMaggio, Dickey, Gehrig, Gordon and Selkirk hit balls out of the park. Dozens of youngsters positioned themselves beyond the outfield walls and battled over the precious souvenirs.

The Greenville Spinners players sat behind the Yankees dugout. The following night, they were scheduled to play an exhibition game against the Jersey City Skeeters of the International League at Meadowbrook. They watched the big leaguers closely, hoping to learn something that might improve their chances of future success.

A heavy downpour passed through the ballpark around the time of the first pitch. *The Greenville News* pointed out that approximately $2 million in payroll was represented in the personnel on the field that day. Playing a meaningless exhibition game on a soggy surface placed New York and Brooklyn's high-dollar assets at risk of serious injury.

The umpires called the Yankees' John McGraw and Brooklyn Manager Leo Durocher to home plate to discuss calling off the game. Durocher was in his first year as the player-manager of the Dodgers, having been hired by General Manager Larry McPhail to bring about a turnaround in a team that had suffered six straight losing seasons. Durocher was known as a tenacious, scrappy player, and his managerial style emulated those same aggressive qualities. His competitive philosophy was epitomized by a legendary quote attributed to him: "Nice guys finish last."

McCarthy was inclined to try to play the game, but Durocher saw absolutely no need to take the risk, and he became enraged over the prospect of playing. The fans watched as the red-faced Dodger manager screamed at umpire crew chief Charlie Moran. Sensing that playing the game was in question, fans began to chant loudly, "Play ball! Play ball!"

Moran had been calling major league games since 1918 and was known around the league as "Uncle Charlie." He listened patiently to Durocher's rants and carefully weighed his options. He looked around at the thousands of fans that packed Meadowbrook Park and made one final appeal to Durocher to convince him to allow his players to take the field. Durocher finally relented, and Moran held his mask up in the air and shouted at the top of his lungs, "Play ball!" The crowd erupted in a roar of approval.

It may have been tempting for McCarthy to rest a few of his stars and not risk injury on the slippery playing surface, but he did not. The position players included in the Yankee lineup card that McCarthy exchanged at home plate that day represented the best the Yankees had to offer:

1.	Frankie Crosetti	Shortstop
2.	Red Rolfe	Third base
3.	Tommy Henrich	Right field
4.	Joe DiMaggio	Center field
5.	Lou Gehrig	First base
6.	Bill Dickey	Catcher
7.	George Selkirk	Left field
8.	Joe Gordon	Second base
9.	Bump Hadley	Pitcher

Brooklyn used a five-hit third inning to tally four runs and take a lead they would never relinquish. The Yankees responded in the bottom of the third with two runs—the first off an inside-the-park home run by Frankie Crosetti. Tommy Henrich followed with a triple, and DiMaggio drove him home with a sharply hit double that careened off the left field fence.

DiMaggio did not disappoint the fans that day. He went two for two with a pair of doubles. He showed off his arm when he fired a perfect strike to gun down a Dodger runner at home plate and made a long running catch of a deep fly ball in center field.

The Yankees arrived in Greenville the night before the game, well past midnight. They were playing their ninth consecutive exhibition on the road. It's safe to assume DiMaggio and his teammates were a bit road weary. Any evidence of that weariness was not present in DiMaggio's effort at Meadowbrook. He operated from a personal code of conduct that required him to always give his best. When asked once why he went all-out to catch a fly ball in a game that meant nothing in the standings, DiMaggio said simply, "I played my best every day. You never know when someone may be seeing you play for the first time."

Gehrig struggled in the game. In two plate appearances, he hit a weak pop foul and a groundout to first. Dave Tillinghast of the *Greenville Piedmont* wrote, "Gehrig's feebleness at bat on both occasions elicited sympathy."

Dickey, considered to be the best catcher in the game at the time, also struggled at the plate with an 0-2 performance that included a strikeout. He did bring the crowd to its feet when he gunned down the Dodgers' Pete Coscarart as he attempted to steal second base.

Rain halted the game twice, leaving the field even more treacherous than it was at first pitch. Brooklyn scored an additional run in the top of the fourth to go ahead 5-2. After the Yanks batted in the bottom of the fifth, the skies opened again, and this time, the umpires had no choice but to call the game.

Meadowbrook's small rooftop press box spilled over that day as the local media were joined by a band of 14 New York writers who had been traveling with the Yankees during their exhibition tour. The New York contingent banged out game summaries that hit the wires shortly after the game was called. The lead in Associated Press story on the game read:

Greenville, S.C., April 12—The Brooklyn Dodgers and a rainstorm both soaked the New York Yankees yesterday. Brooklyn did it for the second straight time, 5-2, in a game cut to five innings by rain.

The 1939 Yankees were one of the most dominant teams in the history of Major League Baseball. They finished 17 games ahead of the Boston Red Sox and defeated the Cincinnati Reds in four straight games to win their 11th World Series championship. They are the only team to outscore their opponents by more than 400 runs in a season.

On May 2, 1939, the iron man of baseball, Lou Gehrig, went to manager Joe McCarthy and asked to be removed from the starting lineup. Gehrig had started 2,130 consecutive games, a remarkable record of endurance that was not broken until 1995 by Baltimore's Cal Ripken. Gehrig played through bone fractures, the flu and many other ailments on his way to establishing the consecutive game streak. After removing himself from the lineup, Gehrig traveled to the Mayo Clinic and was diagnosed with amyotrophic lateral sclerosis, known throughout North America today as Lou Gehrig's disease.

A capacity crowd of 61,808 filled Yankee Stadium on July 4, 1939, for Lou Gehrig Day. In between games of a doubleheader with the Senators, the Yankee great was showered with gifts and accolades, including the retirement of his jersey number. Babe Ruth was on hand to speak in honor of his former teammate.

Gehrig requested that Sid Mercer, a veteran sports writer, speak on his behalf. Mercer began his talk, and the crowd started chanting, "We want Gehrig!" Lou reluctantly stepped to the microphone and delivered an emotional speech that has been referred to as the Gettysburg Address of baseball. Despite his misfortune, Gehrig said, "I consider myself the luckiest man on the face of this earth." On June 2, 1941, 17 days after his 38th birthday, Gehrig passed away.

In 1941, DiMaggio permanently established himself as a baseball immortal when he hit safely in 56 consecutive games. While many of baseball's greatest records have fallen, DiMaggio's 56-game hitting streak remains, considered by many to be a record that will never be broken. The Yankees won nine World Series during DiMaggio's 13-year career. He was an All-Star every year he played, and his #5 jersey has been permanently retired by the Yankees.

Spinners owner Joe Cambria was in Greenville for the exhibition. He was proud of his new ballpark and the high-profile matchup he arranged for the citizens of Greenville. He smiled when he heard of Yankee manager McCarthy's praise for his ballpark. "It's one of the dandiest Class B League parks in the country," McCarthy said. Cambria was also pleased to keep 15 percent of the healthy gate receipts from the contest.

The Yankees' 10-car chartered train left the Southern Railway depot at 7:30 p.m. bound for Charlotte. Hundreds of fans stood alongside the tracks to catch a final glimpse of their baseball heroes. As the steam locomotive chugged its way out of Greenville, its engineer blew the train's whistle, a sound that marked the end of a historic day in Greenville's baseball history. For years to come, at places like Tucker's Soda Shop in West Greenville and Carpenter Bros. Drugs on Main Street, stories about the time the '39 Yankees played at Meadowbrook were told and retold.

5
Mike and Reggie

I'm tellin' you, this baseball is a great life.

—Reggie Otero

It was a little past 11 p.m. on Saturday when Reggie Otero and Mike Guerra walked out of the Rivoli Theatre in downtown Greenville in April of 1939. They had just seen Buck Jones star in the film *Law of the Texan*. Most of the dialogue in the black-and-white Western was a mystery to the two Spanish-speaking natives of Cuba, yet they enjoyed seeing the man in the tall white Stetson hat corral a band of outlaws.

The Washington Senators had assigned Otero and Guerra to the Greenville Spinners for the 1939 season. Earlier in the week, they sat with their Spinner teammates and watched the New York Yankees and Brooklyn Dodgers play a rain-shortened exhibition game at Meadowbrook Park.

As the two Cubans strolled down Main Street, they talked of what they learned from the big leaguers. Otero, a slick-fielding first baseman, had studied the actions of Yankee first baseman Lou Gehrig. Guerra, a catcher, kept a watchful eye on the movements of Bill Dickey. Gehrig and Dickey represented the pinnacle of baseball success that the two Cubans aspired to achieve. Their dreams of baseball stardom were not so much about personal glory, but rather the joy they would experience if they were able to share the financial rewards of American baseball with their loved ones back in Cuba.

Most Greenvillians had retired for the evening, and the farther the two men walked, the more alone they became. They stopped and sat on a bench outside the entrance to their hotel. Their thoughts drifted toward home. Eight hundred miles separated Otero and Guerra from the comfort of family and friends. Fried chicken, mashed potatoes and boiled peanuts replaced seasoned pork, rice and beans, and plantains as their dietary staples. Everyone around them spoke an unfamiliar language. They were strangers in a foreign land, connected to their teammates and the community only through baseball. As they sat on the bench, they longed for the warm ocean breezes and salty air of their homeland.

This late-night conversation between Otero and Guerra was part of a long-term friendship. Their paths had first crossed as teenagers in the Cuban Leagues, and both brought their baseball skills to America in 1936. Their lives and families would forever be intertwined as Guerra married Otero's older sister Carmen in 1940, and Otero selected Guerra to serve as godfather to his firstborn son in 1956.

Fermín "Mike" Guerra was born on October 11, 1912, in La Habana, Cuba. His family migrated to Cuba from the Canary Islands and was part of an immigrant population known as isleños (islanders). The isleños were a poor working class that typically ended up performing manual labor jobs.

Fermín was put to work at a very young age, which left no time for formal schooling. He learned to play baseball in vacant lots and also worked as a batboy for the Almendares Blues, a Cuban professional team, which he would later manage for 15 years. He built a reputation among the Cuban sandlots as a fiery competitor.[1]

Guerra began playing in Cuba's semi-pro baseball circuit as a teenager. While playing for the Santa Clara Leopards, he caught the pitches of Cuban legend Luis Tiant Sr., whose son Luis Jr. was a three-time 20-game winner during an 18-year major league career.

The right-handed Guerra was only 5'7" and 150 pounds, not the typical build for a catcher. He compensated for his size with excellent skills behind the plate, a strong throwing arm and an aggressive spirit. His performance in the Cuban leagues caught the eye of Joseph Cambria, who told Guerra he thought he could play in the United States.

In 1949, while with the Philadelphia Athletics, Guerra recalled the story of Cambria's recruiting. Speaking with a reporter from the *Scranton Tribune*, he said: "As a young boy, I play ball in Havana and am very happy. I no want to leave Cuba, ever. One day Joe Cambria of Washington Senators comes to see me play in Havana. I no speak English then so he tell my friend, who speaks good English that he want me to play in United States."

Guerra said his friend advised him that he would have a good time playing ball in the United States and that he would make a lot of money. After considerable thought, he accepted Cambria's offer.

He was sent first to Albany in the International League but ended up spending most of the 1936 season with the Trenton/York Senators. Near the end of the season, the 24-year-old catcher was called up by the Senators and inserted into the lineup for the second game of a doubleheader against the Chicago White Sox. Guerra failed miserably in his major league debut, going 0-3 and making an embarrassing mental error behind the plate. *The Washington Post* referred to his performance as "a downright horrible debut." Guerra had to wait eight years before he got a second chance in the majors.

In 1937, the Senators assigned him to Salisbury in the Class D League where he played for two seasons. In 1939, Guerra reported to Greenville with the Class B Spinners and joined his friend Reggie Otero.

Reggie Jose Otero Gómez was born on October 7, 1915, in Havana. Details of Otero's early life are lacking, but most likely he followed a path similar to Guerra, learning to play baseball in the sandlots of Havana. Early on, Otero fell in love with playing first base. He enjoyed being involved with the quick infield action, and he practiced his footwork and fielding skills endlessly. First base was the only position Reggie played throughout his American and Cuban careers.

Otero was also signed by Cambria in 1936 and followed his friend Guerra to Albany and Trenton/York in his first season in the United States. He was sent back to Trenton in 1937 and the following year played for the Class D St. Augustine Saints where he hit .308 and earned a promotion to Class B Greenville for the '39 season.

Reggie Jose Otero Gómez
(Courtesy of Hortensia Otero)

Joe Cambria's inaugural Greenville Spinners team had been a disappointment. A last-place finish in the Sally League left Cambria indebted to the good citizens of

Greenville. He was on a mission to field a team that would bring pride to the city. Of course, more wins also meant higher attendance and more profits for the shrewd owner.

Cambria spent the off-season plotting out needed changes in the makeup of his team. He began by not renewing manager Jiggs Donahue's contract. Donahue was a likeable fellow, but he fell short of Cambria's expectations as a field general.

Scoop Latimer of *The Greenville News* offered Cambria his suggestion for the next boss of the Spinners. He strongly recommended that Cambria hire Pat Crawford. The 36-year-old Crawford played for the Spinners from 1925 to 1927 and spent four years in the majors, including his final season in 1934 with the World Series champion St. Louis Cardinals. Latimer told Cambria there had never been a more popular player to come through Greenville.

Crawford was born in Society Hill, S.C., and raised in nearby Sumter. He attended Davidson College and spent off-seasons teaching and coaching in North Carolina high schools, where according to one local newspaper, he established himself as a "mentor and idol of high school athletes."[2]

Crawford had retired from baseball, and Cambria hoped that the attraction of returning to Greenville would lure him out of retirement. Cambria extended the offer to Crawford and waited anxiously for his response. Crawford sent a telegram rejecting the Baltimore baseball mogul's proposal, telling him that while Greenville still had a warm place in his heart, other interests prohibited him from accepting the opportunity. He politely thanked Cambria for his consideration.

Crawford had recently opened a boys' summer camp in Morehead City, N.C., that he and his wife operated for several decades. Crawford lived to age 92, at which point he was the last surviving member of St. Louis Cardinals' famed "Gas House Gang."

Cambria eventually hired Ohio native Alexander Boyd "Red" Mc-Coll as his new manager. The 44-year-old journeyman minor league pitcher had spent most of his career playing in various Southern towns including Nashville, Knoxville, Memphis, Mobile and Chattanooga. He played parts of two seasons (1933-34) with the Washington Senators where he appeared in 46 games and posted a 4-4 record.

McColl was the player-manager of the 1938 Americus Cardinals in the Georgia-Florida League and led the league with a 2.04 ERA. His only other managerial experience was limited to brief stints at Chattanooga, Jacksonville and Charlotte. His record as a manager by 1939 was 132-131.

Spinners secretary John Milton (left), business manager and future Greenville Mayor Kenneth Cass (center) and manager Alex McColl (right) hold a discussion around the batting cage at Meadowbrook Park during the 1939 season.
(From the author's collection)

Calvin Griffith, son of Senators owner Clark Griffith, managed McColl as a player in Chattanooga and said of him, "Alex will make Greenville a swell manager. He's a nice fellow, and the public will like him. He's immensely popular wherever he goes."

The weakest part of the prior year Spinners was their pitching, and Cambria expected that the 44-year-old McColl could not only mentor the team's younger pitchers, but also be a key contributor on the pitching staff. The right-handed McColl was a workhorse pitcher throughout his 26-year minor league career, posting four 20-win seasons and an overall record of 332-263.

Cambria made the announcement of McColl's appointment while he was attending the Minor League Baseball winter meeting in New Orleans. Joining Cambria at the meeting were Spinners secretary John Milton, business manager Kenneth Cass and the ever-present Scoop Latimer. The sports writer chronicled Cambria's activity in New Orleans, saying, ". . . Cambria has been busy as a bee at the convention, buzzing around with the big wigs and the bushers, trying to buy and trade for players he knows will help Greenville."

Cambria also planned to use his Cuban pipeline to improve the talent pool in Greenville. In addition to Otero and Guerra, he retained Cuban pitcher Jorge Comellas, who had appeared in 11 games and posted a 3-4 record for the Spinners in 1938.

Guerra battled veteran Herb Crompton for the Spinners' starting catcher role. Crompton had made it to the big leagues for a proverbial cup of coffee in 1937 before returning to Greenville in 1938 where he hit .282. Crompton had the edge when it came to power at the plate, but Guerra demonstrated that he could use his speed to stretch singles into doubles and doubles into triples. He handled his duties behind the plate with precision and skill and had a rifle arm to second base. Perhaps the thing that McColl found most attractive about Guerra was his passion for the game. Guerra in Spanish means war, and every day the fiery catcher suited up to play, McColl could count on Guerra to protect home plate with every ounce of his diminutive frame and never back away from a fight.

Power-hitting Joe Zagami was Otero's competition at first base. Zagami belted 16 home runs and batted .309 for the Class D Easton (Md.) Browns the previous season. The 5'11" 160-pound Otero lacked the power that was expected from a first baseman, but in the eyes of his manager, Otero's magical fielding skills equalized his inability to hit home runs.

Otero played first base with charisma. When he dug a throw out of the dirt, he raised his glove high with a little wave. He was adept at making backhanded plays and racing to the bag for the unassisted putout. He was quick to flash a broad smile and tip his cap to the appreciative Meadowbrook fans. Early in the season, Scoop Latimer started calling him "Flash" and penned a detailed description of the Cuban first baseman's play:

> The spectator sits on pins and needles as Otero goes after high or low throws, ground and balls, but the handsome young Cuban relieves the tension by snatching the ball with a little piece of leather that's only a distant cousin to a regular first baseman's scoop . . . How he does it, is one of the mysteries of baseball, but his hand snaps at a target like a turtle going for a darting fish . . . It's a treat to see him play, and when the season is over he'll have fewest errors perhaps, of any other first baseman in the country in a similar number of games.

The '39 Spinners opened their 140-game season on April 18 in Greenville against rival Spartanburg. Batting second and playing first base on opening day was Otero. McColl opted for the more experienced Compton to start behind the plate. The Spinners delighted the opening night crowd of 5,000 with an 8-3 win.

In their third game of the season, Otero suffered a deep laceration on his foot when a Spartanburg player spiked him on a close play at first base. Otero was rushed to nearby Greenville General Hospital where he received several stitches on his injured foot.

The Spinners won three of their first four games, and McColl was pleased with his team's play but disappointed in the offensive performance of his catcher, Compton. In their fifth game, a road matchup against the Savannah Indians, McColl inserted Guerra behind the plate, and he responded with a 4-5 night to help lead the Spinners to their fifth victory in six games. The next night, Guerra was back in the starting lineup.

1939 Greenville Spinners: Bottom row, far right—Mike Guerra; Top row, fourth from left, Reggie Otero; fifth from left, Alex McColl (manager) and far right, Kenneth Cass (business manager)
(Courtesy of the Greenville County Historical Society—William B. Coxe Collection)

On May 4, with the Spinners hovering around the .500 mark, they hosted the Columbia Red Birds. It was Otero's first game back in the lineup after his injury. The Spinners trailed 8-7 in the bottom of the ninth when Guerra came to the plate with runners on first and second. He proceeded to smack a double off the left field fence that scored two runs and gave the Spinners a 9-8 come-from-behind win. From this point forward, Guerra remained a fixture in the Spinners starting lineup. Otero also had a successful night at the plate going 2-5 and playing flawless first base. Team owner Cambria, happened to be at Meadowbrook Park that night and was all smiles over the performance of his two young Cuban prospects.

The 1939 season fell short of Cambria's expectations. The Spinners remained near the top of the league in hitting but near the bottom in pitching. They finished with a disappointing 64-76 record and fifth place in the Sally League, 20 games behind first place Columbia. Their team batting average was .301, but only one pitcher, player-manager McColl, had an ERA below 4.00.

Guerra batted .321 and finished second in the Sally League in triples with 17, an unlikely feat for a catcher. He was named to the Sally League All-Star team. Otero batted .325 and had a pristine .988 fielding percentage.

In their next-to-last game of the season, the Spinners were hosting the Augusta Tigers. A group of local fans came up with an idea to show their appreciation for their favorite player, Otero. They had watched Otero all season long make his flashy one-handed snags at first and provide consistent hitting for the Spinners. His broad smile lit up Meadowbrook Park. Before games as he chatted with fans and always had time for adoring youth. His fans knew Otero and his wife would incur expenses to return to Cuba, so they took up a collection to show their gratitude to their favorite player.

In the top of the seventh inning, McColl, who happened to be pitching, walked toward first base. The public address announcer drew the crowd's attention to what was about to happen as McColl handed Otero an envelope containing the cash collected from the fans. An overwhelmed Otero tipped his hat and flashed his signature broad smile as the fans stood and cheered.

On this night, Otera did not disappoint his admirers as he collected three hits and made a tremendous stretch play at first that electrified the crowd. The Greenville fans thought this was the last they would see of their favorite Cuban, however, Otero returned to the Spinners for the 1940 season, once again hitting over .300 and remaining a fan favorite.

Guerra finally made it back to the big leagues in 1944 and spent the next seven seasons as a backup catcher for the Washington Senators, Philadelphia Athletics and Boston Red Sox. His best year in the majors was 1949 when he appeared in 82 games and batted .282 for the Athletics. For his major league career, he hit .242 in 1,750 plate appearances.

Like his friend Otero, Guerra was endearing to the fans. He played for the Chattanooga Lookouts in 1942, and the local paper ran a contest that allowed fans to vote for their favorite Southern League player. Guerra won by a landslide. The paper printed dozens of letters endorsing Guerra, and the following are excerpts from three of those letters:

. . . Guerra is my favorite player because he is a team player—colorful and he has a fighting heart that never gives up. My favorite player is Mike Guerra on account of his catching, throwing, hitting, pepper and all-around hustle.

I like Mike Guerra because he is always trying; he's cool under fire, works his pitchers nicely and hits in the timeliest spots . . .

Fermín "Mike" Guerra
(Courtesy of National Baseball Hall of Fame Library)

Guerra became one of the top stars in Cuban baseball during a 20-year playing career. He was the Most Valuable Player in the 1949-50 Cuban League as a player-manager for the Almendares Blues. He hit .304 and led his team to the league championship. He ranks fourth in the number of years played and fifth in plate appearances in Cuban baseball history.

After his playing days ended, Guerra was a highly successful manager in the Cuban and Venezuelan leagues. He also worked as a scout for the Detroit Tigers from 1960 to 1962. In 1969, Guerra was elected to the Cuban Baseball Hall of Fame.

Guerra left behind a trail of stories about his scrappy, competitive demeanor. Once when managing a game in Cuba, he engaged the opposing manager in a heated verbal exchange. Guerra invited the other manager into his dugout to settle the matter with their fists. Players separated the two coaches before it got out of hand.

Brooklyn Dodger star pitcher Don Newcombe played for Guerra in Cuba in 1948. Midway through the season, Guerra cut Newcombe from the squad. Newcombe admitted he was not playing well that season but was very unhappy with Guerra's decision and vowed to get even. A few months later, Newcombe was at Dodger spring training in Vero Beach, Fla., and the Dodgers were scheduled to play the Philadelphia Athletics. Guerra was catching for the A's, and Newcombe went to the visiting bullpen before the game intent on settling his vendetta against Guerra. Newcombe stood 6'4" and weighed 220 pounds, dwarfing the 5'7" 150-pound Guerra. Witnesses to the exchange said Guerra stood eyeball to eyeball with Newcombe refusing to back down, before teammates stepped in and separated the two angry men.

After two seasons in Greenville, Otero continued on his 17-year journey through the minor leagues. His best years were in the Pacific Coast League where he played for the Los Angeles Angels from 1944 to 1947.

In late 1945, he was called up to the major leagues by the Chicago Cubs and played in 14 games. He went 9-23 and drove in five runs, helping the Cubs clinch the National League pennant. Otero joined the Cubs one day shy of being eligible to play in the '45 World Series against the Detroit Tigers. It was his only trip to the majors as a player.

From 1948 to 1952, Otero played for the Class B Portsmouth Cubs in the Piedmont League where he once again became popular with the local fans. He hit over .300 in four of his five seasons in Portsmouth and served as player-manager in 1952. While managing Portsmouth, he spoke at a local civic club luncheon and shared his views on managing in the minors.

"Young players are like handmade chairs," Otera told his audience. "You make them one day, paint them the next and then spend many, many hours polishing them. That's what the managers in the Piedmont League must do—the polishing."

Otero enjoyed a 13-year career in the Cuban professional leagues. He was considered by many as the "best and most stylish first basemen ever" to play in Cuba. After retiring as a player, Otero continued to influence the Latin game as a manager. He coached the Havana Sugar Kings from 1954 to 1956, and his longtime friend Guerra played catcher on Otero's 1954 team.

He also gained fame for managing in the Venezuelan League from

1955 to 1968 where he led the Industriales de Valencia to three championships and Leones del Caracas to four titles. His seven championships are the most in the league history, which led to Otero's election to the Venezuelan Baseball Hall of Fame.

Reggie Otero, manager of
Industriales de Valencia
(Courtesy of Hortensia Otero)

From 1959 to 1965, Otero was as a member of the Cincinnati Reds coaching staff. He developed a close mentoring relationship with future Reds star Pete Rose. Rose, who began his career as a second baseman, struggled with fielding balls hit to his right and executing the pivot on double plays. Rose played for Otero on the Leones del Caracas Venezuelan League team during the winter of 1964-65, and each day after practice, Otero hit hundreds of grounders to Rose. He was credited with helping Rose master the skills needed to become a major league infielder.

Otero was a member of the Cleveland Indians coaching staff in 1966 before joining the Los Angeles Dodgers as a full-time scout. He became a pioneer in discovering baseball talent in Latin countries. In 1972, he discovered 16-year-old Pedro Guerrero playing on the east coast of the Dominican Republic. He signed Guerrero to a pro contract with the Dodgers, and Guerrero enjoyed a 15-year major league career in which he had a lifetime batting average of .300. Guerrero was the World Series MVP for the Dodgers in 1981 and a five-time All-Star.

––––––––––

Fermín Guerra died on October 9, 1992, after a long battle with heart disease. Roberto González Echevarría closed his informative book, *The Pride of Havana: A History of Cuban Baseball*, by sharing a few thoughts from an in-person interview he conducted with Guerra the year before he died:

> *Guerra looked frail, and a stroke had affected his speech slightly. But he remembered everything and was still upbeat about his fistfight with the immensely bigger Don*

Newcombe: "I was tough," Guerra said. At the end of the interview a grandson chimed in to say that he was so proud that his grandfather had been able to accomplish so much being illiterate. I was startled. This man who had managed successfully in Cuba, and elsewhere, who was a leader in his time, could not read and write? His wife, the sister of Regino "Reggie" Otero, explained with some embarrassment that she had taught Fermín how to write his name to sign contracts and autographs, and then eventually how to read and write a little.

Shortly after the Los Angeles Dodgers captured the 1988 World Series, Reggie Otero suffered a massive heart attack. The damage was unrepairable, and he spent his final days in his home in Hialeah, Florida. One of the perks of being a part of the Dodgers organization was that he shared in the spoils of their World Series championship, which included an off-season team trip to Italy.

Otero's daughter-in-law Hortensia was in his home as Reggie approached his final days. She recalled her father-in-law telling his wife with great pride, "I'm going to take you to Italy." It was almost as if the trip was recompense for all the years he spent traveling the baseball circuit. Otero was unable to fulfill his promise to his wife as he died in his home on October 21, 1988, eight days after the Dodgers won the World Series.

The lives of Regino Otero and Fermín Guerra were woven together by the game they both loved. From the humblest of beginnings, they persevered to ultimately make a significant contribution to baseball in three different countries. Early in their careers, they passed through Meadowbrook Park where they also left their mark on the baseball history of a small Southern community.

For both Guerra and Otero, baseball was a year-round profession. As soon as their American season ended, they were back in Cuba or Venezuela for the start of another season. Once when asked about the difficult grind of playing baseball year-round, Otero enthusiastically told a reporter, "Unless a fellow is sickly or something like that it can't do him any harm. There's only one way to learn baseball and that's to think about it all the time and play as much as possible. And you can do that in Cuba or even Panama. On top of everything else, some of these guys in winter ball get $1,000 a month, an apartment, and the clubs even pay the transportation to Cuba for the players' wives and children. I'm tellin' you this baseball is a great life."

6
War Years

Coming back was difficult, but I had baseball.

—Corporal Lou Brissie

Six-foot four-inch southpaw Lou Brissie was on the mound at Meadowbrook Park pitching for the Camp Croft (Spartanburg, S.C.) All-Stars in May of 1944. Their opponent was the Greenville Army Air Force Base Jay Birds. A few hundred fans paid 40 cents apiece to watch the competition between a collection of servicemen from the two nearby military training bases, many of whom had played professionally in the minor or major leagues.

Brissie was a couple weeks shy of turning 20. He had earned a reputation as a teenage pitching phenom while playing in the area's textile leagues. On the drizzly May evening at Meadowbrook, Brissie confounded the Jaybirds' batters with his overpowering fastball and sharp breaking curve. In six innings of work, he gave up only one hit and struck out 11 of the 19 hitters he faced. The game was curtailed due to rain, with Camp Croft leading 4-0.

Six months later, Brissie was lying prostrate in the freezing mud and snow in Italy's Apennine Mountains fighting for his life. His body had been riddled with shrapnel from a massive German artillery blast.

Leland Victor "Lou" Brissie was born on June 5, 1924, in Anderson, S.C. He spent his first 11 years in Greenville where he attended elementary school at the now historic Hayne School. His father owned a motorcycle repair shop and traveled the Southeast performing in motorcycle stunt shows. Brissie's father eventually lost his business during the Great Depression and moved his family to nearby Ware Shoals where he obtained work as a mechanic at the Riegel Textile Mill.

At age 14, Brissie's skill as a pitcher earned him a spot on the Ware Shoals Riegels men's textile league team. In his debut, he struck out 17 of the first 19 batters he faced. Word spread quickly throughout the textile circuit about the tall slender teenager from Ware Shoals who was a strikeout machine. Professional scouts started to show up whenever he pitched, and after graduating high school, Brissie had multiple offers to play professionally.

The Brooklyn Dodgers enticed him with a $25,000 signing bonus, but his father advised his son not to accept it until he first spoke with Connie Mack of the Philadelphia Athletics. The elder Brissie had heard that Mack was a "gentleman" who treated people fairly and he predicted that his offspring would, "one day grow up to help the old man win another championship."[1]

At the time of Brissie's high school graduation (1941), Cornelius Alexander Mack (born McGillicuddy), whose last name was shortened to "Mack" during his playing days so that it would fit on scorecards, was 79 years old and in his 40th consecutive year as manager and part owner of the Athletics. He had won nine AL pennants and five World Series titles. Doug Skipper, writing for the Society for American Baseball Research, described the venerable baseball legend:

He was known as "The Tall Tactician" and was baseball's grand old gentleman for more than a generation. Statuesque, stately, and slim, he clutched a rolled-up scorecard as he sat or stood ramrod straight in the dugout, attired in a business suit rather than a uniform, a derby or bowler in place of a baseball cap. He carried himself with quiet dignity and commanded the respect of friend and foe. Widely addressed by players and other officials as Mr. Mack, he and the Philadelphia Athletics were so closely linked for 50 years that the team was often dubbed "the Mackmen."

Chick Galloway was the baseball coach at Presbyterian College and a former shortstop with Mack's Philadelphia Athletics. Galloway sent word to his former coach about the talented Brissie. Mack was very familiar with the caliber of baseball played in the Southern textile leagues, having signed several players from the area including Shoeless Joe Jackson in 1908.

In June of 1941, Galloway brought the 17-year-old Brissie to Philadelphia's Shibe Park to meet Mack. It was Brissie's first trip outside of South Carolina and the beginning of a relationship with the legendary baseball executive that would forever shape Brissie's life.

He donned an A's uniform and took to the mound at the empty ballpark. Mack sat near the top row of the grandstand, dressed in his familiar black suit, straw hat and high collar. After Brissie threw for a while, Mack invited him into his office.[2]

Mack was impressed with Brissie's physical talent but knew the youngster had much to learn about the art of pitching and about life. Mack had a bias toward intelligent, disciplined players and believed the all-around development that a young man could receive in college outweighed the benefits of a lengthy journey through the minor leagues.

Mack presented Brissie's father with a proposal. The Philadelphia Athletics would sign Lou to a contract and agree to pay for his college education. After college, he would remain the property of the A's and be invited to their spring training.

Brissie's father appreciated the wisdom of Mack's offer and enthusiastically agreed to the deal. Mack recommended three options for college: Duke, Holy Cross or Presbyterian. The baseball teams at all of these schools were coached by former players of Mack's. Brissie chose Presbyterian because of its proximity to his family in Ware Shoals.

He enrolled at P.C. in the fall of 1941. From the moment the Japanese attacked Pearl Harbor in December of Brissie's freshman year, he felt a strong pull to serve his country. Rather than wait to be drafted, he enlisted in the Army in December of 1942. He reported to Camp Croft for active duty in March of 1943. Pitching for one of the many service teams at Camp Croft in 1944, he won 25 games against a single loss and earned a spot on the camp's traveling All-Star team.

During training at Camp Croft, Brissie was notified that his uncle Robert had been killed in Northern Africa while serving as a private in the 354th Coast Artillery Division. Robert, who was two years older than his nephew, was remembered fondly by Lou as his "first catcher." Robert was buried in a military cemetery in Tunisia.

In June of 1944, Brissie was sent as part of the 88th Infantry Division to assist the Allied forces in Northern Italy. He took with him a letter that his father had received from Connie Mack. The letter instructed Brissie's father to have his son write to Mack while he was in service. Brissie penned his first correspondence to Mack while bunkered in a foxhole in Italy. Mack immediately responded with an encouraging letter that referenced his hope that Brissie would someday be pitching for him in Philadelphia. It was the first of several letters exchanged between Mack and Brissie over the next couple of years.

On a frigid overcast morning of December 7, 1944, Brissie was riding in the back of a military transport truck as it moved slowly along a winding road in the Apennine Mountains, about 10 miles southwest of Bologna. Six other vehicles, each filled with infantrymen, were part of the convoy. The soldiers were returning from a rest station where they had enjoyed the rare opportunity for a shower.[3]

The 88th Division had been fighting in this area for more than a year, and they had suffered nearly 90 percent casualties with over 11,000 men killed, wounded or missing. Brissie, a corporal, was the infantry squad leader for G Company, 351st Infantry Regiment, 88th Infantry Division. Although Brissie was 6'4 ½" and weighed 205 pounds, his Army buddies called him "Slim."

The convoy of trucks came under attack from German artillery. Brissie, along with his fellow soldiers, leapt out of the trucks and ran for cover. The Germans launched a second artillery volley, and an explosion occurred within inches of Brissie. Ira Berkow, in *The Corporal Was a Pitcher*, describes in detail what happened to Brissie during the attack:

Within moments there was: this shell burst with a shriek, the noise shattering to the ear, the earth erupting as if it had been dynamited. Brissie was slammed to the ground by impact, his helmet knocked off, every button on his jacket sent flying. His clothes and boots were in tatters and in an instant his entire body felt as if it had just been struck with a jolt of electricity. Another howling shell exploded, and another. He couldn't move his leg—he could see through the ripped pants that it had been nearly shredded from the knee to the ankle—but he had to move out of the line of fire. His only thought was to not get hit again.

He dragged his body along the snow-covered ground to a nearby creek bed where he blacked out. He lay there, half of his body floating in the icy creek water, before being discovered by a corpsman who had been sent to the area to identify and collect the deceased. The shell that injured Brissie killed 11 American soldiers.

The corpsman noticed a slight movement by Brissie and quickly got him on a stretcher. He was placed across the hood of a Jeep and driven toward a medical unit. On the way, the Jeep was hit by a German mortar, and Brissie was thrown off into the snow. He fractured a vertebra and received additional shrapnel wounds in his right shoulder.[4]

Doctors quickly assessed Brissie's leg and told him amputation was his only option to stop the spread of a potentially fatal infection. He pleaded with the physicians not to amputate explaining that he was a baseball player and that he needed his leg. Brissie was told that he would likely die if they did not amputate, but his response was, "I'll take my chances."

Over the course of the next two years, Brissie endured 23 operations and 40 blood transfusions. He was aided by a pair of physicians who took a personal interest in his case and were willing to go beyond normal procedure in their efforts to reconstruct the corporal's shattered left leg.

He was one of the first soldiers in the Mediterranean Theatre to be given penicillin to help fight infection and was administered heavy doses of the newly discovered antibiotic every three hours for several months. He said that he was so filled with the drug, you could wipe a washcloth across his skin, and it would be yellow.

Throughout his recovery, he kept in touch with Mack who continued to hold out hope that Brissie would one day pitch for his team.

According to an interview with Bill Nowlin of the *Society for American Baseball Research*, Brissie said he received a letter from Mack three weeks after his injury. In the letter, Mack told Brissie that his duty now was to try and get well, and whenever he was ready to play, Mack would see he got the opportunity. He said the letter was a tremendous motivator for him during his long and difficult recovery.

Brissie's story brought the somber reality of war home to the citizens of Greenville and surrounding areas. Baseball took a back seat to the draft, food and gas rations and the everyday fears that came along with a massive world war being fought on two fronts.

————————

Joe Cambria's 1940 Greenville Spinners were vastly improved, posting a record of 77-72 and earning a fourth place finish in the Sally League. Pitching had been the nemesis for Cambria's previous Spinner squads, and in 1940, he bolstered the staff with one of his top Cuban prospects. Agapito Mayor, a 25-year-old native of Sagüa la Grande, Cuba, appeared in 25 games and finished 13-4 with a 2.37 ERA. The left-handed pitcher had a minor league career that spanned across seven seasons from 1940 to 1952 but never made it to the major leagues. Mayor, however, had a prolific 17-year career in Cuba where he won 250 games and was elected to the Cuban Baseball Hall of Fame.

After the 1940 season, Cambria and his questionable player contracting methods landed him squarely in the crosshairs of Major League Baseball Commissioner Kenesaw Mountain Landis. A former federal judge, Landis began serving as the commissioner in January of 1920 and was formally elected to the position a year later. He was charged to bring integrity back to the game after the notorious

Black Sox gambling scandal of 1919.

One of Landis' personal crusades was an attempt to limit the control of major league owners on minor league teams. Before the 1920s, the minor leagues operated independently from the major leagues. Branch Rickey developed the modern-day farm system in the 1930s, giving major league teams tight control of the development of their prospects.

Landis believed the farm system created a closed environment, which gave the owners the ability to conceal players and stifle their advancement opportunities. He wanted to promote free movement within the minor leagues and issued several rulings aimed at creating greater freedom for players to move from team to team.

Landis had heard for years of Cambria's suspect contracting methods, and he looked for ways to limit his influence. Sports Editor Scoop Latimer of *The Greenville News* visited Landis at his Chicago office in August of 1940 and asked the commissioner specifically about Cambria. Landis was coy in his response, but after the visit, Latimer correctly predicted that Cambria's days as a minor league owner were numbered:

> . . . *the tide was turning against the individual or major league syndicates owning a chain of minor league farm clubs. And that Cambria as one of these operators, on a small scale may be one reason for the costly, if not unfriendly gestures toward him.*

Shortly after Latimer's visit with Landis, the commissioner took direct aim at Cambria and issued a ruling stating that an individual who worked as a scout for a major league team could not also own a minor league team. At the time, Cambria scouted for the Washington Senators and spent considerable time in Cuba signing players for his friend and Senators' owner Calvin Griffith. He also owned three minor league teams.

Cambria enjoyed the Latin lifestyle; meanwhile, his minor league teams were struggling financially. Cambria reported that he lost $20,000 in 1940 on his three minor league holdings. Cambria's choice was clear. He made immediate plans to dispose of his ownership in his minor league teams to comply with the ruling.

Cambria sold his interest in the Spinners to his friend Clark Griffith. With Cambria no longer connected to the Spinners, Greenvillians unofficially changed the name of Meadowbrook/Cambria Park to Griffith Park.

The 1941 season opened with an exhibition game between the Senators and the defending American League champion Detroit Tigers. More than 4,000 fans filled Griffith-Meadowbrook Park on the afternoon of Wednesday, April 9. Among the spectators that day was Shoeless Joe Jackson.

The Tigers roster included three future Hall of Famers: Hank Greenberg, Charlie Gehringer and Hal Newhouser. Former Greenville Spinner Mickey Vernon, a favorite with local fans in 1938, returned to Meadowbrook in a Senators uniform. He received a standing ovation when he came to bat for the first time. The Senators defeated the Tigers 5-3 in a rain-shortened seven-inning exhibition. Within a year, both Greenberg and Gehringer were on active military duty. Newhouser attempted to join the service multiple times but was repeatedly turned down due to a damaged heart valve.

The 1941 Spinners disappointed their new owner with a 60-77 record and a seventh place finish in the South Atlantic League. Once the season ended, Griffith looked for a way to exit his investment in Greenville.

On December 7, 1941, the lives of all Americans changed with Japan's surprise attack on Pearl Harbor. The following day the U.S. Senate and House approved the President's request to declare a state of war on Japan. Three days later, Germany and Italy declared war against the United States.

Baseball Commissioner Landis knew that in times of war recreational activities were in question. He deferred a decision on whether to play baseball in 1942 to the President. On January 15, 1942, President Roosevelt wrote Landis a letter known as the famous "Green Light Letter." Roosevelt gave his blessing for the continuance of America's pastime when he wrote:

> *I honestly feel that it would be best for the country to keep baseball going. There will be fewer people unemployed, and everybody will work longer hours and harder than ever before. And that means that they ought to have a chance for recreation and for taking their minds off their work even more than before.*

Griffith had multiple reasons to discontinue his ownership of the Spinners. He wasn't making money, and the war was going to create a scarcity of talent. Also, Griffith already owned a Class B team in Charlotte. Instead of any of these readily available excuses, Griffith blamed a longtime Southern prohibition as the ultimate culprit for ridding himself of the Greenville franchise. He announced in February of 1942 that he intended to sell the Spinners, citing his inability to make a profit due to South Carolina blue laws, which prohibited Sunday baseball. Blue laws were a body of regulations designed to prohibit activities that would dishonor the Sabbath. In a letter to Scoop Latimer, Griffith wrote:

> *I came to this decision after exhausting every means to secure Sunday baseball for Greenville. I communicated with the Governor of South Carolina, the Mayor of Greenville and your Sheriff and one of your State senators. I was advised I should secure the opinion of the Greenville County Attorney which I did. It is his opinion that the law does not permit us to play Sunday baseball.*

Daily headlines in the local papers reminded Greenvillians of the terrors of war. Much of the ink in Scoop Latimer's daily sports column was devoted to excerpts from letters from servicemen with connections to Greenville. Food and gas were being rationed. School age children were taught what to do in the event of an air raid. Box scores and pennant races were less important, but baseball remained a needed diversion.

The hope of professional baseball continuing in Greenville in 1942 was doubtful after Griffith's divestiture, but a few weeks before the start of the Sally League season, a grassroots effort to field a team began to emerge. A group of 11 baseball-loving citizens ponied up enough cash to purchase the rights to the Spinners franchise. The group was led by realtor Lehman A. Mosley and local businessman Jimmy Gaston. Kenneth Cass served as treasurer, Jimmie Daniel acted as secretary and Gaston was the general manager. It was the kind of local community ownership of a minor-league team that put a smile on Commissioner Landis' face.

With both Joe Cambria and Calvin Griffith out of the picture, Greenville's baseball stadium would forever be known as Meadowbrook Park. The ownership of Meadowbrook Park was transferred to the city of Greenville and a five-year extension for free rent was given to the new Spinners owners.

The owners of the Spinners turned to local talent to help fill the roster as so many young baseball prospects were away in the military. Among them was Brandon Mills' star player Joe Anders, who played third base for a portion of the 1942 season before enlisting in the Army and serving in the Asiatic-Pacific Theater. Anders was one of the textile league's most highly regarded stars, and after the war, he played two additional seasons for the Spinners. At the time Anders left for military service, he was batting .326 and reportedly was on the verge of signing a contract with the New York Yankees. Later in life, Anders led several unsuccessful efforts to persuade Major League Baseball officials to reinstate his good friend and mentor Shoeless Joe Jackson.

The Spinners' 1942 season was filled with injuries, loss of players to the draft and declining attendance. Their manager, Eddie Phillips, a native of Buffalo, even threatened to resign midyear, telling his bosses, "Either I get some help or I'm going back to Buffalo." The Spinners finished with a 61-74 record and in a familiar spot near the bottom of the Sally League.

In early 1943, South Atlantic League officials curtailed baseball operations until after the war. Sagging attendance and a short supply of players were obstacles too big to overcome. It marked the second time in the Sally League's history that a world war brought a temporary end to its operations.

Meadowbrook Park was turned over to the city and run by the

Park and Tree Commission. While not as active as it would have been with a professional team, baseball was still played in the five-year-old stadium. Teams from the Negro leagues, textile leagues, high schools and military bases utilized Meadowbrook sporadically throughout the war years. Furman University began playing its home baseball games at Meadowbrook in 1943. Meadowbrook also hosted a variety of community events such as the annual dog show and political rallies during the war years.

Perhaps the most unusual event to be held at Meadowbrook during this era was a simulated air raid on May 18, 1943. The show was sponsored by the Civil Air Patrol and included a live demonstration of what it would look like for a village to be bombarded and destroyed with explosives and chemical weapons. A small village of seven wooden homes was constructed across the outfield of Meadowbrook. It was demolished in the simulation by 27 different explosions. In September of 1944, a similar event was held that included live demonstrations of flamethrowers, bazookas and machine guns. Both events drew capacity crowds.

Great Britain and the United States commemorated military victory in Europe on May 8, 1945. Across cities in the United States and Europe, celebrations were held in recognition of the defeat of the Nazi war machine. That evening, a few hundred White citizens of Greenville gathered in the grandstand at Meadowbrook Park to celebrate VE day. Two military officials from the Greenville Army Air Base delivered speeches, and a local minister offered a prayer of thanksgiving. A similar service for Blacks was held at the Phillis Wheatley Center. Churches throughout Greenville held thanksgiving prayer services on VE day.

The following morning, a large banner headline spread across the front page of *The Greenville News*—GUNS SILENCED IN EUROPE. The sports page headlined a rivalry baseball matchup between Greenville and Parker High at Meadowbrook Park. A crowd in excess of 1,000 people was expected for the 4 p.m. contest. Despite the fact that the war in the Pacific raged on, a sense of relief and normalcy was beginning to reappear in Greenville.

American baseball fans were uncertain how players who had served in the military would perform once they returned from the war. That question was answered with one swing of the bat by Detroit Tigers slugger Hank Greenberg.

Greenberg registered for the draft eight days after the Tigers lost Game 7 of the 1940 World Series. By May of the following year, he was on active duty. His salary as a professional baseball player at the time was $55,000 a year, and it decreased to $21 per week while in the military. When asked about the pay cut, Greenberg said, "I made up my mind to go when I was called. My country comes first."

Greenberg served 47 months in the Army Air Force, the longest tenure of any professional baseball player. He flew B-29 missions over the Himalayas in the China-Burma-India Theater. During his military service, he had played in only one exhibition baseball game.

The Tigers slugger rejoined the starting lineup on July 1, 1945, two weeks after his discharge from service. In his first three at-bats, he went hitless, but in his fourth attempt, he drove a line drive into the leftfield pavilion at Detroit's Briggs Stadium. The 47,729 fans in attendance were so excited, they littered the field with their hats. The home run blast by the former Army Air Force captain sent a message across the country that America's baseball stars were back. In the final 78 games of the '45 season, Greenberg batted .311, slugged 13 home runs and led the Tigers to the AL pennant.

Brissie was recovering from his injuries at the Finney General Hospital in Thomasville, Georgia, during the summer of 1945 when he received an invitation from Connie Mack to visit him again at Shibe Park in Philadelphia. Although he was still unable to walk without crutches, he was eager to meet with Mack and assure him he would return to baseball.

Sports columnist Red Smith, writing at the time for the *Philadelphia Record*, described Brissie's return visit to Shibe Park:

> *In the summer of 1945, Lou Brissie showed up in Shibe Park in Philadelphia, a great big, handsome kid in a soldier suit, swinging along on crutches.*
>
> *He'd been there before. In 1941, when he had just turned seventeen. His coach at Presbyterian College, Chick Galloway, brought him up to Connie Mack as a left-handed pitcher. On the advice of his father and Mack, the kid returned to school. He heard a lot of artillery before he got back to Philadelphia. Now he visited around with the ballplayers. When they asked questions about his pocketful of decorations he'd brought back, he shrugged and changed the subject to baseball. Seeing the helpless way his left leg hung and hearing him talk about getting rid of his crutches so he could start pitching again, it made you cry.*

Mack told the *Sporting News*, "I'll never forget how he looked. I didn't have the heart to tell him how pitiful it appeared. His right leg was broomstick thin. He didn't have the strength to throw. But he kept on trying, balancing himself on one crutch and throwing with his free arm . . . " When Brissie left after several days, Mack said,

"Few [of the players] thought they'd ever see Brissie again."

Brissie returned to Northington General Hospital in Tuscaloosa, Ala., to continue the process of reconstructing his wounded leg. He kept up his correspondence with Mack, and Mack continued to hold out hope of a baseball future for the wounded veteran. Between August 1945 and April 1946, Brissie had five more surgeries, and the surgeon was able to remove additional shrapnel from his leg that others had believed to be unreachable.

He wrote to Scoop Latimer during his convalescence and said, "I'll play again, but it will be quite a while. Don't worry, I want to play ball. If God lets me walk again, I'll play too. That's my ambition. I'll be O.K. in time." Latimer included Brissie's military address and encouraged his readers to send letters of encouragement.

In April 1946, Corporal Brissie received a medical discharge from the Army and returned home to Ware Shoals. He received two Purple Hearts and a Bronze Star for his distinguished military service.

Slowly, Brissie began to walk and throw a baseball. He returned to the mound in the spring, pitching for the Riegel Textile team in a game against Ninety Six. He wore a cumbersome steel brace on his left leg that had been built for him by doctors at Greenville's Shriners Hospital. He threw a complete game but developed a sore arm, most likely caused by his stiff-legged pitching delivery.

By July, Brissie had been throwing regularly in textile games, and he wrote to Mack telling him he was ready to visit him again. This time, his father traveled with him to Philadelphia, and Lou was given the chance to throw batting practice to the A's at Shibe Park. Under the watchful eye of Mack, Brissie threw reasonably well, although his leg throbbed with pain, a feeling that would be with him for the rest of his life.

Two months after their visit to Philadelphia, Lou's father died from an abscess to his liver. He was 44. Brissie told Ira Berkow in *The Corporal Was a Pitcher*, "My dad was my hero. I knew I could never get over this loss. And, at that moment when he died, I really didn't know if I wanted to keep trying to be a pitcher, if I had the heart for it anymore, now that the person who had been my biggest supporter in baseball, and in everything else, was gone. But I knew that I had to, that I couldn't let him down."

The following February, Brissie received a letter inviting him to the Athletics spring training in West Palm Beach, Fla. He had spent the winter months working out in an effort to rebuild the strength he had lost during his recovery. Mack was surprised at Brissie's improved physical appearance as well as the velocity of his pitches.

Taking care of his wounded leg was a lengthy ordeal for Brissie. Before each game, he had to carefully treat and wrap it and attach a magnesium plate around his shin for added protection. After each pitching performance, he had to spend long hours in a whirlpool or bathtub to aid his recovery.

At the end of spring training, Mack assigned Brissie to Savannah in the Sally League for the '47 season. Here Brissie was promised regular work, which was necessary to develop the endurance needed for a starting pitcher. Typically, pitchers ran on their days off to stay in shape, but due to the problems with Brissie's leg, running was not an option. He needed to pitch regularly to stay in top form.

Brissie quickly became a fan favorite in Savannah and drew standing room only crowds at home and on the road. Savannah drew more than 200,000 fans that season, due in large part to Brissie's popularity. He returned to Greenville to pitch against the Spinners at Meadowbrook Park on June 12 and threw an impressive complete game in front of 3,500 fans, giving up only five hits and striking out 13 in the 5-4 Savannah victory.

As he walked off the mound after recording the final out, Brissie tipped his hat in response to the resounding applause from the appreciative crowd. The cheers emanating from Meadowbrook that night were in response not only to a stellar pitching performance, but also the path that Brissie had traveled. The war was over. Their hometown hero had triumphantly returned.

Brissie finished the regular season with a 23-5 record, a league-leading 278 strikeouts and a stellar 1.91 ERA. He won three postseason games and led Savannah to the Sally League championship. He was the league's only unanimous All-Star selection.

Famed American sports writer, Red Smith said of Brissie's performance in Savannah, "If there ever was a man with two sound legs who made a more remarkable record in his first year in any league, the name doesn't come to mind."

At the close of the Savannah Indians season, Brissie got the call from Connie Mack to join the Athletics for their final series against the New York Yankees. On September 28, 1947, the 23-year-old was given his first major league start. The Yankees had already clinched the American League pennant and were scheduled to face the Brooklyn Dodgers in the World Series.

It was a chilly Sunday afternoon in New York, and it was "Old Timers Day" at Yankee Stadium. The 25,085 fans in attendance were treated to a two-inning exhibition game between former American League greats and ex-Yankee stars. Babe Ruth was on hand, although due to his ongoing battle with throat cancer, he did not play. The gate receipts from the game were donated to the Babe Ruth Foundation for youth baseball.

The Yankees starting lineup included three future Hall of Famers: center fielder Joe DiMaggio, shortstop Phil Rizzuto and 21-year-old rookie catcher Yogi Berra. Brissie's batterymate was former Greenville Spinner and native Cuban Mike Guerra, who was in his first season catching for the A's.

Brissie's first pitch from the mound at Yankee Stadium sailed wildly over Guerra's outstretched mitt and rolled to the back stop, drawing a snicker from the Yankee dugout. He settled down and pitched competitively, giving up five runs off of nine hits in seven innings. He struck out five, walked four and threw two wild pitches. The Yankees defeated the A's 5-3, and Brissie was credited with the loss.

The disappointment over his failed first big league appearance motivated Brissie during the off season. He felt he'd let Mack down, and he wanted desperately to redeem himself.

"I was always grateful to Mr. Mack because he didn't look at my disabilities. He looked at my abilities," Brissie said.

When he returned to spring training in 1948, he was stronger and more prepared. He made the big-league squad and was given the opportunity to pitch the second game of an opening day doubleheader against the Boston Red Sox. In the sixth inning, Brissie had a 3-2 count on Boston's star Ted Williams when Williams lined a shot back up the middle that struck Brissie's injured left leg. The account of the game in the *Boston Globe* described the scene at Fenway Park:

The entire ballpark to a man, moaned audibly, and Williams kicked the first base bag in disgust as Brissie writhed on the ground behind the pitcher's mound in obvious real pain. A Red Sox run scored on Williams' blow, the ball caroming crazily to first sacker Ferris Fain, but the fans' joy at

*the marker was subdued over what appeared a possible end
to a game lad's diamond future.*

As players rushed to the mound, Brissie looked up and jokingly asked Williams why he didn't pull the ball to right field. Brissie
stayed in the game and did not render another hit. Williams led off
the top of the ninth inning, and this time Brissie got the best of him,
striking him out on his way to helping the A's to a 4-2 win. He gave
up only four hits and struck out seven in a complete game as he
secured his first major league victory. After the game, several thousand Red Sox fans hung around the Athletics dugout hoping to get a
glimpse of the decorated veteran turned pitcher who had just defeated their beloved Red Sox.

Over the next two seasons, Brissie established himself as a capable
major league pitcher going 14-10 and 16-11 in 1948 and '49, respectively. In 1949, he was selected to the AL All-Star Game, where he
pitched three innings in the game played at Brooklyn's Ebbets Field.
His performance fell off the following season as he went 7-19 and
was relegated to mostly bullpen duty in 1951. Midway through the
'51 season, the A's were in need of hitting and traded Brissie to the
Cleveland Indians as part of a three-team, seven-player trade involving the A's, Indians and Chicago White Sox.

Brissie finished the 1951 season going 4-3 for the pennant-con-
tending Indians, who finished second in the AL behind the Yankees.
In 1952, he was used primarily as a reliever and finished with a 3-2
record and 3.48 ERA.

Typically, during the '52 season, Brissie was limited to less than
three innings of pitching, but on July 1, he was brought into a tie
game in the ninth inning against the St. Louis Browns. About the

same time, the Browns' 46-year-old Satchel Paige also entered the game. Brissie and Paige battled pitch for pitch over the next nine innings with neither allowing a run. In the top of the 19th, Brissie surrendered a run on a walk followed by a sacrifice bunt and a single. The Indians rallied in the bottom of the 19th with two runs to end the marathon event and give Brissie the victory.[5]

Lou Brissie, a native of Ware Shoals, S.C., pitched for the Philadelphia Athletics and Cleveland Indians after being severely wounded in Italy during World War II.
(Courtesy of the National Baseball Hall of Fame Library)

The 1953 season was Brissie's most disappointing as a professional. He fell from grace with Indians General Manager Hank Greenberg and, as a result, was used sparingly. He asked Manager Al Rosen to give him more innings so he could regain his form, but Rosen ignored his request. He vowed 1954 would be a better year, but the Indians had other plans for the 28-year-old.

Brissie was at his home in Greenville in February of 1954 when a reporter from The Associated Press called him to ask how he felt about his contract being sold to the Triple A Indianapolis Indians. It was the first Brissie had heard of the transaction.

Brissie tried unsuccessfully to convince Greenberg to give him another chance with the big league club. Rather than accept the demotion, Brissie, a few months shy of turning 30, retired from baseball. He accumulated a major league record of 44-48 with a 4.07 ERA across seven seasons.[6]

While his stats will never match those of baseball's greatest pitchers, Brissie's courage and determination earned him the respect and admiration of all he encountered. His teammate with the Indians and future Hall of Famer Bob Feller said, "Lou Brissie would have been a Hall of Fame pitcher, if it hadn't been for World War II."

Three weeks after his retirement, Brissie accepted a job as the commissioner of the American Legion Junior Baseball Program and later worked as a scout for the Dodgers and Braves. Eventually he left baseball for a career in employee relations for private companies and later for a South Carolina state employee training agency.

President Dwight Eisenhower selected Brissie to serve on the first President's Physical Fitness Council. He received countless awards in recognition of his bravery and sportsmanship over the years. He gave dozens of inspirational talks at civic clubs, churches and youth organizations, always telling his story with humility and thankfulness. Throughout his life, he frequented veterans' hospitals offering encouragement and counsel to wounded servicemen.

Brissie lost his first wife Dot to cancer in 1967; eight years later, he married Diana Ingate Smith, and the two were happily married until Lou's death on November 25, 2013. "Lou was even more proud of his military service than he was of his baseball accomplishments," Diana Brissie said. "That is why he enjoyed visiting the VA and giving hope and inspiration to those who thought that their lives may be ending."

Rob Brissie is one of Lou's nine grandchildren. He remembers his grandfather as the most humble man he'd ever met and someone who just didn't talk about himself and all his accomplishments. Rob recalled that even in the later years of his grandfather's life, pieces of shrapnel would continue to emerge from his damaged left leg.

Lou Brissie stands between two Marines he met in a restaurant in Augusta, Ga.
(Courtesy of Lamar Garrard)

Lamar Garrard, a baseball historian and close friend of Brissie, said, "Lou was like a big brother to me." Garrard tells a favorite story about his friend that highlights Brissie's true character. "We were having breakfast at a Chick-fil-A one morning, when all of a sudden, without a spoken word, Lou gets up, grabs his two crutches and ambles over to a table where two Marine recruits were sitting," Garrard said. "Lou comes back to our table, and I ask him, 'Did you tell them who you were?' Of course, he did not. I asked why not, and he replied that it was not necessary. He simply handed them a little note he carried along thanking them for their service. That's just how Lou was. No pretense of being a national hero."

Garrard added that he walked over to the table and explained to the recruits about Lou's background. He said they were deeply impressed and asked to have their picture taken with Brissie. The photo was featured in a newsletter from the Philadelphia Athletics Historical Society.

In the 1800s, Danish philosopher Søren Kierkegaard wrote, "Hope is the passion for the possible." For many of the GIs who were there with Brissie throughout his lengthy stints in various military hospitals, the possible was not visible, but for Brissie, the possible was clear—it was a future in baseball. Driven by the promising letters from Connie Mack and a resilience that was common among those of the "Greatest Generation," Brissie refused to let go of his dream of becoming a major league ballplayer.

The United States Navy Memorial Interview Archive recorded a series of interviews with Brissie prior to his death. Brissie summarized for them the importance of holding onto his hope for a future in baseball.

"Coming back was difficult, but I had baseball," Brissie said. "Mr. Mack had told me that when I was ready, he'd give me the opportunity. So, I had a golden opportunity of something out there in the distance to look forward to and that made a lot of difference. It made a lot of difference."[7]

7
Jimmy

Any clean, wholesome sport is Jimmy Gaston's dessert after a hard day's work.

—Scoop Latimer

Jimmy Gaston, president and general manager of the Greenville Spinners, had retired for the evening to his hotel room in downtown Cleveland. Earlier in the day, he had watched the Cleveland Indians defeat the Boston Braves 2-0 in Game 3 of the 1948 World Series. Attending the World Series was one of Gaston's favorite perks of being a minor league baseball executive.

Gaston provided much of the leadership behind a group of local citizens, incorporated as Greenville Baseball, Inc., that acquired the Spinners franchise from Washington Senators owner Calvin Griffith in 1942. Gaston operated a local finance and insurance company but spent much of his time shouldering the operational responsibilities of the local baseball team.

Professional baseball returned to Meadowbrook Park in 1946, and the Spinners were now an affiliate of the Brooklyn Dodgers. They were enjoying the fruits of the post-war recovery as attendance exceeded 120,000 in 1947 and 1948. Gaston and his fellow investors anticipated continued success in 1949.

Around midnight, Gaston was awakened by a long-distance phone call. The voice on the other end of the line informed him of some devastating news. Meadowbrook Park was in flames.

Fire was the ultimate enemy of ballparks like Meadowbrook.[1] The main grandstand was constructed primarily of wood that had aged and dried over the park's 10-year life. It served as an abundant source of kindling susceptible to quick ignition.

On the evening of October 7, 1948, two Greenville patrolmen noticed a small fire inside Meadowbrook's right field fence. By the time they called it in, the fire had spread to the main grandstand, and by 11 p.m., it was burning out of control. Massive flames engulfed the wooden structure, reaching upward of 40-50 feet into the air. The heat emanating from the blaze pushed observers back several hundred yards. Strong winds blew that evening, fanning the fire with a fresh supply of oxygen and limiting firefighters' ability to control the spread. Firemen fought the extremely hot fire for over four hours, but while Meadowbrook was burning, two additional fire alarms sounded within the city, drawing crews and trucks away from the ballpark.

On the evening of October 7, 1948, Meadowbrook Park caught fire, and the main grandstand was destroyed.
(Courtesy of Firefighting in Greenville 1840-1990 by William D. Browning Jr.)

A front-page photo of the burnt-out ballpark appeared in the *Greenville Piedmont* the day after the fire. The photo caption read:

> *Meadowbrook Park grandstand familiar to thousands of Greenville Spinner baseball fans, was only debris today ... following a Thursday night fire which started along the rightfield fence and spread rapidly through the frame stands, almost completely demolishing them. In the picture above . . . one of the beams which supported the roof curves downward through the center of the camera's view, misshapen by the heat. City officials estimated the damages at approximately $50,000, only partly covered by insurance, although no accurate estimate could be made pending the return to the city of James B. Gaston, President of Greenville Baseball Inc., lessee of the park, who is attending the World Series.*

Gaston was helpless to do anything from Cleveland other than hope and pray that the ballpark would not be a total loss. Over the past two years, the Spinners helped fund significant enhancements to Meadowbrook, including new box seats and improved lighting. When Gaston made it back to Greenville, he learned the disheartening details of the fire's devastation.

The entire wooden grandstand and most of the new light poles and transformers had been destroyed. The concrete foundation and dugouts were intact, but the structure itself would need to be totally rebuilt. The outfield bleachers that were reserved for White spectators had been removed before the fire and were being used for football games at Sirrine Stadium while the bleachers reserved for Black patrons along the left field line were unharmed. All the Spinners' baseball equipment was incinerated.

The city maintained approximately $10,000 of insurance on the structure, well below the estimated cost of repairs. The Spinners' insurance coverage on their baseball equipment was also inadequate to cover replacement.

Greenville Baseball, Inc. had no cash reserves as it operated on a tight budget. Any meager profits were distributed annually to its shareholders. Convincing city council to fund a rebuild of the ballpark presented a unique set of political and financial challenges. For professional baseball to return in Greenville in the spring of 1949, a Herculean effort and a minor miracle would have to take place—just the kind of challenge Jimmy Gaston thrived upon.

———————

James Bostwick "Jimmy" Gaston Jr. was born in Gainesville, Ga., in 1893. His father was a federal judge and one of Georgia's most influential political leaders. According to Jimmy Gaston's grandson, George Gaston, Jimmy spent much of his life fighting to emerge from the large shadow cast by his father's many accomplishments.

Gaston attended Staunton (Va.) Military School and later the University of Georgia. He played baseball at both schools and developed a lifelong love for the game. He was an outgoing entrepreneur who moved from one deal to the next, never afraid to "bet it all" on his latest can't-miss idea. His grandson said he preferred to spend other people's money as opposed to his own.

Gaston was short in stature but established a presence wherever he went. A writer who observed him gathered with fellow Sally League officials in a meeting in Asheville, N.C., described Gaston as "a small debonair man with a grey, pencil thin mustache and a

Windsor-knotted tie" and said he was "in sharp contrast to the rest."

He was loquacious and bold, never afraid to ask for a favor. Through the Spinners' affiliation with the Brooklyn Dodgers, Gaston became acquainted with legendary baseball pioneer and Dodgers GM, Branch Rickey. According to his grandson, Gaston once asked Rickey for an automobile. Gaston's son had returned home from service in World War II, and his father wanted to get him a car to use when he finished school at Newberry College.

Cars were scarce in Greenville after the war, but Gaston figured they would be more readily available in New York, so he called Rickey and told him of his desire to gift a car to his son. A few days later, Rickey's brother Frank personally delivered a new Studebaker Commodore to Greenville for Gaston to give to his son. The Commodore would have been considered a luxury vehicle in the day and not one people would generally expect a college student to own. According to George Gaston, his father enjoyed the immediate status the vehicle afforded him on Newberry's campus.

Gaston would have to use all his persuasive skills and political savvy to orchestrate the rebuilding of Meadowbrook in less than five months. He held nothing back as he began to resurrect Meadowbrook from its ashes.

A debate arose among city officials about possibly relocating the stadium to a site less prone to flooding. This discussion did nothing but cause the rebuilding efforts to lose precious time. A formal proposal emerged to have the city rebuild the stadium out of concrete and steel, to limit future risk of fire. The estimated cost of such a structure was over $100,000. Council members, who were already skeptical about saving the ballpark, shot down that idea with the speed of a Bob Feller fastball.

One Greenvillian suggested local citizens donate money to reconstruct the park and have it become a memorial to New York Yankee great Babe Ruth who had died two months before fire destroyed Meadowbrook. That idea also fizzled on the drawing board.

Meanwhile, Gaston submitted his own proposal, requesting the city rebuild the park and then lease it back to Greenville Baseball, Inc. with lease payments ultimately funding the reconstruction costs. He suggested a rent of $5,000 per year for 10 years. The city countered with a proposal to not only have the Greenville Baseball, Inc. pay the annual rent of $5,000, but also contribute a five-cent tax on every admission. Based on prior year attendance, this would add another $5,000 per year to the city's coffers.

Gaston vehemently opposed the proposal, calling the additional admission tax absurd. He went public with his opposition in *The Greenville News* where he stated that if the city insisted on the tax, he would have to tell Sally League officials and the Brooklyn Dodgers that the Spinners would be forced to move to another city.

On December 8, 1948, city council backed off the admissions tax and agreed to rebuild the grandstand at Meadowbrook and enter a 10-year lease with Greenville Baseball, Inc. at rent not to exceed $5,000 per year. The costs to rebuild were to be covered by the city's operating fund. At the end of the lease, ownership of the ballpark and its lighting system would revert to the city. Kenneth Cass, former business manager of the Spinners and baseball enthusiast, was now serving as mayor of Greenville, and he most likely wielded some influence on his fellow city leaders in helping convince them to rebuild the park under mutually agreeable financial terms.

As construction got underway, Gaston was on the job site daily. *The Greenville News* reported that Gaston fell over scaffolding on the site while he was giving specific direction to electricians. He injured his shoulder and spent the next day at home recovering. The following day, he returned to the park attending to the details of his reclamation project.

Remarkably, Meadowbrook Park was back open for business on Saturday, April 9, 1949, as the Spinners hosted the Asheville Tourists in an exhibition game. Nobody deserved more credit for the park's rebirth than "little Jimmy Gaston." The Spinners lost their opener 13-12 but looked forward to a scheduled exhibition game against the Brooklyn Dodgers the following Monday afternoon.

The game with the Dodgers was to be Gaston's triumphant celebration of the reopening of the ballpark, but Mother Nature had a different plan. Rain forced the cancellation of the game that would have brought future Hall of Famers Jackie Robinson, Pee Wee Reese, Roy Campanella and Duke Snider to Meadowbrook.

Two years earlier, Robinson became the first Black to play for a major league team, giving hope to millions of Black Americans across the country. Marion Butler lived in a Black neighborhood adjacent to Meadowbrook and was 6 years old at the time of Robinson's scheduled appearance in Greenville.

"My mama was a big baseball fan, and of course Jackie Robinson was our hero. My mama took me out of school and took me to the game, and we stood in the rain for hours waiting for Jackie and the Dodgers to play baseball," Butler recalled. "Jackie came out of the dugout for just a short time, but then he went back inside. I remember crying like a baby when the game got cancelled."

The Dodgers spent the night in Greenville aboard their train at the Southern Railway Station and departed the next day for Charlotte to play an exhibition against the Washington Senators.

The 1949 Spinners roster included Tommy Lasorda, a 22-year-old left-handed pitcher from Norristown, Pa. The future Los Angeles Dodgers manager and baseball Hall of Famer went 7-7 with a 2.93 ERA in 178 innings, but more importantly, he met his wife while pitching in Greenville. According to the account in *Tommy Lasorda, My Way*:

> *... one night he saw a young woman in the stands and asked her friend if they would go eat after the game. As soon as the last out was made, Tommy showered and then met the ladies in the parking lot and introduced himself. He asked Joan Miller for her number, but her mother interceded. "I told her mother that Jo would make me a 20-game winner," Tommy recalls ... The two went to lunch at a local kitchenette. Tommy was in love. "I looked at her and told her that she may think I was crazy, but that I was going to marry her ... Nobody thought it would work," said Tommy. "An Italian Catholic from the north and a Southern Baptist?" But Tommy was nothing if not determined.*

Lasorda shared with Dan Foster of *The Greenville News* his most vivid memory of his playing days in Greenville. On a hot summer day when he was not scheduled to pitch, Lasorda went to Paris Mountain State Park for an afternoon of swimming and sunbathing. He fell asleep and suffered a severe case of sunburn. When he got to the park that evening, he was told he was going to pitch. "So, I put on a sweatshirt and those flannels, and pitched," Lasorda said. "I nearly died."

Baseball Hall of Famer Tommy Lasorda (front row, far right) pitched for
the 1949 Greenville Spinners. As manager of the Los Angeles Dodgers,
Lasorda won two World Series championships.
(Courtesy of Dean Kennet)

Lasorda returned many times to Greenville where he visited with
relatives and friends and helped with fundraising for a local Catholic
high school. In 2014, after being named to the Greenville Baseball
Hall of Fame, Lasorda spoke to Bob Castello of *The Greenville News*
about his time in Greenville: "I really enjoyed playing there. The fans
really liked the baseball players. It was a nice city."

A legendary story that was passed along by Gaston to his son
claimed that Lasorda approached Gaston in 1949 to explain that he
was scheduled to pitch on the day he planned to get married. Lasorda requested a day off, but Gaston refused. As the story goes, Gaston
told Lasorda to tell his future wife that Gaston would pay for a wedding reception at the Poinsett Hotel to make it up to her. Gaston's

grandson said it is possible the story is true but not likely that his grandfather would have funded such an elaborate affair entirely out of his own pocket. Lasorda died in January of 2021. He and his wife Joan were married for 70 years.

The 1949 Greenville Spinners finished 82-72 and third in the Sally League, but attendance dropped 30 percent, and Gaston and his fellow investors became concerned over their diminishing financial returns. On top of the poor financial year, the worst flood in a quarter of a century hit Greenville while Gaston was away attending the '49 World Series. Six inches of rain fell during a 24-hour period, and surging waters from the Reedy River left Meadowbrook Park and surrounding areas submerged. Gaston had left his new 1949 Ford convertible parked under the grandstand at Meadowbrook; the flood waters covered it, marking the second year in a row disaster struck Meadowbrook while he was attending the World Series.

As the unofficial spokesperson for the Spinners, Gaston was a frequent visitor to Scoop Latimer's "green and gold room" where he was typically boasting about the potential of his Spinners team. In 1946, he proclaimed to Latimer that the Spinners were the best Greenville team since Manager Frank Walker's 1926 Sally League championship team. He boldly predicted his team would win the pennant, but in the final standings, Greenville was in third place behind the Columbus Cardinals and Columbia Reds.

Gaston saw a 1947 wire photo of Joe DiMaggio standing beside a charter plane used by the Yankees and boasted to Latimer that he was negotiating with an airline company to fly the Spinners to their games in Jacksonville. There is no way to know if this promise ever materialized, but it would have been very unlikely given the ongoing financial struggles encountered by the Spinners.

Jimmy Gaston (left) sits in the stands at Meadowbrook Park
with Shoeless Joe Jackson.
(Courtesy of Ballparkbiz.com)

Gaston was the ultimate sportsman. Scoop Latimer said of him, "Any clean wholesome sport is Jimmy Gaston's dessert after a hard day's work." He refereed amateur boxing events, supported youth sports in the area and considered himself an "unofficial" baseball scout, as he was constantly sending word up to his major league contacts about area prospects. Regardless of whether Gaston had any official baseball scouting roles, he often spoke proudly of one of his most famous baseball discoveries.

One morning Gaston stopped by the post office in Greenville where he recognized the young girl working behind the counter. He had seen her attending baseball games at Meadowbrook with her father. She introduced herself as Elizabeth Mahon, and the two engaged in conversation about baseball. Gaston learned that she was also playing softball for the Mills Mill girls team, which had played at Meadowbrook earlier that year.

Gaston learned that Mahon was one of the stars of her team and a very gifted athlete, which prompted him to reach out to Jimmy Hamilton, a scout with the Chicago Cubs and friend of Cubs owner Philip Wrigley. It was Wrigley who established the All-American Girls Professional Baseball League (AAGPBL) in 1943 to help fill a void created by the absence of so many baseball-playing males who were serving in the military. Originally, the league played a modified version of fast-pitch softball, but in 1948, pitchers switched to an overhand delivery, and the game began to closely resemble baseball.

Gaston returned to the post office with an offer for the young female baseball star. In an interview with Jim Sargent in 2008, Mahon recalled the encounter with Gaston, saying one day Gaston asked her, "Lib, how would you like to go up north and play ball for money?"[2]

Within days of Gaston's offer, Mahon and her teammate and friend Viola Thompson were on a train headed to spring training in Peru, Ind., with hopes of being selected for a spot on the roster of one of the AAGPBL teams. Mahon was assigned to the Minneapolis Millerettes and spent only three weeks with them before she was sent to the Kenosha (Wis.) Comets. She was an infielder in the AAGPBL from 1944 to 1952 and had her best season in 1945 when she led the league with 79 RBIs. She was selected to the league's All-Star team in 1946 and '49. Mahon died in 2001 at age 82 and was inducted posthumously into the South Carolina Athletic Hall of Fame.

Mahon's friend Viola Thompson pitched four years in the AAGPBL with three different teams, including the 1944 league champion Memphis Chicks. The switch to overhand throwing in 1948 forced her out of the AAGPBL, and she joined the National Girls Baseball League of Chicago where she played until 1952.

Thompson served as an adviser to filmmaker Penny Marshall for the making of the 1992 sports comedy *A League of Their Own* starring Geena Davis, Tom Hanks and Madonna, which depicted life in the AAGPBL. Actual clips of Thompson's playing days appear during the credits at the end of the movie. Thompson was inducted into the South Carolina Athletic Hall of Fame in 1996 and died in 2017, two days before her 96th birthday.

———————

Greenville drew more than 100,000 fans for three consecutive years (1947-1949) and contended for the league championship in both '48 and '49. During that three-year period, the Spinners rosters included 11 players who played in the major leagues. None was more colorful than Everett Lamar Bridges, a short, stocky 21-year-old shortstop who batted in the lead off position for the '48 team.

Bridges became known as "Rocky" while playing in Greenville. He credited Meadowbrook's public address announcer with giving him the name: "He thought Lamar sounded lousy and started calling me Rocky. For quite a while I thought it was because of my build. Then I realized it fit my game."[3]

Bridges appeared in all 154 of the Spinners games in '48 and led the Sally League with a remarkable 626 plate appearances. He broke into the major leagues in 1951 with the Brooklyn Dodgers where he backed up Jackie Robinson and Pee Wee Reese. He spent 11 seasons as a utility infielder with the seven different major league teams.

He was known for a sharp self-deprecating sense of humor and was rarely photographed without a large chaw of tobacco in his cheek. In 1964, *Sports Illustrated* referred to Bridges as "one of the best stand-up comics in the history of baseball."

He joked about his playing career in which he held a lifetime average of .247, saying, "I am the only man in the history of the game who began his career in a slump and stayed in it." He was far better than he gave himself credit for and managed to earn a spot on the 1958 American League All-Star team. Regarding that experience, he quipped, "I never got in the game, but I sat on the bench with Mickey Mantle, Ted Williams, and Yogi Berra. I gave 'em instruction on how to sit."[4]

After his playing days ended, Bridges spent seven seasons as a big-league coach with the Angels and Giants and 21 years as a minor league manager. He closed his career as a roving instructor for the Pittsburgh Pirates.

After Bridges passed away in 2015, longtime Pirates manager Jim Leyland said, "He is one of those guys who had a reputation more for being a character than his baseball knowledge. But he knew the game. He was sharp as a tack. When I asked him about a player, I could go to the bank with his answer. If he said a guy couldn't play, he couldn't. If he said a guy could play, he could. There was no debate."[5]

Attendance dropped 50 percent for the Spinners in 1950 during a 68-85 season and a sixth place finish in the Sally League. Fans attending games at Meadowbrook complained to police about increasing incidents of disorderly conduct, including cursing and pestering of spectators. On June 9, the personal belongings of the Savannah Indians players and coaches, including $234 in cash, were stolen from their locker room at Meadowbrook.

Jimmy Gaston was unsuccessful in repeated attempts to get local officials to relax blue laws that would allow the Spinners to play

Sunday games. Adding to the team's challenges was the fact that the reinstatement of the military draft for the Korean War had depleted the pool of available players for minor league teams like Greenville. All these issues, along with declining financial profits, led Gaston and his fellow investors to put the Spinners up for sale after the 1950 season.

In the midst of its financial difficulties, the Class A South Atlantic League booted Greenville out and replaced them with a team from Montgomery, Ala., citing Greenville's inability to post a required $5,000 bond. Gaston immediately began discussions with the Class B Tri-State League as a possible landing spot for the Spinners in the '51 season.

After meeting with Sally League officials in Macon, Ga., Gaston told Scoop Latimer: "I went to the meeting with a $5,000 check [and was] prepared to post it and I also said we could guarantee $15,000 in the bank to resume operations." Apparently, Sally League officials were not convinced by the fast-talking Greenville businessman who told Latimer, "I've been voted out of the league."

Gaston began to sell off existing player contracts and told Latimer the proceeds were being used to pay off "overhanging debts" of the team, further evidence of the team's troubled financial situation. Gaston refused to let professional baseball die in Greenville. He secured admission to the Tri-State League for the 1951 season and made a desperate trip to Florida for spring training to sign as many players as possible, all the while courting investors to purchase the stock of the team.

Only 17 days before the opening of the season, Gaston announced the details of the sale of the Spinners franchise to three local businessmen, Pete Bybee, B. Jack Foster and W.W. (Bill) Jones. Bybee was one of the original stockholders in Greenville Baseball, Inc. and was joint owner of the Sanitary Café. Jones was head of the Peoples Guardian Life Insurance Company, and Foster owned a local laundry business. Within a few weeks, both Jones and Bybee sold their ownership stakes to Foster, leaving Foster as the sole owner of the team.

Gaston was retained as the Spinners' general manager and vice president, and he continued to work frantically to ensure that the team was operational for the upcoming season. He was handicapped by the lack of a working agreement with a major league team as he scoured the country trying to find capable players willing to play for Greenville.

Eventually, Gaston assembled a 25-player roster in time for the opening game at Greenwood on April 16. The hurried assembly of the team translated into poor performance on the field as the Spinners lost their first 12 games and finished 38-98, last among the eight teams in the Tri-State League. Local fans showed their disapproval at the box office as the team drew only 37,564 fans, an average of 552 per home game.

After the Spinners lost their first 10 games, Gaston announced his resignation as general manager, and Foster assumed control of the team. Foster said he had put a significant amount of money in the team and that complete control of the team would enable him to run it the best he could "in the best interest of the team and the fans." Later in the year, Foster added Bob Hunter, owner of a local tire business, as a partner in his baseball venture.

Typical of the disastrous 1951 Spinners season were the events of the evening of August 2. The Spinners had scheduled a "Booster Night" and provided free admission to the game, which was washed out by a violent thunderstorm in the second inning. Scoop Latimer described the scene at Meadowbrook as floodwaters overtook the ballpark:

Swirling muddy water, forming a lake from streams surging down the meadow and Mayberry Street, inundated the playing field and began flowing into sections of the grandstand. Hundreds, growing apprehensive, shed their shoes and stockings and began to wade to cars.

Latimer went on to say in his account that "the generous owners Foster and Hunter couldn't even give the fans a game free, meaning just about everything bad had broken for the Spinner management this season." Foster and Hunter reported a financial loss of $44,000 in their first year but said they were willing to try their hand at baseball for an additional season.

The new owners attempted a series of promotions in 1952 improve attendance including an appearance by baseball comedian Max Patkin. It was the first of 10 appearances at Meadowbrook Park by Patkin who later became known as the "Clown Prince of Baseball." At the height of his popularity in 1988, Patkin appeared as himself alongside Kevin Costner in the popular baseball movie *Bull Durham*.

Despite the various promotions, attendance improved only slightly as the Spinners finished 63-76 and sixth in the Tri-State League. As expected, Foster and Hunter put the team up for sale at the end of the season. The assets of the club consisted of 23 player contracts, two sets of uniforms, baseball equipment, a team bus and office equipment. Liabilities were not disclosed but were speculated to be significant.

No buyers could be found, and the owners folded their baseball operations in early 1953, leaving Greenville without professional baseball once again. Hunter and Foster maintained the lease on Meadowbrook and allowed it to be used throughout 1953 for a variety of events including college and high school baseball games as well as textile and Negro league contests.

In 1954, Hobart Ford, a dentist from Newport, Tenn., fronted the necessary funds to re-establish the Spinners' baseball operations. Ford had been a part owner of the Charlotte Hornets, Knoxville Smokies and Morristown Red Sox and was looking to expand his minor league operations to Greenville. Interestingly, Ford fielded a team in Morristown in 1953 that included 16 Cuban players, compliments of Meadowbrook Park's founding father, Joseph Cambria.

The 1954 Spinners included a handful of local players, including recent Clemson graduate Dick Hendley, who served as the team's player-manager for a portion of the season. Attendance improved significantly despite the team's losing record, but by midseason, the leadership of the Tri-State League temporarily took over ownership of the Spinners citing poor management and a backlog of unpaid debts, thus leaving Greenville once again on the brink of losing professional baseball.

This time, it was Mayor Kenneth Cass who spearheaded a citizen-led drive to keep the Spinners alive. Cass and a group of local businessmen formed a stock corporation under the name of Greenville Baseball, Inc. and sold shares to the public. More than 400 citizens purchased stock, giving the Spinners franchise the capital it needed for the 1955 season.

Textile League legend Earl Wooten served as the 1955 Spinners player-manager, and the quality of talent on the team got a boost from a one-year affiliation with the Milwaukee Braves. Playing in the Tri-State League, the Spinners finished second with a 60-55 record and won the first half of a split season. They were swept in a three-game playoff against Spartanburg, winners of the second half, which decided the official league champion. At the end of the season, the fledging Tri-State League dissolved, and Spinners executives unsuccessfully petitioned the South Atlantic League for reentry. With no league to play in, professional baseball once again exited Greenville in 1956 and did not return until 1961.

Jimmy Gaston moved to Augusta, Ga., in the summer of 1951 but could not stay away from baseball. In the spring of 1952, he accepted a position as business manager of the Drummondville (Canada) Cubs in the Class D Provincial League. He later served as general manager of a Class B team in the Carolina League that split time between Wilson and Kinston, N.C. He also worked at Fort Gordon in Augusta as its recreational director.

Gaston made his last of three unsuccessful attempts for political office in 1954 when he ran as a Republican for the U.S. Senate, a race that was eventually won by a write-in candidate, Strom Thurmond. Gaston died in 1958 at age 64.

While his accomplishments or legacy may not have been as impressive as his well-known father, little Jimmy Gaston left a significant mark on professional baseball in Greenville. Without the resolve and fortitude of this local sportsman, businessman and would-be politician, it is not likely pro baseball would have survived through two wars, a devastating fire and persistent flooding from the Reedy River.

8
Coach

I don't know what my life would have been without Coach Phillips.

—Mike McCall

When Meadowbrook Park opened in 1938, it quickly became a second home for 10-year-old Bill Phillips. He lived about a mile and a half away, easy walking distance for the energetic, baseball-loving young boy.

Once his chores and homework were complete, he made a beeline for the front gate at Meadowbrook. He secured a job as batboy for the Spinners, and he quickly endeared himself to the professional players and coaches with his passion for the game and willingness to retrieve baseballs from all areas of Meadowbrook.

Most everyone's favorite Spinner on the '38 team was first baseman Mickey Vernon, but a player from a different position was responsible for the permanent direction of Phillips' baseball aspirations. One of the Spinners' catchers took a personal interest in the young batboy and gave him a worn-out catcher's mitt, along with a few tips on how to handle himself behind the plate. The glove and the encouragement inspired Phillips' dream to become a major league catcher.

Phillips moved on from his days as a batboy but stayed deeply connected to Meadowbrook over the next three decades. He played at Meadowbrook as a high school, college and professional player and coached numerous high school and American Legion games in the historic ballpark. Few Greenvillians have had a closer connection to Meadowbrook than Bill Phillips.

William Beacham "Bill" Phillips was born in Greenville on December 2, 1928. His father, John Phillips, was originally from Morven, N.C., and first came to Greenville to train for military service in World War I at Camp Sevier. He eventually returned to Greenville and worked as a painter. He and his wife, Docia, a devoutly religious woman, had four sons and two daughters. John had played amateur baseball in North Carolina and transferred a love for the game to his children.

From an early age, the Phillips boys were sports enthusiasts, playing whatever game was in season, but always favoring baseball. In the years to come, the Phillips name would become synonymous with baseball in the Greenville community.

Bill was the youngest of the four boys. His oldest brother John began working for *The Greenville News* as a 10-year-old delivering newspapers. By the time he was 16, John was working full time in the press room and spent a total of 54 years with the paper. His early work efforts helped his younger brothers focus their energies on sports.

Brothers Jack and Alva were outstanding multisport athletes at Greenville High. Jack was a member of Greenville High's 1942 state championship basketball team and played one season of professional baseball with the Greenville Spinners before serving 47 years as a Methodist minister at various churches throughout South Carolina.

Alva was captain of the 1943 state championship football team at Greenville High, and his baseball skills earned him a contract with the Chicago Cubs in 1944. He played five years of minor league baseball, before returning to Greenville to become the athletic director at

Monaghan Mill, a position that paid him more handsomely than his minor league salary. Alva was known throughout the community as a successful American Legion baseball coach, high school and college official and part owner of a popular downtown sporting goods store.

Randy Phillips, Alva's youngest son and Bill's nephew, worked as a hitting instructor and scout for nearly 30 years with the Red Sox, Blue Jays, Pirates and Braves organizations, as well as MLB International. He recalled his family's deep connection to Meadowbrook Park.

"My father used to hang around Meadowbrook when he was a little kid. He'd play pepper with the players, shag fly balls and just hang out," he said. "Then Uncle Bill started hanging out there and that's when he was given the catcher's mitt by one of the players and that's what turned him into a catcher." Randy added that his childhood was similar to that of his father and uncle as he said he spent countless hours at Meadowbrook "chasing foul balls, scarfing up cracked bats and running errands for players."

Randy's older brother Al also spent many of his formative childhood years roaming through every nook and cranny of Meadowbrook and has a wealth of treasured memories from the old ballpark. To this day, he can recite with exacting detail the dimensions of the park's outfield wall. "It was 435 to center, 310 down the lines, 389 to left center and 390 to right center," according to Al.

Like his Uncle Bill, Al played catcher and had a successful high school, American Legion and collegiate baseball career followed by a brief stint in the Reds' farm system. "My Uncle Bill gave me my first catcher's equipment, and I owe him a lot for all he taught me," Al said.

When Alva was a senior at Greenville High in 1944, the school had been without a baseball team for several years. Alva went to Slick Moore, the school's athletic director, and told him he had a group of guys who wanted to play baseball. "Slick told my Daddy, 'You got the players together, so you coach them,'" Randy said.

Alva Phillips became the student/player-coach for his high school baseball squad. The team wore hand-me-down football jerseys and played their home games at Meadowbrook. Among his fellow class-mates that Alva convinced to join the 1944 team was Cally Gault, who later served as the head football coach at Presbyterian College from 1963 to 1984.

Bill followed in his brothers' footsteps, excelling in football, bas-ketball and baseball at Greenville High. During the summer, his skills as a catcher were in high demand in the competitive textile baseball leagues. He established a reputation as one of the area's brightest young baseball talents. During his senior year, he also began dating his future wife of 63 years, Bette Ann Fowler.

"Our first date was to the football awards banquet in December," Bette Ann recalled. "It was the big event of the year, and I was hon-ored to be his date. Bill won the most valuable player award that night. That was the night it all started for us."

Phillips was a highly sought-after football prospect, but his skills on the baseball diamond caught the attention of Connie Mack of the Philadelphia Athletics. The Phillies' owner/manager invited the promising 18-year-old catcher to Philadelphia for a tryout at Shibe Park. Given Mack's penchant for encouraging prospects to attend college, he likely steered Phillips in the same direction that he guided Lou Brissie in 1941, as Phillips opted to attend Furman University where he played baseball and basketball for Coach J. Lyles Alley.

Hugh Glymph, a childhood friend, first met Phillips when the two were fourth grade classmates. Glymph was a baseball teammate of Phillips on little league, high school, textile and college teams.

"Bill just had a great understanding of the game from a very young age," Glymph recalled of his childhood friend. "He had a tremendous arm and was the best catcher you've ever seen, and he was just one of the finest human beings you could ever know."

Bill Phillips (far right) leaves the dugout at Meadowbrook Park while playing for the 1946 Greenville High Red Raiders with teammates from left to right, Don Wham, Bill Kerr, Hugh Glymph and Robert Brown.
(Courtesy of the family of William B. Phillips)

Phillips was named to the 1948 All-Southern Conference baseball team and upon graduation, Connie Mack signed him to a contract with the Athletics. He spent a shortened first year with Savannah in the Sally League followed by a full season with Fayetteville in the Class B Carolina League, before joining the Greenville Spinners for the 1951 and '52 seasons. The 1951 Spinners were now playing in the Tri-State League, and the Korean War was in full swing, which forced the Spinners to draw heavily on local baseball talent to complete their roster.

Phillips gained a reputation for his solid defensive play as a catcher and his sportsmanship on and off the field. He also had a fiery competitive side as evidenced by an incident at Meadowbrook in June of 1952.

In the top of the eighth inning in a game against Knoxville, the Smokies' first baseman and player-manager Fred Gerkin was at bat. Gerkin was a 31-year-old World War II veteran and journeyman minor leaguer. The New York Giants, parent club of the Smokies, moved Gerkin from the Triple A Minneapolis Millers to Class B Knoxville in the middle of the '52 season to help shake up a team they believed was underperforming. From the day he arrived, Gerkin flashed his competitiveness every chance he got, berating umpires over questionable calls and chastising players for their mistakes, all to the delight of the Knoxville fans.

Gerkin was batting left-handed against the Spinners' right-handed pitcher Ray Suit. Phillips was catching. The first pitch to Gerkin brushed him off the plate. Gerkin shot an angry look toward Suit and then turned and threatened Phillips. According to Phillips' son Steve, Gerkin said, "If he does that again, I'm going to break this 'blankety-blank' bat over your head."

Never one to back down from a challenge, Phillips gave Suit the sign for another high and tight fastball that knocked Gerkin to the dirt. Gerkin sprang to his feet and started swinging at Phillips as both benches cleared.

"I was listening to it on the radio, and I heard them say, 'Phillips is on top of him, and he can't move,'" recalled Phillips' wife Bette Ann.

"I was at home expecting so I wasn't at the game, but I got in my car and hurried down to the ballpark. I guess I thought I was going to protect my husband."

Scoop Latimer from *The Greenville News* described the efforts to calm the donnybrook:

> *The Star-Spangled Banner was blared over the loud speaker, but even the National Anthem and the presence of policeman failed to quell the trouble at once. Order was restored after about ten minutes of pleading by men and music.*

Gerkin, Phillips and Suit were ejected from the game, and after further review by league officials, Gerkin also received a two-day suspension, endearing him even further with the Knoxville fans.

Phillips served a two-year stint in the military and then played one additional season for the Spinners in 1955 before a back injury ended his playing career. He returned to Greenville High in 1955 as a teacher and coach, eventually moving into the position of head basketball and baseball coach while also serving as assistant football coach. During the summer months, he coached the Greenville American Legion baseball team which was comprised primarily of players from Greenville and Carolina High.

Phillips won state championships in basketball in 1964 and '65 and several conference championships in baseball. His contributions as a longtime successful American Legion coach earned him a special night in his honor as he was awarded Greenville's "Key to the City." Phillips coached multiple sports successfully, but baseball remained his first love, and many of his former players recall his influence as a teacher of the game.

"It was the little things that he taught us that were so impactful," former Greenville High player Mike McCall said. "One day, at practice, he did a demonstration for us on fielding and explained the importance of getting our glove on the ground. He showed us how moving it up was a simple quick reflex action as opposed to having to use muscles to move the glove down."

Mike McCall started playing baseball for Coach Phillips as an eighth grader at Greenville High in 1960. His older brother Jackie was already a starter for the Red Raiders, and Mike quickly established himself in the Raider infield alongside his older brother. McCall played at Clemson and in the Phillies minor league organization for two years and said he learned more about baseball from Coach Phillips than at any other level where he played.

Dr. Tom Latham, a prominent Greenville physician, played outfield for Greenville High in the mid-'60s and echoed McCall's sentiments about Phillips' baseball wisdom.

"He was so good at the fundamentals of the game," Latham recalled. "He taught me the correct way to bunt and how to throw the ball properly from the outfield with back spin instead of side spin."

Latham played at Furman where he earned All-Southern Conference honors in 1970. He noted that Phillips continued to influence his baseball career beyond his days at Greenville High.

"My sophomore year at Furman, I hit .314 but dropped to .248 my junior year," Latham said. "Over that summer, [Phillips] recognized that I was standing about six to eight inches too close to the plate. He moved me back, and the next year I hit .298 and made the all-conference team."

Lester Erwin was a starter on the 1965 Red Raider baseball team and one of 10 players on that team who eventually played at the collegiate level. He recalled an incident when Coach Phillips' knowledge of the game, along with his competitive spirit, created a baseball oddity.

"I remember a game where we had a controversial play at first base, and coach got in an argument with a young umpire," Erwin said. "He lit him up pretty good as he explained the proper interpretation of the rules. I guess you would say he won the argument because the umpire just threw up his hands up and walked out the gate, and so we played the rest of that game without that umpire."

Meadowbrook Park served as the home field for Greenville High

Coach Bill Phillips stands on the steps of the first base dugout at Meadowbrook Park.

(Courtesy of the family of William B. Phillips)

and the Greenville American Legion teams during most of the park's 34-year existence. Erwin appreciated the opportunity he got to play in the historic ballpark as a youth.

"The first time I walked into Meadowbrook, I fell in love with it," Erwin said. "I know it got a little run down as it got older, but to me, it was as perfect a ballpark as you would ever want to play in."

Phillips left Greenville High in 1969 to become the athletic director and head football and baseball coach at nearby Wade Hampton High School. He inherited a Generals baseball program that had not experienced much success. He quickly built a winner, capturing the school's first region championship in 1971 with a team that included Phillips' oldest son, Steve.

Don Moore, a standout pitcher for Wade Hampton from 1969 to 1971, recalled Phillips' impact on the Generals baseball program. "He was a calming influence on us," Moore said. "He always seemed to know what to say to the players and just how to say it. I think he made us confident and relaxed at the same time." Moore, who was the most valuable player on the Generals baseball team for three consecutive years, said of Phillips, "I know he made me a better pitcher."

Phillips' prize baseball pupil was Dickie Dietz, a future major league catcher with the Giants, Dodgers and Braves. As an eighth grader, Dietz was struggling in school, and his mother used to joke, saying she would drop him at the front door of the school, and he would leave out the back door.

"I remember Daddy telling the story that Dickie was sort of incorrigible as a young boy," Steve Phillips recalled. "He said they had sort of given up on Dickie at school around the time he was in eighth grade, and one day he [Dietz] was walking across the Church Street bridge, and Daddy went to him and talked to him. He told Dickie, 'If you are going to make it, we are going to have to work together.' He gave him a pep talk, and Daddy pretty much took Dickie in and became almost like a father to him."

Dietz played football, basketball and baseball at Greenville High and was a two-time all-state football performer at halfback for the Red Raiders and a three-time all-conference baseball catcher. *The Greenville News* reported that in more than 200 high school, American Legion and textile league games, Dietz hit an impressive .426.

While Phillips was unable to fulfill his own dream of becoming a major league catcher, he saw in Dietz all the skills needed to reach the big leagues. Phillips invested heavily in his protégé as he attempted to transfer all his baseball knowledge to Dietz. Steve Phillips recalled that his father spent many long hours at Meadowbrook giving Dietz one-on-one instruction.

The extra investments paid off as Dietz had 15 of the 16 major league clubs clamoring to sign him. Dietz was married during his senior year in high school, which made him ineligible for his final year of high school athletics. He was playing for Monaghan Mill in the Western Carolina Textile League while he waited for his high school class to graduate so he could officially become a professional.

In June of 1960, Dietz signed as an amateur free agent with the San Francisco Giants. Coach Phillips assisted the 18-year-old Dietz with his contract negotiations, which resulted in Dietz getting a $90,000 signing bonus (approximately $800,000 in 2021 dollars). It was the largest signing bonus ever for a baseball player from South Carolina and *The San Francisco Examiner* reported that it was likely the largest bonus the Giants had ever paid to a player at that time.

A photo appeared in *The Greenville News* the day after Dietz signed with the Giants showing him in the home of Bill and Bette Ann Phillips. He was seated at the Phillips' dining room table with pen in hand, flanked by his wife and infant daughter Robin, his mother and Giants scout, Tim Murchison. Coach Phillips stood directly behind Dietz wearing a broad smile as he watched his protégé ink the record-breaking contract. Dietz told Gene Granger of *The Greenville News* that day, "It feels great . . . just like a dream come true."

The 6-foot-1, 195-pound right-handed catcher was assigned to the Class D Artesia (N.M.) Giants. Before he left Greenville, he promised Coach Phillips' son Steve that he would send him the ball from his first professional home run. On Saturday evening, June 25, 1960,

Dietz belted a 425-foot blast over the left center field fence in Artesia. Five days later, the ball arrived at the Phillips' house as promised.

Dietz had his best year in the minors in 1963. As a 19-year-old playing for El Paso in the Double A Texas League, Dietz hit .354 with 35 home runs and 101 RBIs. He edged out future major league players Jim Beauchamp and Rico Carty for the league batting title. Dietz had a remarkable .551 on base percentage and demonstrated excellent control of the strike zone with 159 walks against only 89 strikeouts.

At age 24, Dietz advanced to the major leagues in June of 1966. The following year, he made the all-rookie team, and in 1968, he hit .272 while appearing in 98 games for the Giants.

Dietz became San Francisco's starting catcher in 1970, and playing regularly helped him enjoy his best year in the majors. By the All-Star break, he was hitting .337 with 18 home runs and 77 RBIs. National League Manager Gil Hodges selected Dietz as an alternate for the 1970 All-Star Game. Joining Dietz in the July classic were 19 future Hall of Famers.

He wrote a column for his hometown paper sharing his impressions from the All-Star event. "Probably the most interesting thing that happened to me today was when I got to the ballpark and went in the locker room. Guess where my locker is?" Dietz wrote. "It's between [Hank] Aaron and [Willie] Mays."

With the National League trailing 3-1 in the top of the seventh inning, Hodges inserted Dietz in the lineup in place of starting catcher Johnny Bench. In the bottom of the ninth, Dietz blasted a solo home run over the center field wall off Jim "Catfish" Hunter.

Dietz's homer sparked a dramatic National League rally that sent the game into extra innings. In the bottom of the 12th, Pete Rose scored the winning run for the National League when he bowled over American League catcher Ray Fosse. Dietz was standing in the on-deck circle when the epic home plate collision occurred.

Dietz finished the 1970 season hitting .300 with 22 home runs, 107 RBIs, 109 walks and an on-base percentage of .426. He remains the only catcher in the history of the major leagues to record 100 walks and 100 RBIs and hit .300 in a season.

Dietz served as the player representative for the Giants, and he took an aggressive stance in support of the 1972 players strike that delayed the start of the season. Once the strike ended, the Giants placed Dietz on waivers. He was picked up by the Los Angeles Dodgers for the '72 season and spent a final year with the Atlanta Braves in 1973 where he played in 83 games and hit a respectable .295. Dietz was released by the Braves who already had two other younger catching prospects. Surprisingly, no other team picked up the veteran Dietz, ending his eight-year major league career at age 31.

Dietz was one of 24 player representatives who authorized the 1972 strike. Twelve of those player reps were either released or traded by their teams following the player walkout. Some believe Dietz's career was shortened because of being blackballed from baseball due to his active role in the strike.[1] He finished his big league career with a lifetime batting average of .261.

Randy Phillips was a friend of Dietz, and the two shared many conversations about baseball and in particular hitting. "He had a nice and simple stance and swing—not a lot of moving parts and not a lot that could go wrong. From a very young age, he was a disciplined hitter with a great eye," Phillips said. As a 19-year-old, Dietz walked an incredible 159 times while appearing in 109 games for the El Paso Sun Kings. Phillips added, "To be a good hitter, you gotta be tough, and Dickie was a tough competitor in the batter's box and on the field."

Dickie Dietz was a native of Greenville and played in the major leagues for the San Francisco Giants, Los Angeles Dodgers and Atlanta Braves from 1966 to 1973.
(Courtesy of National Baseball Hall of Fame Library)

Mike Lum played with Dietz in Atlanta in 1973 and remembered him as a likeable teammate. "He was a down-to-earth guy," Lum recalled. "He was very approachable and just a guy who had a lot of fun playing the game. He was fun to be around and a guy who really loved life."

Phillips remained a mentor to Dietz beyond his high school days. On one occasion when Dietz was in the major leagues and stuck in a hitting slump, he asked his old coach to watch him play in a game on television.

"Sure enough, Daddy saw something in Dickie's swing that day and called him and gave him some advice," Steve Phillips recalled. "The very next day, Dickie hit a home run."

Dietz was one of three of Phillips' players who had successful major league careers. Bob Patterson, a former pitcher at Wade Hampton, pitched 13 years in the major leagues with five different teams. Infielder Doug Strange, also a former Wade Hampton player, played nine years in the majors with five teams.

Over the course of his 31-year career in coaching, Phillips touched the lives of hundreds of student athletes who continue to speak of him today with a deep sense of respect and appreciation.

"Everyone who played for him had the utmost respect for him," Lester Erwin said of Phillips. "You didn't want to let him down or do anything that would cause him to get upset with you." Erwin became a high school teacher and baseball coach, and his Carolina High School team won the state 3A baseball championship in 1983.

"My father worked as a milkman, and he left the house at 5 a.m. and didn't return home 'til after dark," Mike McCall said. "I feel pretty sure I saw more of Coach Phillips than I saw of my dad as a youth."

Dr. Tom Latham, added a common sentiment of many of Phillips' former players saying, "He was like a second dad to me."

As much as he loved baseball, Phillips' greatest passion came from his Christian faith. Several of his former players attested to his Christian example, saying the very worst words that ever came out of his mouth when he was angry were "John Brown." An opposing player in a Spinners game once claimed to an umpire that Phillips had cursed at him. The umpire quickly dismissed the assertion, saying, "Everybody here knows that boy doesn't cuss."

Phillips found the Fellowship of Christian Athletes (FCA) the ideal platform for sharing his faith. He started student FCA chapters at Greenville and Wade Hampton High and earned a reputation in the community as a developer and molder of young men. In February of 1968, the Greenville Women's Club invited him to speak at its weekly coffee hour. In his remarks, Phillips shared his personal faith journey.

"I do not come to you as one who is perfect," he told the group. "I do not come to you as one who is holier than thou. I do not come to you as a saintly person. I was wrapped up in sports. Baseball is a thrill to me. Basketball is a thrill to me. I love to win, but I looked back and said, 'What have I done for Jesus Christ? What boys have I turned away? What boys have I helped?' I asked God to call the signals of my life."

His wife Bette Ann was in the audience that day and recalled being "so very proud" of her husband and the example he set for all the young men he coached.

Former player Mike McCall said his childhood home was not far from Coach Phillips' home and remembered his coach regularly extending an invitation to him. "He would ask me just about every week if I wanted to go to church with him," McCall said. "He said he would come pick me up, but in all those times he asked, I never said yes."

In 2012, McCall attended Coach Phillips' funeral. He said he had not been a regular church attendee, and his wife had been encouraging him to consider going. On the way home from the funeral, McCall turned to his wife and said, "Pick a church, and we will go Sunday." His wife questioned him as to why now, and McCall said simply, "Because Coach wants me to."

It was the beginning of a spiritual rebirth for McCall, one that he attributes directly to the lifelong influence of his former coach. Fighting back tears, McCall summarized the impact of Phillips on his life, saying, "He was a just a great man, and I don't know what my life would have been without Coach Phillips."

There was no player Phillips had invested more time and energy in than Dickie Dietz. Phillips' tutelage of Dietz's early baseball career was the catalyst for Dietz's ultimate rise to success in the major leagues. Phillips had done everything in his power to put Dietz on the path to baseball success, but one day, it occurred to Phillips that he had neglected to share with his former star player what he valued most.

Both Phillips' son Steve and wife Bette Ann recalled that Phillips visited Dietz and told him he had shared "just about everything important in his life" with him, but he had neglected to share "the most important thing of all." Phillips then shared his Christian testimony with Dietz, and when he came home, he told his wife that the two of them got down on their knees, and Dickie prayed to accept Christ. When Dietz died from a heart attack in 2005, Phillips and his son Steve co-officiated his funeral.

In retirement, Phillips stayed involved with his church, which he had attended for more than 50 years and served as a Sunday school teacher and deacon. He also remained active in the local FCA chapter. A great source of joy during his retirement years were the regular encounters he had with his former players.

Ronnie Moore played high school and American Legion baseball for Phillips from 1957 to 1960 and later became a successful coach, winning three boys basketball state championships at J.L. Mann High School. Moore said he often ran into Coach Phillips in the grocery store, and they would stand in the aisle and talk for a long time, recalling memories of high school and American Legion games. Moore said, "Looking back at what he did and how he coached and how he treated people definitely impacted my own journey as a coach and athletic administrator."

The other place where many of his former players and students encountered Phillips was at funerals. If a former player lost a loved one, Phillips was committed to attend the funeral and pay his respects. Joel Shaw, who played football for Phillips in 1978 at Wade Hampton, said, "For over 20 years, he probably went to two or three funerals a week. That's how he stayed in touch with people and let them know he still cared."

It was once suggested to Phillips that perhaps he didn't need to attend all those funerals and that his players would understand if he just sent a card or gave them a call. To which he responded, "Oh, no, I couldn't stop going. I have seen how much it means to them to see me during their time of grief. I have to go."

Phillips retired from a distinguished career in athletics and education in 1986. He, along with his brother Alva and nephew Randy, was elected to the Greenville Baseball Hall of Fame. He received the state's highest honor, The Order of the Palmetto, in 1994.

Archie Black, a local Greenville attorney who played baseball and football on some of Phillips' earliest Greenville High teams, was only a few years younger than Phillips when he played for him, and yet he said he always viewed him as "a father figure." He remained a close friend to Phillips and said, "All my life, out of respect, I always called him Coach."

In retirement, "Coach" never quit coaching. When his grandson Matthew became a member of a Little League team, Phillips drove to Columbia three to four days a week to help coach the team. Phillips also helped with his grandson's high school baseball team, once again commuting to Columbia multiple times a week to teach the game he loved.

Only days before his death in 2012, Phillips was visited in the hospital by a family friend who informed him that her grandson was playing baseball and was a pitcher. Although critically ill at the time, Phillips asked if someone could bring him an orange. From his hospital bed, he used the orange to demonstrate the proper grip for a variety of pitches. He told his visitor to be sure to pass along his instruction to her grandson. Phillips died shortly after this meeting at age 83.

Phillips' wife, Bette Ann, shared a story, illustrating that her husband's legacy as a coach continues beyond his death. She was recently on a FaceTime call watching her 3-year-old great-grandson William swing a plastic baseball bat when she turned to her son Danny, who was with her, and said, "You know what Coach would say if he were watching this, don't you? He would say get that bat off your shoulder and up in the air. Be ready to hit that ball."

9
Ted and Mickey

The best hitter I ever saw was Ted Williams.

—Mickey Mantle

This kid [Mickey Mantle] ain't logical. He's too good. It's very confusing.
—Casey Stengel

Ted Williams showered in the small empty locker room underneath the grandstand section of Meadowbrook Park. He slipped on a sport coat, grabbed his travel bag and walked out of the main entrance of the park.

His work for the day was finished. The Red Sox had scored 15 runs in the first three innings of their April 1956 exhibition game against the Philadelphia Phillies, and Boston Manager Mike "Pinky" Higgins pulled his superstar from the game before the start of the fourth inning.

Williams singled in the first inning, hit a towering three-run home run in the second and drew a walk in his final at-bat. After Higgins removed him from the game, Williams headed to the locker room to get ahead of what he knew would be a post-game rush on the limited showering capacity in Meadowbrook's cozy home locker room.

The 37-year-old future first-ballot Hall of Famer left the ballpark while his teammates completed their 21-1 thumping of the Phils. He walked north on Hudson Street toward Washington Street and in the direction of the Southern Train Depot.

A young boy spotted Williams walking along Mayberry Street, and quickly word spread throughout the network of hero-worshiping youngsters who had assembled that day in and around Meadowbrook Park. Within a few minutes, Williams became a baseball version of the Pied Piper as a long line of youth was following him on his walk to the train station.

Williams stopped at the corner of Hudson and Washington streets and patiently signed his name for every single youngster.

Two years later, a raucous group of fans leaned over Meadowbrook's grandstand wall and pleaded for an autograph from New York Yankees superstar Mickey Mantle. The man known simply as "The Mick" leaned against the batting cage seemingly oblivious to the impassioned demands for his signature. Mantle was in town for an April 1958 exhibition game with the Phillies, and he seemed far more concerned about getting his cuts in the cage than fulfilling the requests of the zealous fans. One angry fan, hoping to strike a chord with Mantle shouted, "Ted Williams told us you wouldn't sign any autographs." Mantle was unphased.

He finished his time in the batting cage where he launched balls out of Meadowbrook batting right- and left-handed. He walked slowly over to the three-foot cinder block wall that surrounded the infield and flashed his signature smile at the throng of adoring fans. He perched himself on top of the wall and signed his name to balls, bats, programs, hats and anything else that was stuck in his face for nearly an hour.

Professional baseball disappeared once again in Greenville from 1956 to 1961. The Tri-State League folded after the 1955 season, and the Sally League refused Greenville's request for readmittance, blaming their denial on the club's financial instability.

Ownership of the team remained with the Greenville Baseball Club, Inc., which at this time was comprised of several hundred individual stockholders who had purchased shares through a last-ditch community effort to keep professional baseball alive in Greenville in 1955. The organization was overseen by a group of executives that included Greenville's most influential baseball supporter, Mayor Kenneth Cass, along with local businessmen Sam Roane Jr. and Steve Kelly.

The corporation maintained its lease of the ballpark with the city and utilized it for a variety of local sporting and community events. Sterling High School played its home football and baseball games in Meadowbrook during this era as did the Greenville Black Spinners and the Greenville American Legion baseball team. Furman University played baseball games at the park until it moved its campus five miles north of downtown off Poinsett Highway in 1958. Meadowbrook was also the site of an annual summer textile league All-Star game that drew the top talent from the highly competitive area textile leagues.

A quarter-mile, fan-shaped dirt track was installed around the baseball field at Meadowbrook in the spring of 1956 in response to the growing popularity of stock car racing. It hosted NASCAR-sanctioned races on Thursday evenings that included appearances by future NASCAR Grand National Series Champion Ned Jarrett and Ralph Earnhardt, father of legendary NASCAR racer Dale Earnhardt. Additional racing events, including midget cars and motorcycles, were added to the well-attended Thursday night events.

In July of 1956, the park's most unusual doubleheader began with a baseball game between Benedict College and the Greenville Negro All-Star team. It was followed by a stock car race featuring several local Black drivers.

Leo Carrillo, who played Pancho on the popular TV show *The Cisco Kid*, and a group of more than 200 cowboys and cowgirls held a series of Texas rodeo shows at Meadowbrook in May of 1957. In June of 1957, the Lone Ranger and his trusted horse Silver joined with TV wonder dog Lassie for two Saturday shows at Meadowbrook. Sam Snyder's Water Follies also appeared at the ballpark in 1957 and included swimming, diving and dancing in what was claimed to be the world's largest portable pools. Traveling circus shows, along with the local horse and dog shows, continued to fill available dates at Meadowbrook during the absence of professional baseball.

While many of these events drew large crowds, the largest audiences were reserved for a series of four Major League Baseball exhibition games between 1955 and 1958. The driving force behind securing and promoting these successful games was Steve Kelly, secretary of Greenville Baseball, Inc. Kelly had relocated to Greenville in 1947 after retiring from an engineering career in Buffalo, NY. On his first visit to Greenville, he and his wife attended the annual Greenville-Parker football game, and Kelly told *The Greenville News'* Gil Rowland, "Any town that would support two football teams like that looked like a darned good town to me, so I decided to settle here."

Kelly bought a home in Spartanburg and quickly left retirement behind as he opened a laundry business in Greenville. He plunged head-first into the civic and social affairs of the community with the energy and enthusiasm of someone much younger. He served on the board of directors of the Greenville County Humane Society, the Greenville County American Red Cross, the Greenville Hearing and Speech Center and the United Fund. The son of Irish immigrant parents, Kelly also single-handedly organized an annual St. Patrick's Day parade and celebration in Greenville.

Kelly became known around town as man who could "get things done." He loved baseball almost as much as he loved Ireland, and his passion for the game earned him the nickname "Mr. Baseball." He told Rowland that he lived daily by a motto given to him by his Irish mother, "Go forth, my son, and meet the day with a twinkle in your eye, a smile on your face, a song in your heart and a kindly word on your lips for everybody."

The first exhibition Kelly helped organize was held on Monday, April 4, 1955, and pitted the American League's Boston Red Sox against the National League's Philadelphia Phillies. The Red Sox were without Ted Williams who was engaged in a contract dispute. Red Sox Manager Higgins, fully expecting the absence of Williams to affect the attendance at Meadowbrook, made a side bet with his assistant coach Del Baker that the game would not draw more than 3,000 fans.

Higgins realized quickly that he was going to lose his wager. Local baseball fans filled every available seat in the stadium, forcing ushers to allow the overflowing fans to sit dangerously inside the wall around the infield. By game time, an estimated 6,000 fans jammed Meadowbrook and watched the Red Sox beat the Phillies 9-7. It was the largest crowd of the Red Sox and Phils spring exhibition games to date, which all but guaranteed the two teams would likely return to Greenville. By October, team officials had confirmed their plans for a second exhibition game in Greenville the following spring.

A train carrying the Red Sox and Phillies pulled into Greenville's Washington Street depot a little past midnight on Tuesday April

10, 1956. The teams stayed aboard the train overnight, sleeping in a collection of customized Pullman cars. Earlier that day, the Phillies' future Hall of Fame pitcher Robin Roberts had pitched a complete game and led his team to a 2-1 win over the Red Sox in Montgomery, Ala. Around 8 a.m. the next day, the Phillies went to the Poinsett Hotel, and the Red Sox made their way to The Hotel Greenville where they were given access to rooms and fed a hearty breakfast. They reported to Meadowbrook at 11:30 a.m. for pregame workouts.

Ted Williams ended his holdout with the Red Sox in May of 1955 but missed the first month of the season as he tended to personal matters related to a divorce from his first wife, Doris. He finished the year hitting .356 but lacked enough plate appearances to qualify for the batting title, which went to the Detroit Tigers' Al Kaline with a .340 average. When Williams arrived in Greenville in 1956, he had the highest lifetime batting average among active players (.348) and was arguably the best hitter in professional baseball.

———————

Theodore Samuel Williams was born August 30, 1918, in San Diego. His mother, May Venzor Williams, was born in Mexico. She was devoutly religious and worked as a foot soldier for the Salvation Army. To the detriment of her family, she often spent from sunup to sundown attempting to save the souls of the destitute on the streets of San Diego. She was known around town as "Salvation May." Williams' father operated a passport photography business, battled alcoholism and was rarely around. He was once described as someone who would ask to be excused from the dinner table and then go missing for the next two or three days. Ted and his younger brother Danny were latchkey kids.[1]

Baseball became the outlet for Ted's childhood loneliness. He spent hours in his backyard or at a nearby playground fine tuning his home-run swing, "always concentrating on striking the lower half of the ball with an uppercut motion to gain greater loft."[2] Williams played high school and American Legion baseball in San Diego and began his professional career in 1936 with the San Diego Padres of the Pacific Coast League. The Boston Red Sox purchased Williams' contract in 1937, and after a year at their minor league affiliate in Minneapolis, he joined the Red Sox and began his historic 19-year major league career.

As a young boy, Williams said, "All I want out of life is that when I walk down the street folks will say, 'There goes the greatest hitter that ever lived.'" Williams' achievement of his childhood aspiration will always be subject to debate, but his numbers certainly put him on a very short list of those who deserve to be considered the greatest hitter of all time. He holds a lifetime batting average of .344, is the last player to hit over .400 in a season (1941)—and only once in 19 seasons (1959) did he fail to hit .300. He has the highest on-base percentage of any player (.482), a result of his remarkable discipline at the plate and his 20/10 vision. Whenever a catcher complained to an umpire for not calling a pitch a strike with Williams at the plate, on more than one occasion the umpire shut down the argument by saying, "If Mr. Williams didn't swing at it, it wasn't a strike."[3]

Williams developed a reputation for being aloof. He was known for private acts of kindness and generosity, but publicly he was ill-tempered and best described as a "cranky professional." He dealt with some deep-seated anger from his childhood, and the target for much of his anger was the Boston media. Williams said in his autobiography, *My Turn at Bat*, "Oh how I hated that Boston press." He believed that the local media had turned the fans against him.

The writers exacted a level of revenge on Williams by not selecting him for the MVP award in 1942 or '47, both years in which he won the American League Triple Crown. Williams hit .406 in in 1941 but also missed out on the MVP award that year as it went to Joe DiMaggio, who hit safely in 56 consecutive games.

His relationship with fans wasn't much better. Williams committed an 11th inning error in a game in 1956 and was showered with a chorus of *boos*. He turned to the fans in the outfield stands at Fenway Park and spit at them. At the end of the inning, Williams emerged from the dugout and spat at the Boston fans a second time. Williams homered in his last at-bat of his professional career. As he returned to the dugout after rounding the bases, he refused to acknowledge the cheering crowd, emblematic of his tumultuous relationship with the Boston fans.

Williams gave up four and half years of his best baseball years serving as a Marine combat aviator in World War II and the Korean War and is the only player in the Baseball Hall of Fame to have served in both of those wars.

In the spring of 1956, Williams was 38 years old but showed no signs of losing his ability to hit a baseball. Greenvillians packed Meadowbrook Park early on the morning of April 10 to get a glimpse of the man known throughout the game as "The Splendid Splinter."

Greenville native Mike McCall was eight years old when his father allowed him to skip school to see the Red Sox and Phillies 1956 exhibition. McCall said his father "could talk his way into just about any situation," and somehow with his young son in tow, he talked his way into the Red Sox locker room prior to the game.

McCall's father had purchased a 10-cent scorecard as he entered Meadowbrook that day. He handed the program, along with a blue pen, to his son and instructed him to politely ask the Red Sox players for their autograph. The young boy secured eight signatures, including that of Ted Williams.

As a former minor league player and lifelong baseball enthusiast, McCall appreciates the significance of that scorecard and has carefully maintained it over the past 65 years. He intends to pass it down to his son, along with the story about the day he stood beside the great Ted Williams in the locker room at Meadowbrook Park.

Williams always drew a crowd of admiring onlookers when he stepped into the batting cage. Even Mickey Mantle admitted that he frequently stood outside the cage and watched closely as Williams took practice swings. The capacity crowd of 6,000 looked on as Williams seemed to effortlessly loft ball after ball over Meadowbrook's outfield wall. A throng of young boys battled behind the wall in an effort to secure a souvenir from Williams' bat.

In his first at-bat, Williams laced an off-speed pitch from the Phillies' Saul Rogovin up the middle for a single. Williams came to the plate in the second inning with two men on base. Rogovin mistakenly left a pitch up in the strike zone, and Williams unleashed his powerful swing, driving the ball deep over the right center field wall. The ball cleared the banks of the Reedy River and the railroad tracks beyond the outfield wall, landing on top of an adjacent warehouse roof.

Williams' home run that day has become legendary among Greenvillians who claim to have been at the game. Each time the story is told about Williams' blast, the ball seems to move a little farther from home plate. Local baseball enthusiast Randy Phillips joked, "Eventually that ball is going to end up in Asheville." No one was around that day with a tape measure to gauge the exact length of Williams' home run, but assuming it at least cleared the river and the railroad tracks, it most likely traveled over 450 feet.

Meadowbrook Park and surrounding area, April 1954. In an exhibition game in April of 1956, Ted Williams hit a home run over the right field wall that, according to witnesses, landed atop the warehouse building on the far side of the Reedy River.
(Courtesy of the Greenville County Historical Society—Joe Jordan Collection)

Williams made his final plate appearance in the third inning, and the Phillies attempted a radical shift of their infield in response to his tendency to pull the ball. Center fielder Richie Ashburn moved into short right field; second baseman Ted Kazanski played in the normal spot of first baseman Stan Lopata who had moved close to the foul line. Shortstop Granny Hamner was approximately a yard

162

on the first base side of second. Third baseman Willie Jones moved to the normal shortstop position.

The first time Williams saw such a shift like this was in 1946 against the Cleveland Indians. He had gotten four hits and eight RBIs and scored four runs in the first game of a doubleheader, and then he doubled in his first at-bat in the second game. The next time Williams stepped up to the plate, Indian player-manager Lou Boudreau moved six fielders to the right side of the field, leaving the left fielder as the only player on the left side of the field. Williams laughed when he saw the unusual shift and proceeded to hit a ball right at Boudreau, who, as a shortstop, had moved between the first and second basemen. Williams joked after the game, saying, "If they start doing that against me, I'll start hitting right-handed."[4] As evidenced by Williams' batting record, the shifts were not effective in stopping the prolific pull-hitting Red Sox star.

With the Phillies' infield skewed heavily to the right side, relief pitcher Marino Pieretti threw cautiously to Williams in his third and final at-bat. Williams drew a walk, and the Mead-

Boston Red Sox star Ted Williams appeared in exhibition games at Meadowbrook Park in 1956 and '57. Williams hit home runs in both contests.
(From the author's collection)

owbrook fans voiced their displeasure over not getting to see Williams strike another mighty blow. When he came back to the dugout at the end of the inning, manager Higgins told him to hit the showers and take the rest of the afternoon off.

Former Greenville Spinner and two-time American League batting champ (1946 and '53) Mickey Vernon had joined the Red Sox as a backup first baseman. Vernon was a fan favorite during his 1938 season with the Spinners and received a resounding ovation when he was introduced to the fans at Meadowbrook. Vernon got one hit in three at-bats in the game.

Williams, Jimmy Piersall, Jackie Jensen, Faye Thornberry and Frank Malzone belted home runs for the Red Sox in their 21-1 victory. Future Hall of Fame umpire Jocko Conlan was part of the umpiring crew that called the game.

Williams ended the 1956 season with a .346 batting average, but the Red Sox finished a disappointing 13 games behind the Yankees and in fourth place, a position all too familiar to Williams and his teammates.

The success of the '56 game in Greenville resulted in a third exhibition between the two teams the following year. The city was also offered a Sunday afternoon game in 1957 between the New York Yankees and New York Giants, but local blue laws prohibited such an event on a Sunday, and Greenville missed out on the opportunity to host two April exhibitions.

Both the Red Sox and the Phillies broke spring training on Monday, April 8, and headed north by train the next day to Greenville for their first in a series of exhibitions. Following an all-night train ride, the players on both teams ate breakfast at the Poinsett Hotel and the The Hotel Greenville before reporting for batting practice at 11:30 a.m.

The Phillies had two minority players on their roster who were not allowed access to the local hotels, as Greenville was still very much a segregated community in 1957. The players, John Kennedy and Cuban-born Chico Fernandez, were taken to the Phillis Wheatley Center, a Black community center, where they showered and were fed breakfast prior to the game.

A capacity crowd was on hand on a cool spring day, and fans without reserved seats were allowed to sit on the ground inside the outfield wall. Any ball hit into the outfield crowd was ruled a ground-rule double. When it became apparent that no additional spectators were going to be admitted to the game, approximately 600 fans broke through the fence in right field, knocking down the gate attendant as they rushed into the ballpark.

Former major league pitcher and Greenville resident Lou Brissie was on hand and met with Williams outside the Red Sox dugout prior to the game. The two likely recalled the incident in 1946 when Williams hit a line drive up the middle that caromed off Brissie's leg. Williams had hit the same leg that Brissie had nearly lost due to a German artillery blast during World War II. Williams said he had an awful feeling when he hit the decorated war hero and was very thankful he had not inflicted any further damage to Brissie's leg.[5]

Williams was escorted to home plate by Mayor Cass and Miss Greenville, Peggy White, as part of the pregame festivities. A photo appeared the next day in *The Greenville News* showing Williams standing near home plate with his hat over his heart alongside Mayor Cass and Miss Greenville.

Williams was uncharacteristically friendly with *The Greenville News* Sports Editor Jim Anderson during his 1957 visit. Anderson wrote, "Ted Williams turned on his personal charm. Surely this was not the man pictured some places as eating sports writers. He could not have been more pleasant and agreeable had he been a promoter wanting free advertising."

Williams summarized his hitting philosophy for Anderson saying, "First thing is to get a bat of the right weight. Then a batter should get a comfortable stance at the plate. He should not stand too far back. The entire plate must be protected with the swing of the bat. Each person should have his own individual swing. Take 20 of the greatest hitters—not any two of them hit exactly alike."

He concluded his conversation on hitting with the following request: "Do this please, Jim. In what you say about my batting, will you ask the kids who are interested to write to Hillerich & Bradsby Co. at Louisville and ask for my tips on hitting? They'll be glad to send to any boy who writes them."

In his first plate appearance of the game, Williams demonstrated his hitting technique to perfection, blasting a home run to right field off Phillies pitcher Harvey Haddix. The Red Sox defeated the Phils 6-3 and moved on to Charlotte for their next exhibition.

Hy Hurwitz from the Boston Globe was one of several reporters traveling with the team. At the end of his game story, Hurwitz heaped praises on the success of the Greenville exhibition:

> There were 5,166 paid in today's overflow crowd . . . It was a big haul at the box office . . . They get $3.50 for box seats and $2.50 for reserved grandstand and $1.25 for bleacher tickets . . . This town is booming . . . Most of the income is from the textile industry, which once flourished in New England.

Williams had another prolific year for the Red Sox, batting a league-leading .388. He finished second behind the Yankees' Mickey

Mantle in the balloting for the league MVP, and the Red Sox once again ended the season in third place, 16 games behind the first place Yankees.

Greenvillians expected a repeat of the Red Sox-Phillies exhibition in the spring of 1958, but a scheduling mix-up ended any chance of Boston returning to Greenville. Not to worry, the New York Yankees replaced the Red Sox, and their game with the Phillies was scheduled for April 7.

––––––––––––

Eight-year-old Jimmy Grantham had difficulty going to sleep on Easter Sunday evening in 1958. His parents had informed him that the next day he and his older brother Leighton were going to attend an exhibition baseball game between the New York Yankees and Philadelphia Phillies. Although the young Grantham was a self-proclaimed Milwaukee Braves fan, and his Braves had defeated the Yankees in the '57 World Series, he recognized the significance of the opportunity that awaited him. The most storied baseball team in the game was coming to his city. More than six decades after attending the exhibition, Grantham remembers what impressed him most about that day.

"The pinstripes," he said emphatically in reference to the Yankees' trademark uniform design. "Those Yankee pinstripes represented the zenith of professional baseball, and they were right here in my hometown."

A devoted baseball fan and lover of "old ballparks," Grantham still treasures the memories of that day in Meadowbrook when he got an up-close view of the team that represented the most historic and successful franchise in all of sports. He said that day "was like Christmas and my birthday all rolled into one." He has carefully maintained the scorecard from the game, which reveals an incomplete attempt by Grantham and his brother to score the game. No doubt the events of the day were too much of a distraction for the two young baseball fans.

The professional teams arrived by train around midnight on Easter Sunday and slept in their Pullman sleeping cars. The next morning, the Yankees headed to The Hotel Greenville, and the Phillies to the Poinsett Hotel for an 8 a.m. breakfast, but not before they were greeted by a couple of young female fans.

Jean Vigodsky was in the eighth grade at Hughes Middle School when the Yankees came to town. She was a diehard Yankees fan who inherited her love of sports from her father. She collected baseball cards and enjoyed watching the Yankees on the baseball "Game of the Week."

Vigodsky organized a Mickey Mantle fan club in honor of her favorite Yankee and invited six of her friends to join, bringing total membership up to a maximum of seven, a tribute to Mickey's jersey number.

"When we heard the Yankees were coming to Greenville, we decided we had to get to the train station as early as possible because we figured everyone in town would be there waiting to see the Yankees," Vigodsky recalled.

Sarah Ann Cathey Cano was a classmate of Vigodsky's and a member of the Mantle fan club. Cano's father, a local dentist, took the two girls to the Southern Railway Train Station early on the morning of April 7 to greet the Yankees.

"When we got there, we were the only ones there," Vigodsky said. "We got to meet nearly every one of the players, and they were so gracious. Yogi Berra, Moose Skowron and all of them got off the train and signed my autograph book. I even got Casey Stengel's autograph."

None was more kind to the two teenage girls than their hero Mickey Mantle. Dressed in a tailored suit, white shirt and striped tie, Mantle stood between the girls and wrapped an arm around each of their shoulders while Cano's father snapped the photo.

"I remember I had such a crush on him," Cano said of Mantle. "When he got off the train, he was standing by himself, and we just went over and talked with him and got our picture made. He didn't seem to be in a hurry at all, and we were so thrilled."

New York Yankees star center fielder Mickey Mantle (center) poses with young fans Sarah Ann Cathey Cano and Jean Vigodsky at Southern Train Depot on Washington Street in Greenville on April 7, 1958.
(Courtesy of Sarah Ann Cathey Cano)

Later that evening, Cano wrote in her diary, "Today was a wonderful day. Daddy, Jean and I went down to the train station early so we could get autographs of the Yankees. . . Mickey Mantle put his arms around me and Ethel while Daddy took our picture. Later we went to the ballgame. The Yankees won 20-1. Mickey Mantle hit a home run." The following day, she wrote, "Today is a usual day, but I couldn't think as well because I was still excited about the game."

At The Hotel Greenville, Mantle ate breakfast at a table with teammates Whitey Ford and Enos "Country" Slaughter. Manager Casey Stengel sat two tables away and politely answered questions from the *Greenville Piedmont's* Dan Foster. Looking over at Mantle, he told Foster, "Mantle is an amazing player. Certain days, there's no one in baseball who can hit a baseball as far as he can, either left-handed or right-handed . . . If he has a good year, that's bad on the other teams."

The Yankees' Black players, Elston Howard and Harry Simpson, along with the Phillies' Chico Fernandez and Dan Herrera, were not allowed to join their teammates in the downtown Greenville hotels and were escorted to the Phillis Wheatley Center by its director J. Edgar Smith. The four players delivered words of encouragement to a gathering of local young Black athletes at the community center.

Four days prior to the game, organizer Steve Kelly announced that he had arranged with the clubs' managers to have a contingent of players visit the patients at the Shriners Hospital for Children. It was announced that the Yankees would send Mickey Mantle, Moose Skowron and a player to be determined. The Phillies representatives were scheduled to be future Hall of Fame pitcher Robin Roberts, catcher Stan Lopata and one additional player.

Kelly told the *Greenville Piedmont* about his conversations with the Yankees' Stengel and the Phillies' Mayo Smith regarding the hospital visit. "Both were delighted to arrange the visit for the kids, which is typical of the cooperation we've been getting from club officials in getting ready for the game," Kelly said.

Roberts and Yankee pitcher Bob Turley, along with Yankee third baseman Andy Carey and Phillies catcher Andy Seminick, were pictured in the afternoon paper meeting with smiling youth at the hospital. Baseballs autographed by the entire Yankees and Phillies teams were sent to the hospital and passed around among the patients.

Temperatures at game time were in the low 60s, about 10 degrees cooler than normal, and a strong 20 mph wind blew toward right field, making it feel much cooler. The official paid attendance for the game was 6,993, but eventually, the gates were left unattended, and it was estimated that approximately 9,000 fans filled Meadowbrook Park for the exhibition.

As in 1956 and '57 exhibitions, excess fans were allowed to sit five to six deep inside the outfield wall. Fans without tickets sat atop box cars that lined the railroad tracks along the Reedy River and the outfield walls. Perhaps the most ingenious of onlookers were five fans who reclined in the raised bucket of a yellow bulldozer beside the right field foul pole.

Miss Greenville, Martha Gray, dressed in a purple dress and purple shoes, presented Yankee manager Stengel with a bouquet of flowers. Mayor Cass attempted to introduce Stengel to the crowd but struggled to divert Stengel's attention away from Miss Greenville. The Yankee skipper was overheard to say to Ms. Gray, "I hope you follow us daily."

Stengel did manage to part company with Miss Greenville for a few minutes prior to the game and huddled his Yankee team on the infield for a pep talk. He was disappointed in their 3-2 extra inning loss the day before to the Phillies in Columbia and attempted to light a fire in his talented team.

Honorary batboys included future major leaguer, Dickie Dietz, who wore his Greenville High Red Raider uniform and posed for pictures prior to the game with Yankee second baseman Bobby Richardson.

Richardson, a native of Sumter, S.C., recalled an unusual event that occurred prior to the game related to the post-baseball career of his teammate, Bob Turley.

"We were taking batting practice, and a ball went over toward the edge of the wall in foul territory. A fan reached over to get the ball, and Bob Turley pushed the fellow a bit, and the guy fell over on the field," Richardson said. "Before the game was over, there was an arrest warrant out for Turley."

Richardson explained that, in the off season, Turley sold insurance, and he used that story from Greenville to sell each of his Yankee teammates a personal liability insurance policy. After retiring from baseball, Turley became a successful financial planner and insurance executive and was one of the co-founders of the A.L. Williams Insurance Company, later called Primerica Financial Services.

Several photos in the *The Greenville News* the next day showed many of the players obliging the autograph-seeking fans. Richardson was Mantle's teammate from 1955 to 1966 and a close friend. When told about the graciousness Mantle extended to autograph seekers that day at Meadowbrook, Richardson commented, "That's just who he was. He would do anything in the world for you. Unfortunately, so much that has been written about Mickey doesn't portray that good side of Mickey."

Richardson recalled numerous incidents where Mantle quietly helped someone without fanfare or public recognition. He said Mantle visited him in South Carolina on four occasions, once helping him raise enough money to build a new YMCA in Sumter.

Mickey Charles Mantle was born in Spavinaw, Okla., on October 20, 1931. His father, Elvin "Mutt" Mantle, named his son in honor of the major league's best catcher at the time, Mickey Cochrane. Mutt moved his family to Commerce, Okla., when Mickey was three and took a job in a zinc mine.

Mutt dreamed of Mickey becoming a big league ballplayer and from an early age groomed his right-handed son to also hit left-handed. Mutt's efforts paid off as Mantle eventually became the greatest switch-hitter of all time.

Blessed with natural athletic ability, Mantle excelled early on as a multisport athlete but ultimately focused his attention on baseball. He was playing for a local semi-pro baseball team when he was discovered by Yankee scout Tom Greenwade. Mantle graduated high school in 1949, and Greenwade immediately signed him to a contract with the Yankees Class A affiliate in Independence, Kan.

Mantle found himself in the Yankees' spring training in 1951, as a 19-year-old being touted by Stengel as the heir apparent to Joe DiMaggio. Stengel said of Mantle, "He has more speed than any slugger I've ever seen, and more slug than any other speedster—and nobody has had more of 'em together. This kid ain't logical. He's too good. It's very confusing."[6]

Almost overnight, Mantle became the most famous baseball player in America. As noted on a website dedicated to his life:

America needed a baseball hero in 1951. Mickey Mantle became that hero. With television sets appearing in every American home, we were able to watch Mickey and the Yan-

kees virtually every Saturday on the Game of the Week and practically every October in the World Series.[7]

Mantle severely injured his right knee chasing down a Willie Mays fly ball in the 1951 World Series, and it was the first of several injuries that forced him to play with severe pain throughout his career. He still managed to lead the Yankees to 12 American League pennants and seven World Series championships during his 18-year career. He was a three-time American League MVP and won the Triple Crown in 1956. Mantle was a first ballot selection into the National Baseball Hall of Fame in 1974.

Mantle's activities off the field and battle with alcoholism are well documented, but those who knew him best like to remember his better qualities. Close friend and teammate Whitey Ford said Mantle was "a superstar who never acted like one. He was a humble man who was kind and friendly to all his teammates, even the rawest rookie. He was idolized by all the other players."[8]

———————

Twelve-year-old Butch Scott was one of hundreds of youngsters at Meadowbrook Park when the '58 Yankees came to town. Scott and his father were diehard Yankee fans, which he attributed to the Yankees' frequent television appearances on baseball's Game of the Week.

Scott was a veteran of many trips to Meadowbrook, a place where he said his father used to drop him off with his friends and let them "roam all over the ballpark." Scott and his dad were among the first to arrive at Meadowbrook, and as soon as they passed through the gate, the young boy sprinted straight to the Yankees' third base dugout. He crawled up on the roof to get as close as possible to his baseball heroes. He had a 10-cent scorecard and pen in hand and used all the childhood spunk he could muster to collect signatures from the Yankee players.

Scott was thrilled to get the autograph of his hero, Mickey Mantle, but it was manager Casey Stengel who provided the young boy with an unforgettable baseball memory. By game time, Scott's scorecard not only had Mantle's signature, but also included the autographs of 10 other Yankee players. Missing from his collection was Stengel's *John Hancock*. As the Yankee manager stepped out of the dugout and headed toward home plate to exchange his lineup card, Scott pleaded for his autograph. Stengel turned toward Scott and said, "How about you give me your autograph?"

What happened next most likely made Scott the envy of every young fan in the ballpark. "He lifted me off the roof of the dugout and onto the field," Scott recalled. "He handed me the lineup card and told me to walk with him to home plate where we gave it to the umpire."

Before he sent Scott back to the stands, Stengel scribbled his signature across the back of the young boy's scorecard. The next day *The Greenville News* Sports Editor Jim Anderson made a brief reference to Stengel's pregame interchange with Scott.

It's been 63 years since Scott walked the Yankee lineup card to home plate in front of his father, his friends and 9,000 Greenville baseball fans. The broad smile on Scott's face as he retells the story indicates that the passage of time has not diminished the joy of a boy's fondest baseball memory.

Don Larsen was the starting pitcher for the Yankees in Greenville. Two years earlier, Larsen pitched the only perfect World Series game in history. Curt Simmons took the mound for the Phillies.

The Yankees blasted six home runs and demolished their National League opponent 20-1. Much to the delight of the Greenville fans, Mantle went 5-for-5 with a home run, three doubles and a single. Moose Skowron hit two home runs, and Elston Howard and Don Larsen also hit balls out of Meadowbrook.

Philadelphia Phillies shortstop Granny Hamner (#2) is caught in a run-down in the Phillies and New York Yankees exhibition game at Meadow-brook Park on April 7, 1958.
(Courtesy of the Greenville County Historical Society—Joe Jordan Collection)

In the bottom of the fourth inning, Yankee outfielder Harry "Suit-case" Simpson was hit on the wrist by a Simmons' fastball. Joe Trimble from the *New York Daily News* was one of 10 reporters traveling with the Yankees and incorrectly reported that Simmons was rushed to a local Negro hospital for X-rays. Trimble made a logical assumption that at the time Greenville had segregated healthcare facilities, but in fact, four years earlier, the local Negro hospital was closed, and Black patients were allowed to be treated at Greenville General Hospital. X-rays at Greenville General revealed that Simpson had suffered a broken wrist.

Both teams received approximately $4,000 for their trip to Greenville and based on the success of the event, vowed they would like to return the following year, a promise that was not fulfilled.

Mantle, Williams and their Yankees and Red Sox teammates signed hundreds of autographs on their visits to Greenville. Much of the memorabilia containing those signatures has disappeared over the years, victims of attic purgings, estate sales or just general neglect. Fortunately, some of those signatures remain as treasured family relics, and the stories that go with them give voice to an era when Meadowbrook Park hosted the very best in the game.

10
Big Chief

The best medicine in the world is to smile and keep a good humor.
—Urbana Blanco Estevis

Camilo Estevis stood atop the pitcher's mound at Meadowbrook Park on a warm June evening in 1962. It was the top of the 10th inning, and Estevis had gone the distance, limiting the Macon Peaches to two earned runs. He had struck out seven and walked a couple.

Estevis was in search of his fifth victory in six starts since being sent to Greenville from the Dodgers AAA farm team in Omaha. His pitching skills, along with his winsome personality, made him a fan favorite among the Meadowbrook faithful. Paid attendance was a mere 462, and fewer than that remained as the Tuesday night game dragged into extra innings.

The top of the order was due up for Macon, which meant that Estevis would face its cocky 21-year-old second baseman, Pete Rose. The Greenville fans began to chide Rose with chants of "R-o-s-i-e, R-o-s-i-e, R-o-s-i-e," as he stepped into the batter's box. Earlier in the season, a Sally League beat reporter had tagged Rose with the nickname "Hollywood," but it was the following year that Rose picked up a name that stuck with him throughout his career.

Rose was playing for the Cincinnati Reds in a spring training game against the Yankees when he sprinted to first base after drawing a walk. The Yankees' Whitey Ford and Mickey Mantle yelled at him from the dugout, "there goes Charlie Hustle."[1] The next day, a

New York paper featured a headline that read, "Charlie Hustle Beats Yanks." It was the same year that Rose began his 23-year major league career in which he broke Ty Cobb's record for most hits.

Estevis said he and Rose developed a friendly rivalry during their time in the Sally League. "Sometimes we would see each other on the street prior to a ballgame, and he would point at me and hold up four fingers and rub his stomach," Estevis said. "He was telling me that he was going to get fat on my pitching and go four for four against me later that night." Estevis said he typically responded by smiling at Rose and pointing to his head, which was his way of saying he was going to "outsmart Rose that night" with his "crafty pitching style."

Estevis was 6'2" and 200 pounds but was not an overpowering pitcher. He said his fastball topped out at 85 mph only if he "was throwing downwind in a hurricane." He prided himself on his ability to keep hitters off balance by changing speeds and throwing a sharp "nickel curve." Estevis also said he was known for his skill at "painting the black," referring to his ability to spot pitches on the corners of home plate.

Macon was one of the stronger hitting clubs in the league. It sent 10 players off the 1962 roster to the majors. Macon was managed by 28-year-old Dave Bristol, who had a successful career as a manager with the Reds, Brewers, Expos, Braves and Giants. In April, the Peaches beat the Spinners 32-5, setting a Sally League record for runs scored in a game.

Rose had doubled off Estevis earlier in the game for his only hit in three attempts. Estevis was beginning to show signs of throwing well over 100 pitches across his nine innings of work. Rose singled in the 10th, and Estevis gave up a three-run homer as Macon defeated Greenville, 8-3. Estevis would have to wait until late July to get a chance to exact revenge on Rose and the Peaches.

180

In May of 1962, the AAA Omaha Dodgers' manager Danny Ozark found himself with one too many pitchers on his roster. Estevis was the odd man out, and the Dodgers gave him a bus ticket to Greenville. It would be the fourth stop in his minor league career that began in 1960 when he joined the Dodgers organization as one of their most promising young arms.

Estevis was born in 1938 in Edinburg, Texas, and spent his childhood in the small communities of the Rio Grande Valley section of southern Texas. His father served as a sniper in General George Patton's Third Army during World War II. He earned a Purple Heart for service in the Western Allied invasion of France that included fighting in the Battle of the Bulge. Estevis said his father "really never came home from the war," stating that he left his mother, his two sisters and him and moved to Montana shortly after returning to the States. "I was probably 7 or 8, and my sisters were 5 and 2 when my dad walked out on us," he recalled.

Estevis' mother knew she needed help raising two young daughters and a son. She sent Camilo to live with his paternal grandmother and uncle on a nearby sharecropper's farm/ranch. He was one of nine children (six boys and three girls) living on the ranch, and he said, "All of us had to do our part in farming cotton and a variety of vegetables and handling the chores around the ranch."

Several of his cousins were good athletes, and it was on the ranch that Camilo first connected with baseball. "My uncle always provided about an acre of the land where we could play when we were finished working," Estevis said.

An older cousin, Francisco, became an accomplished baseball

player in high school and college, and Camilo said, "He was the one who taught me the game and made me a thrower. Thanks to him and his reputation, I became well known in the area."

Coming out of Edinburg High School, Estevis had the chance to play professional baseball. The Pittsburgh Pirates offered him a $20,000 signing bonus, but his uncle instructed him to call his father to seek advice on whether to turn professional.

"It was only like the third or fourth time I had ever spoken with my father," Estevis said. "He had dropped out of third grade, and he told me that when he went looking for a job after the war, he was always asked about his education. He said people laughed at him when he had to admit he didn't even graduate high school."

With encouragement from his father, Estevis set a goal of becoming the first member of his family to obtain a college degree. He enrolled initially at Pan American University in his hometown of Edinburg but transferred his sophomore year to New Mexico Highlands University where he played for John Donnelly, a man Estevis said was a key influence and mentor to him. Donnelly was a native New Yorker and a graduate of St. John's University. Estevis affectionately referred to him as "Father John."

At Highlands, Estevis established himself as one of the most dominant pitchers in the NAIA ranks with a three-year record of 31-6. His senior year, he posted a 0.90 ERA and led the NAIA in strikeouts. Estevis was also an outstanding hitter, with a .440 average his senior year. In 1959, with college degree in hand, Estevis signed with the Los Angeles Dodgers for what the local papers said was a "sizeable bonus."

When Estevis' signing was announced, Highlands Coach Donnelly told the *Valley Morning Star*, "We have accomplished the things which we set out to do in this order: 1. Camilo has his college degree. 2. He has a real good shot in professional baseball with a good organization and a good classification. 3. His bonus is a sufficient size to enable him to purchase his own home . . ."

The Dodgers sent Estevis to the Reno Silver Foxes in the Class C California League. Word spread among the Silver Foxes that an "Indian from New Mexico" was on his way to join the team. Estevis has high cheekbones and a dark complexion, but he is not a Native American. He says, "I am a proud Texan."

The first time Estevis pitched in Reno, third-string catcher Mike Stubbins from Uhrichsville, Ohio, was assigned as his batterymate. "Mike couldn't pronounce my name, so he came out to the mound and said, 'I'm going to just call you Big Chief,'" Estevis said. Estevis went along with it, and the nickname followed him throughout his career.

Estevis went 5-3 in Reno in 12 appearances but was hit twice on the same foot by line drives and missed six and a half weeks with a broken right foot. One of Estevis' most notable teammates in Reno was second baseman Bobby Cox who became a Hall of Fame manager with the Atlanta Braves.

The following spring, "Big Chief" was promoted to the AA Atlanta Crackers. In Atlanta, Estevis began to master the craft of pitching under the watchful eye of Rube Walker, the team's manager. Walker was later best known as the pitching coach for the New York Mets from 1968 to 1981, where he oversaw a staff that included such notables as Tom Seaver, Nolan Ryan, Jerry Koosman, and Ron Darling.

Estevis won his first five starts with the Crackers before misfortune struck again, this time in the form of a knot on his wrist that required surgery. When he returned, he never regained his early season form and finished 5-5.

Estevis started the 1962 season in AAA Omaha before joining Greenville on May 16. The Spinners pitching staff was badly in need of help, and the Dodgers believed it was the best spot for Estevis to get the regular work he needed.

———————

Professional baseball returned to Greenville in the spring of 1961 when the Los Angeles Dodgers relocated their Class A Sally League affiliate from Macon, Ga. Professional baseball had been absent from Meadowbrook for four years, and when Dodgers executives arrived in Greenville to inspect the ballpark, they found obvious signs of neglect. The playing surface was worn and in need of care, and the dugouts had been filled in with concrete to install an oval stock car track in 1956.

The city and the Dodgers made sizeable investments to ready the park for an April 18 home opener. The Dodgers sprung for a new $7,500 scoreboard, the first at Meadowbrook to feature electric lights. The entire ballpark received a fresh coat of paint. Box seats were painted red and remaining seats green, and the outside façade was painted blue. New bleacher seats were installed along the outfield lines. A batting cage used in the Dodgers' former home at Brooklyn's Ebbets Field was shipped to Greenville.

The Dodgers sponsored a "name the team competition," allowing Greenvillians to vote for either "Dodgers" or "Spinners" as the team's mascot. In a close race, "Spinners" won. The city granted the Dodgers a five-year lease for Meadowbrook, and city council approved the playing of 10 Sunday afternoon games, a first for a city that had historically adhered to blue laws that limited activities such as baseball on Sunday afternoons out of respect for the Christian Sabbath. Two years later, the Fox Theatre on Main Street began showing movies on Sunday evenings further signifying that church would no longer be the only show in town on Sundays in Greenville.

The Dodgers sent 28-year-old Charlie Senger to serve as general manager of the club. Senger was a native of Brooklyn, N.Y., and a former baseball and basketball player at Florida Southern. After a brief stint in the minor leagues as a knuckleball pitcher, Senger was hired by the Dodgers organization. He came to Greenville from the Class D Panama City Fliers where he served as GM for a team that led the league in attendance. He was viewed as an energetic go-getter who plunged headfirst into the Greenville community. He moved his wife and infant son to the Terrace Apartments, joined a local textile basketball team, and in a short time became well known throughout the city as he served as the Dodgers' official advance man.

Thirty-five-year-old Roy Hartsfield was tabbed as the manager of the Spinners. Like Senger, Hartsfield came to Greenville from Panama City where he led the Fliers to the Class D Alabama-Florida League championship in 1960. Hartsfield was an Atlanta native and an outstanding football, basketball and baseball player at West Fulton High School. He was offered a football scholarship at the University of Georgia but opted to play professional baseball. After a year with the Atlanta Crackers as a starting shortstop, he enlisted in the Navy during World War II. In 1946 and '47, he played for the Charleston Rebels of the Sally League and appeared in several games at Meadowbrook Park. He continued his minor league career after the war and eventually made it to the big leagues in 1950. Over the course of the next three years, he appeared in 265 games for the Boston Braves.

Hartsfield got his first managerial position in 1958 as the player/

manager for the Class D Iowa Bruins, and he moved several times within the Dodgers organization as a minor league and major league coach. By the time he arrived in Greenville in 1961, he was a knowledgeable, well-respected baseball man. He got his only chance as a major league manager when he was named as the first skipper of the Toronto Blue Jays in 1976. He coached three years for the expansion Blue Jays and compiled a record of 166-318.

Greenville's baseball fans expressed their gratitude for the return of professional baseball at the turnstiles as they helped the Spinners lead the league in attendance. The Spinners drew 100,101 in 1961 and were the only team in the Class A level to eclipse 100,000 fans. They finished 72-66 and third in the Sally League behind the Asheville Tourists. Asheville ran away with the league championship and was led by future Hall of Famer Willie Stargell.

The 1962 Spinners were in last place, 13 games behind the league-leading Macon Peaches when Estevis arrived in Greenville in May. The local fans were losing interest fast, and attendance suffered. On Estevis' first night with the team, only 337 fans came out to watch the Spinners lose to Asheville.

Estevis' initial start was on the road against the Knoxville Smokies. He pitched nine solid innings, giving up two runs and striking out 11 in the Spinners 6-2 win. He followed that performance with another complete-game victory against Augusta. In his third appearance, he once again went the distance but lost 2-1, setting up a memorable night that would cement his relationship with the local fans.

Wednesday night, June 6, was "Kid's Night" at Meadowbrook. All youth were admitted free and given a chance to win one of several prizes that included a Shetland pony, complete with saddle and bridle. An overflow crowd of 6,553 showed up to watch "Big Chief" pitch for the Spinners against the Charlotte Hornets, an affiliate of the Minnesota Twins. Seventeen of the players from the '62 Hornets eventually played in the big leagues, including three-time American League batting champion and future Hall of Famer Tony Oliva.

Inspired by frequent chants of "Chief, Chief, Chief" from the large crowd, Estevis pitched his best game thus far, giving up one earned run, striking out seven and going the distance again in the Spinners' 6-4 win. He held Oliva to a single hit in five at-bats. *The Greenville News* said of his performance, "Estevis is the 'medicine man' that the ailing Spinners needed to fight out of the Sally League cellar."

Later in the summer, Estevis beat the Twins again on a humid July Sunday afternoon game. That day, he held Oliva hitless in four at-bats on his way to a four-hit complete-game victory. In the bottom of the fifth inning, Estevis helped his cause when he belted a two-run home run to secure the 5-1 win before a disappointing crowd of 658.

"Tony Oliva was a beautiful person and a helluva hitter," Estevis said of the future Twins star. "We used to visit after the games that year, and he told me, 'I just can't hit you as hard as I want to.'"

On July 31, in a game at Macon, Estevis got an opportunity to avenge his earlier loss to Pete Rose and the Peaches. Estevis scattered seven hits across nine innings as he won his 13th game against four losses. Rose went two for four in the Peaches' 13-4 loss.

Led by the pitching of Estevis and the hitting of first baseman Mel Corbo, the Spinners mounted a late-season fight to gain a spot in the Sally League playoffs. They defeated the Macon Peaches three consecutive games in mid-August and followed that with three straight wins over league-leading Savannah. As they were fighting for the

1962 Greenville Spinners: Front row—batboys Ellis Beddingfield and John Mauldin. Second row—Manager Roy Hartsfield, Hector Valle, Richard Hunt, Robert Cotton, William Berrier, Hugh Pepper, Robert Arrighi, Richard Crowe, Braxton Baily, Donald Ross. Back row—President and General Manager Charles Senger, Jose Cesar, Domingo Carrasquel, Melvin Corbo, Camilo Estevis, Sheldon Brodsky, Philip Brown, William Kalmes, Ford Young, Ray Apple, Samuel Hitcher, Sherman Jones and Trainer William Snell

(From the author's collection)

fourth and final playoff spot, they lost a crucial series to Asheville and finished in fifth place. Attendance dropped nearly 50 percent from the prior year as the Spinners drew 59,000 fans in 1962.

Estevis led the Sally League with 18 wins against eight losses and struck out 147 in 214 innings pitched. He started 25 games, completed 24 and had an ERA of 2.95. He also hit .299 with three home runs. In addition to Oliva and Rose, the 1962 Sally League rosters featured several well-known future major leaguers including, Gene Alley (Asheville), Tommy Helms and Art Shamsky (Macon), Ken Berry and Don Buford (Savannah) and Jim Northrup (Knoxville).

Future Basketball Hall of Famer Dave DeBusschere pitched for the '62 Savannah White Sox, going 10-1 on the season. In a game between Greenville and Savannah at Meadowbrook during the '62 season, an umpire was late in arriving and DeBusschere was pressed into service as the base umpire for a couple of innings.

Estevis' wife gave birth to their first daughter in early June while he was winning games for the Spinners. Once his wife and infant daughter were able to travel from their home in Pharr, Texas, they joined him in Greenville for the remainder of the season.

"I really enjoyed my time in Greenville," Estevis recalled. "The people were so very good to me. I remember being invited to barbecues at people's homes on Sundays after games. I was treated very well in Greenville."

In early November, the Dodgers organization covertly backed a moving van up to the front entrance of Meadowbrook, loaded all their baseball equipment and took it to their Vero Beach, Fla. training facility. Greenville Mayor David Traxler said he had not been given any notice by the organization of its intent to depart Greenville and break the final three years of their five-year lease for the ballpark.

The Dodgers eventually sent a formal letter to Mayor Traxler, blaming their decision to exit Greenville on the Sally League's plans to move up to AA classification. *The Greenville News* Sports Editor Jim Anderson responded to the Dodgers' surprise exit by writing a scathing column in the form of an open letter addressed to Fresco Thompson, the Dodgers' Director of Farm Clubs. Anderson wrote:

> *There is a right and a wrong way to do things. The Dodgers chose the wrong way ... Not one person in the Dodger organization has spoken one word to the local fans to say their support has been appreciated. The only supposition is, therefore, that the Dodgers feel they did not have good support.*

… It was untimely of you to say one day you were dropping out of the Sally League because you could not field a Double A team, and then the next day sign with the Texas League to have a Double A team in Albuquerque, N.M. … What is regretted in the dissociation of yourself and this city, is simply the manner in which no clear-cut statements were issued, no courtesy shown your lessor, no concern given at all to baseball fans, and the entire matter treated as something rather humorous by the "hatchet man" you sent here to affect the pullout.

The Dodgers abrupt departure in the fall of 1962 left Greenville once again without a professional baseball team.

In 1963, Estevis was assigned to play for the Dodgers' newly formed AA team in Albuquerque, N.M. He went 16-12 in 38 appearances with a 3.74 ERA. He boasted a 4-0 record against the league's best hitting team, the El Paso Sun Kings. Estevis led the league in victories (16), strikeouts (196) and complete games (19) for a team that finished fifth in a six-team league. He was selected to the Texas League All-Star Game, and although he didn't pitch in the game because he had pitched the night before, he was selected to pinch hit in the third inning and delivered a hit.

Despite being one of the best pitchers in the Texas League in 1963, Estevis was informed by the Dodgers in September that he would not be invited to spring training. The Dodgers had made sizeable investments in several other younger pitchers, which led to their decision to release the 25-year-old Estevis.

Estevis' contract was purchased by the Chicago White Sox who assigned him to Indianapolis to start the '64 season. After a serious elbow injury, he was sent to Lynchburg where he finished the season. Estevis said the White Sox gave up on him after that year, and he spent the following two years pitching for Veracruz in the Mexican League before retiring permanently from baseball.

Playing minor league baseball in the segregated South in the early '60s had its challenges for Blacks and Latin players. Estevis said he was fortunate to avoid some of the more severe treatment others received.

"In all my time in the minor leagues, I only remember one time when I got a raw deal. It was in a restaurant in Arkansas," he said. "The owner didn't want to serve me, and so I said, that's his privilege, and I left. That night at the game, I am surrounded by kids who want my autograph. One of them is restaurant owner's son. So, as I am autographing the little's guys booklet, I tell him, 'I hope you don't grow up to be like your father.' He looked up at me and then at his father who grabbed him and pulled him away. That's the only incident like that I can recall from my career."

After retiring from baseball, Estevis had his college degree to fall back on and enjoyed a successful career working primarily as an adult education counselor and placement officer. He speaks proudly of his two daughters, both of whom earned advanced degrees and have rewarding careers. Estevis became a scratch golfer, which filled his need for competition. Today, he says his outdoor activities are limited to gardening and yard work.

At 83, Estevis' baseball memories remain vivid. He recalls with exacting detail specifics about games from nearly 60 years earlier. He has no regrets or hard feelings about a baseball career that did not pan out as he had hoped. In fact, when he speaks about his minor league career, his words are filled more with joy and thankfulness for the good times rather than bitterness or regret about his misfortunes.

Estevis attributes his positive attitude to his grandmother, Urbana Blanco Estevis, who raised him on the farm in the Rio Grande Valley. She always told me, "The best medicine in the world is to smile and keep a good humor."

11
Greasy Corner

Black teams, representing Black communities, formed a replica of major league baseball, separate and unequal in everything but athletic ability.

—*Invisible Men: Life in Baseball's Negro Leagues*

On a warm June morning in 2021, John Calvin Whiteside returned for a visit to Mayberry Park. He stood in a familiar spot on the grass covered infield, halfway between second and third base. More than 50 years have passed since Whiteside was a slick fielding shortstop for his high school team, the Sterling Tigers. Sterling practiced at Mayberry Park and played its home games at the adjacent Meadowbrook Park.

Whiteside grew up a couple of blocks away in Greasy Corner, one of three Black neighborhoods that surrounded Meadowbrook Park. The intersection of North Hudson, Birnie and North Calhoun marked the center of Greasy Corner. The neighborhood's borders extended northeast along Hudson Street to the banks of the Reedy River where it converged with the Southern Side community. Greasy Corner encompassed both Meadowbrook and Mayberry Parks. To the west, it ran along Gower and Birnie streets before intersecting with the West Greenville community. It spread east toward downtown Greenville, stopping at Pendleton and Augusta streets.

No one knows for certain how Greasy Corner acquired its name. Most say it started when a Piedmont-Northern train crashed into a truck carrying a load of pigs at the Greasy Corner intersection. Others point to either a series of gas stations or "greasy spoon" cafés that populated the neighborhood.

Greasy Corner was a self-contained community. Residents purchased food and household goods from a collection of "mom and pop" grocery/convenience stores, like Michaels or Sijons on Hudson Street. Robert Hudson's barbershop in the heart of Greasy Corner was a gathering spot for the male population. Several beauty shops and small cafés were spread throughout. Entertainment options included the Harlem Theatre on Hudson Street near the Reedy River or the Five Spot on Birnie Street, a combination pool and dance hall. Talley's liquor store and a couple of locals who operated stills and sold moonshine out of their homes provided residents with alcoholic refreshments. Burials were handled by one of two funeral homes located on opposite ends of Calhoun Street.

Residents included educators, physicians, business owners and a large contingent who earned their living in trades such as bricklaying or concrete finishing. Others either walked or caught the bus to the more affluent homes in Greenville where they provided domestic services. Houses ranged from spacious three- and four-bedroom wooden homes with welcoming front porches to small single room "shotgun" houses, which were often leased to the Black residents by White landlords. Once the workday was complete, residents were drawn to the Greasy Corner intersection where they socialized well into the evening.

Four long-serving churches formed the spiritual nucleus of the community. Tabernacle Baptist Church, Israel Chapel CME Church, Pilgrim Rest Baptist Church and St. Anthony's Catholic Church were centers of spiritual nourishment and a social hub for the families of

Greasy Corner. Other neighboring churches, including Mountain-view Baptist, the United House of Prayer, Allen Temple AME and Israel Metropolitan CME Church, also have a long history of service in the area.

Children attended the Union School at the intersection of Markley and Calhoun streets or the Gower Street School. These schools were typically overcrowded and under-resourced with facilities far inferior to their White counterparts.

Whiteside's grandmother, Sue Pearl Booker, was the matriarch of Greasy Corner. She was an educator who, according to Whiteside, taught many of the local Black children how to read and write. Her watchful oversight over the comings and goings of the neighborhood earned her the title of the "Mayor of Greasy Corner." She took great pride in her neighborhood and was regarded by city officials as a respected spokesperson for her community. Longtime Police Chief Harold Jennings considered her a trusted friend, and the two worked to keep Greasy Corner as safe as possible. Whiteside said of his grandmother: "She used to like to say that she could speak to aristocrats, bureaucrats, Democrats and even alley cats."

The youth of Greasy Corner enjoyed skating down the hill on Birnie Street or walking along the train tracks collecting pieces of

John Whiteside, captain of the 1967 Sterling High School baseball team, slides into third base in a game at Meadowbrook Park.
(Courtesy of The Torch, 1967 Sterling High School Yearbook)

coal that had fallen from the trains. On hot days, they often swam in the murky waters of the Reedy River. One former resident remembered that many of the local textile mills dumped chemical waste in the Reedy and said, "When we were swimming in it, we could look up the river and see different colored water heading toward us. We knew it was time to get out when we saw that."

Sports and especially baseball were important to the community. "Baseball was a way of life around our neighborhood," Whiteside says with enthusiasm. "It was a game we loved, and as kids, we played baseball all day long. It was such a big part of our lives."

Whiteside was one of many youth from the surrounding neighborhoods who chased down baseballs beyond the boundaries of Meadowbrook Park, sometimes even jumping into the Reedy River to retrieve the souvenir. "We would take the balls and sell them to the White parents going into the game, and they gave them to their children. We would get anywhere from 25 cents to a dollar for a ball, which would give us money to go to a movie, plus buy us something at the concession stand," Whiteside remembered. "Sometimes we would take the ball to the gate at Meadowbrook, and if we gave it back, they would let us in the game free."

Whiteside and his friends often watched games at Meadowbrook standing atop a small hill outside the park and peering over the left field wall. "I remember standing on that hill watching Willie Stargell hit one over the right field wall and over the Reedy River," Whiteside's cousin, Marion Butler, said about a memorable home run the future Hall of Famer hit in 1961 while playing for the Asheville Tourists.

On that June morning when Whiteside returned to his shortstop position at Mayberry Park, the sounds of heavy construction equipment could be heard as workers graded the land for the planned 60-

acre, $40 million Unity Park. The new park is in part an attempt by the city to right some of the past wrongs related to the inadequacy of recreational facilities offered to Greenville's Blacks during segregation. Whiteside smiles at the irony of the massive construction in an area where the city's investment was so minimal during the days of his childhood.

"The infield at Mayberry was lots of lumps and bumps. We'd have to pick up rocks and glass out of the infield before practice," Whiteside said. "We had a single merry-go-round that held about three of us, a swing set and one seesaw."

Whiteside referenced a tiny building near the entrance to the park that housed a single folding ping pong table. "That was our community recreation center," he joked. A grassy area behind the left field fence served as a dumping ground for rocks and debris from city projects.

Whiteside turned toward Mayberry's third base line and pointed to the location of a police shooting range that was built in 1938, within a few feet of the baseball field. "Can you believe they would put a shooting range right there with all these kids running around here?" he asks in disbelief.

Police officers practiced their marksmanship by firing at targets affixed to a series of telephone poles within the range. Whiteside and other local kids dug lead slugs from the poles and carted them across the street to Goodlett's junkyard in exchange for a few coins. If they were well-behaved, the junkyard's owner, O.M. "Cutie" Goodlett gave the boys a look at his pet monkey that he kept in a cage in his office.

The distance between the outfield fence of Mayberry Park and the concrete outfield wall of Meadowbrook Park was a few hundred feet. In terms of access for Blacks, there was a vast chasm between the two parks, a divide that had been built over years of legalized racial segregation.

For most of Meadowbrook's life, it was a place Blacks were allowed to use only on selected dates and times, and their access came with a series of restrictions. If a Black resident attended a "non-Black" event, they were forced to sit in the designated "colored section" along the third base line. Separate, but certainly not equal, concession and restroom facilities were provided. Members of Black teams playing at Meadowbrook dressed in their uniforms prior to arriving at Meadowbrook as they were not allowed to use the park's locker rooms.

"Meadowbrook was a big-time park for us, and we enjoyed getting the chance to play there. It had real lights, not just a few light bulbs on a pole like we had at Mayberry," Whiteside said.

Whiteside remembers combing box scores as a youth to find how his favorite major league players fared and listening to games on the radio, but the real heroes of his youth were not Williams, DiMaggio or Mantle. His love for the game was most influenced by men he knew, not just men he read about—players such as his cousin Marion "Baldy" Butler, Frank "Rabbit" Johnson, June Furman, Babe Smith, Herbert "Big Hank" Roberts, Richard "Chop Chop" Curry, Ernest "Chic" Bolen, Max "Bear" Chapman, "Tater" Foster, Lawrence "Smokey" Blakely, Cornell "Corn" Blakely and Rico Dawson. Several of these men transferred their knowledge of the game's fundamentals to Whiteside and dozens of others as they continued to live in the neighborhood and coach local youth teams, further solidifying their baseball legacies.

The pictures of Greenville's early Black baseball stars didn't appear on baseball cards. Their exploits on the diamond were rarely covered by the local media. Their opportunities for advancement were limit-ed in a segregated world. Nearly all of them spent the prime of their baseball careers playing on loosely organized semi-pro teams or community softball teams, yet their stories remain legendary around the neighborhoods surrounding Meadowbrook Park. The players and the teams they played on are an important and often overlooked part of the rich baseball history of the Greenville community.

———————

Like many other American cities, Greenville's Black community built its own baseball world. Author Donn Rogosin, in his book *Invisible Men, Life in Baseball's Negro Leagues*, explains that these base-ball subcultures were built out of necessity.

> *Baseball has long been called America's game. It was not just white America's game, it was a game loved by all races, but due to the segregated society that emerged in America during reconstruction, Black communities were forced to build their own baseball world.*
>
> *In segregated America, great Black baseball players were forced to exhibit their talents behind a rigid color barrier— victims of the unwritten law that no Black man was allowed in the major leagues. Men of extraordinary athletic ability passed their lives in obscurity, absent from the sport pages of the white newspapers, obliterated from American sports history.*
>
> *Confronted by an intolerant society, the Black athlete and the Black community built their own sports world Black teams were formed and later, black leagues. . . . Black teams,*

representing Black communities, formed a replica of major-league baseball, separate and unequal in everything but athletic ability.

Baseball was played nonstop by youth at Mayberry Park or on any other open field within the Black neighborhoods of Greenville. Adults played baseball, as well as softball, on evenings and weekends.

Meadowbrook Park became the home field for games for the following Black teams: The Sterling High School Tigers, The Greenville Black Spinners, The Greenville Red Socks, the St. Anthony Braves and the Greenville Negro All-Stars. The most prominent of the semipro teams was the Greenville Black Spinners.

The first reference to an organized Black baseball team in Greenville dates to 1910 when *The Greenville News* reported on a game between the Greenville Giants and a similar team from Anderson. The Giants were referred to as "Greenville's fast colored team" and one of "the best colored teams in the state." The team disappeared around the time World War I began but made a brief reappearance in the late 1940s.

Marion C. "Kingfish" Clark was born in Greenville in 1887. He had a strong entrepreneurial spirit and a love for his community and its people. He was a self-taught chef and café owner. His wife, the former Emma Shumate, operated a beauty shop. Clark was concerned that Blacks in his community suffered from a deficit of leisure and recreational activities, which led him to open a series of billiard parlors, and with the help of his friend Mark Durham, he organized the Greenville Black Spinners in 1921.

The Black Spinners were a collection of mostly local players who competed against teams like the Spartanburg Sluggers, Easley

Browns, Asheville Blues, Charlotte Black Hornets and the Raleigh Tigers. Initially, home games were played on the baseball field on Perry Avenue and later at Graham Field; Meadowbrook became the Black Spinners' official home when it opened in 1938. Many of the Black Spinners games were scheduled for Monday evenings when the park was not being used by Greenville's White professional team.

Infrequent and brief accounts of Black Spinners contests appeared in *The Greenville News* from 1921 to 1969. Advertisements for the games always included the following statement: "A special section will be reserved for white fans at the game." Most often, this meant that the entire grandstand section on the third base side was reserved for Whites. The games drew large crowds, particularly those against archrival Spartanburg. Whenever gate receipts were significant enough, players were paid small amounts of money for their play.

In 1939, the Catholic Diocese of Charleston purchased six acres on Gower Street and built a church and school focused on serving Greenville's Black community. The church is operated by the Franciscan order and became known as St. Anthony's of Padua, in honor of the patron saint of the poor. The church and school have remained a vibrant part of Greenville's West End community for over 80 years.

The Franciscans built a baseball field on their property, and it was home for a women's softball team, youth teams and the St. Anthony's Braves, an adult baseball team that competed in the local semi-pro circuit. Recorded accounts show Braves' games played between 1945 and 1955. Many of the same area players who played for the Black Spinners also played for the Braves.

For a short time in the mid-'50s, an additional Black semi-pro team known as the Greenville Black Red Socks appeared, and like

St. Anthony's, it relied upon many of the same local players to fill out its roster. Also, during a period in the '50s and '60s, Negro All-Star teams were formed with a collection of the best players from Greenville and surrounding areas. They competed against similar All-Star teams from cities such as Charlotte and Columbia. In 1954, *The Greenville News* noted that the local All-Star team was a farm club of the Indianapolis Clowns of the Negro American League.

Sterling High School fielded its first baseball team in 1955 under the direction of its longtime athletic coach, Joe Mathis. While Mathis was better known for his football coaching ability, he leaned on advice from some of the other more knowledgeable local baseball enthusiasts to help identify the best talent at Sterling. Meadowbrook Park was Sterling's home field from 1955 until the federally mandated integration of public schools in Greenville County in 1971 led to Sterling's closure along with the county's four other Black high schools.

Meadowbrook also became a stopover for traveling Negro League teams. The Kansas City Monarchs appeared at Meadowbrook in 1955, 1961 and 1962. The Monarchs' opponent in their August 16, 1962 visit to Meadowbrook was the Harlem Stars, a team that featured legendary Hall of Fame pitcher Leroy "Satchel" Paige. The 56-year-old Paige hurled three scoreless innings before a sparse crowd of 528 as Harlem defeated Kansas City 8-4.

The Indianapolis Clowns of the Negro American League played at Meadowbrook eight times between 1953 and 1970. The 1953 appearance of the Clowns showcased their second baseman Toni Stone, the first female player in the Negro Leagues.

A barnstorming group of Negro Major League All-Stars played a series of exhibition games throughout the Southeast in 1960 and stopped at Meadowbrook on the evening of October 20. The game featured the Milwaukee Braves' Hank Aaron, who went on to break Babe Ruth's career home run record, along with the LA Dodgers' Maury Wills, Cincinnati's Vada Pinson and Cleveland's Jim "Mudcat" Grant. *The Greenville News* promoted the game, yet no account of the game's results appeared the following day in either the morning or evening papers.

Cornell Blakely was born in 1928 and grew up in West Greenville. By the time he was nine, he had earned a job as batboy for the Greenville Black Spinners, and by age 15, he found himself playing left field for the semi-pro team alongside mostly grown men from the local Black community. He also played for the Asheville Blues and the St. Anthony's Braves. In 2009, in connection with a project by the Greenville County Library to recognize the history of Black baseball in Greenville, Blakely recalled his days of playing the semi-pro circuit.

"The crowds were fantastic. It was a livelihood for me. There were a lot of good players. It was a sport we loved, and you played because you knew you were good, and you played with hopes," Blakely said.

Blakely caught the attention of Greenville Spinners General Manager Jimmy Gaston, who used his personal friendship with Brooklyn Dodgers owner Branch Rickey to get Blakely an invitation to the Dodgers spring training in Vero Beach in 1950. The 22-year-old Blakely stood 5'4" and weighed 118 pounds when he reported to the Dodgers training camp. He was Greenville's version of the Negro League superstar "Cool Papa Bell"—small in stature, but able to make things happen on the basepaths with his speed and aggressive-

1943 Greenville Black Spinners. First Row: Unidentified, Frank "Rabbit" Johnson, Cornell Blakely, Robert Bolling, Ralph Shumate. Middle Row: William Yates, Laurence Blakely, June Griffin. Third Row: Robert Dogan, Bill Hill, Max "Bear" Chatman, Horace Pearson, "Tato" Foster, Hank Herbert.

ness. An article in *The Greenville News* announced Blakely's opportunity with the Dodgers and claimed Blakely was faster than Sam Jethro, formerly of the Brooklyn organization but recently purchased by the Boston Braves. The article noted that Jethro was reputed to be the fastest man in organized baseball at that time.

A highlight of Blakely's trip to Dodgertown was the opportunity to meet Jackie Robinson, but unfortunately his desire to follow in Robinson's footsteps to the major leagues ended in Vero Beach. Blakely hoped for a second chance to tryout with the Dodgers and kept a letter dated October 23, 1950, from Spencer Harris, the Dodgers' spring training supervisor, that hinted at a second opportunity.

That promise was never fulfilled, ending the young Greenvillian's dream of becoming a big leaguer. Fortunately for Blakely, he had a "back-up dream."

Blakely performed in the Sterling High School choir, glee club, quartet and band. He turned down music scholarships to three colleges to pursue a baseball career. He received private voice lessons at Furman University and told *The Greenville News* in 1973, "I was the first Black person to get that opportunity at Furman at that time."

After his failed attempt with the Dodgers, Blakely moved to Detroit to pursue a career in music. He took a job at Chrysler Motors and later Ford Motor Company to help pay the bills while he began to write songs and play the R&B nightclub circuit with the likes of future well-known artists Wilson Pickett, Brenda Lee and Little Anthony and the Imperials.

In 1960, Blakely quit his job at Ford and devoted himself full time to his musical aspirations. He went on the road singing in nightclubs throughout Michigan and told *The Greenville News'* Jim McAllister, "I was making a living at it—making as much as I did at Ford and working less." Berry Gordy Jr., the founder of the Motown Record Corporation took notice of Blakely and recorded five of his songs including his biggest hit "I've Got That Feeling," which featured Martha and the Vandellas singing backup. Several of Blakely's songs received attention in the Billboard ratings, but cash sales were not significant enough to earn a full-time living.

While in Detroit, Blakely also worked in the early '60s as an advance man for the Motor Town Review, a collection of concert tours for Motown artists, promoting acts for such stars as Diana Ross and the Supremes and Marvin Gaye. In an interview with Jimmy Cornelison of *The Greenville News* in 1998, Blakely said of that job, "They were just a bunch of kids. Diana Ross and the others weren't stars yet. Mary Wells and Smokey Robinson were the headliners. The others were just put on the show to fill it."

Blakely returned to Greenville in 1962 with hopes to start his own record label while continuing to perform and promote music shows. To provide a steady income for his family, he took a job as a disc jockey at WBBR in Travelers Rest, marking the beginning of a successful career in radio broadcasting that would span nearly five decades. In 1966, he became the first Black on-air personality for WHYZ and eventually worked for several local radio stations including the popular top-40 station WQOK. He was a familiar on-air personality throughout the Upstate and was known by many as "Bouncing Cornell Blakely" or simply as "Corn." His final days as a broadcaster were spent in Newberry where he owned and operated WKMG. He signed off each of his radio broadcasts with a distinctive farewell: "This is my old man's son Corn telling everybody to not smoke in bed for the ashes that hit the floor may be your own."

Blakely died in 2013 at the age of 85.

James Edward Kowans grew up on McCall Street in Greasy Corner. From a young age, he viewed life as his stage. He was a free-spirited youth who made his presence known wherever he landed.

This innate sense of showmanship likely caused him to change his name as an adult. James Kowans just was not flashy enough for his style, so somewhere in early adulthood, he took his mother's last name and added a first name he borrowed from a neighborhood friend who had left Greasy Corner and gone to New York in the '60s. James Kowans became known as Rico Dawson.

Dawson flashed his style, along with his athletic ability, on the baseball fields of Mayberry and Meadowbrook Parks. He played shortstop for Sterling High School in the early '60s, but according to John Whiteside, he had a "second baseman's arm," which may have been Dawson's only weakness as a player.

"Rico could really play the game," Whiteside recalled. "He could hit the ball with power, and he could really run the bases."

The Greenville News claimed that Dawson hit over .400 in each of the three seasons he played for Sterling and was the school's first player to hit over .500 in a season. He played a year at South Carolina State in 1964 and led the conference in home runs, RBIs and fielding percentage.

What made Dawson so memorable around the neighborhood was the extra bit of flash that he brought to the game. "Rico always had to be a little different. If everybody on the team had their shirt tucked in, he would have his pulled out," Whiteside said. "There was definitely a little 'hot dog' in him."

Marion Butler, a teammate of Dawson's at Sterling, remembers an incident involving Dawson's desire to be different. "We had just gotten new uniforms, and Rico went and cut his socks up so they looked more like what the big league players wore," Butler said. "When Coach Mathis saw what he had done, he told Rico, 'You owe me for a new pair of socks.'"

Dawson dropped out of SC State and returned to Greasy Corner where he played for the Black Spinners in the semi-pro circuit. In a 1976 interview with United Press International, Dawson recalled an exhibition game in Meadowbrook Park in the late '60s when the Black Spinners' opponent was the Indianapolis Clowns. "I had a real good day, and they were the type of club that if you were good against them, they wanted you to be with them," he said. "So, I was offered a contract for $4 a day."

The Indianapolis Clowns began playing in the Negro Leagues in the 1930s. Hank Aaron played for the Clowns in 1953 before he signed with the Milwaukee Braves. After Major League Baseball was fully integrated, the Clowns became baseball's version of the Harlem Globetrotters, entertaining fans with showmanship and comedy on the diamond. The Clowns were the last Negro League team to disband in 1989.

Dawson played with the Clowns in 1969 and '70, and his association with them led to his appearance on the biggest stage of his life. He said in an interview with United Press International in 1976 that a casting director from Universal Studios reached out to Ed Hamman, owner of Indianapolis Clowns, for the names of some players who might be a good fit for a new movie about life in the Negro leagues. The owner gave Dawson's name to the casting director.

"I was working at Oaklawn Correctional Center when I got the call from my Uncle Mace Chapman of Greenville, who said Universal Studios was trying to get in touch with me," Dawson told Jim McAllister of *The Greenville News*, shortly before the movie was released. "I told him to stop jiving me. I knew it was a joke. It was lunchtime, and I wasn't much in the mood for a joke."

Dawson was selected to play the role of second baseman Willie Lee Shively in Universal's 1976 sports/comedy film *The Bingo Long Traveling All-Stars & Motor Kings*. Dawson was part of a star-studded cast that included Billy Dee Williams, Richard Pryor and James Earl Jones. He had no acting experience, but he said, "They just wanted me to be myself, so that's what I did."

Initially, Dawson's part did not require much talking, but he told

McAllister: "After they found out I had such a great sense of humor, they changed my part and made it a lot bigger. I just kept everybody alive on the set with my wisecracking . . . had everybody rolling in stiches."

Dawson said he and Richard Pryor became good friends on the set and that at one point in reference to Dawson's antics, Pryor said to the movie's director John Badham, "I thought you hired me to tell the jokes." The movie was a box office success, grossing $33 million on a $9 million budget.

Dawson had hopes of advancing his movie career, but that did not materialize. He continued to play baseball in and around his old neighborhood, primarily for an informal local team organized and coached by his uncle, Mace Chapman.

Mace Chapman, better known to locals as "Peter Rabbit," operated the Rabbit Trap, a Greasy Corner convenience store and game room at 408 Calhoun Street, near the Greasy Corner intersection. Most knew that the store was really a front for the sale of illegal "ball tickets." Chapman, originally from Greasy Corner, moved to California and often spoke of his baseball exploits as a pitcher in the Long Beach area. He returned to Greenville in 1970 and established himself as one of his old neighborhood's most colorful and well-known residents. He was a unique combination of entrepreneur, promoter and athlete. He wore a trademark beard because he said he once heard that a man spends three years of his life shaving, and he had better things to do with his time.

For many years, Chapman fielded a traveling baseball team known as "Free at Last." Chapman was Greasy Corner's version of Satchel Paige as he pitched for Free at Last well into his 60s.

Free at Last played its home games on Saturday and Sunday afternoons at what was left of Meadowbrook Park after its devasting fire in 1972. The games were a popular social event for the local Black community, with some of them drawing two or three thousand fans. Beer and bets flowed freely among the patrons. Local radio personality Cornell Blakely served as announcer for many of the games. Home games were typically followed by a party at Chapman's store that included a disc jockey and free beer for both teams. The team traveled to nearby cities to play other community-based teams and played several games against the inmates at the Central Correctional Institution in Columbia.

Rick Aldridge was a standout catcher at Wade Hampton High School in the mid-'70s and got invited to join the Chapman's team while he was playing college baseball at Spartanburg Methodist. Aldridge was one of two Whites who were regular players on Free at Last. Everybody on the team had a nickname, and Aldridge quickly became known simply as "White Boy." Over a 15-year period, he said he spent many of his summer weekends playing catcher for Free at Last while building lifelong friendships with many of his teammates. His memories of Rico Dawson are consistent with all who knew him and saw him play.

"Rico was a great baseball player. He was only about 5'7"—but he could hit with power, and if he hit a ball in the infield that took two hops, there wasn't anybody who was going to throw him out," Aldridge recalled. "He had a great personality and was fun to be around. We had a lot of great times playing together on those teams."

Dawson died in 2014 at the age of 71, but local social media posts often feature fond memories of the colorful baseball player/Hollywood star from Greasy Corner.

If you ask John Whiteside to list the five best Black players who played at Mayberry and Meadowbrook, he confesses that his list is subject to a bit of partiality. He says his top five must include his cousin Marion "Baldy" Butler. He describes his cousin and former Sterling High School standout as having the kind of skills that would cause a scout today to tag him as a "five-tool player."

"Baldy could hit, he could field, he could run and he could throw a strike to home plate from center field. He was just a great baseball player, and I believe one of the best to ever come out of our neighborhood," Whiteside says.

Butler, who earned his nickname as a result of being born without any hair, grew up on Birnie Street in Greasy Corner and fell in love with baseball at a young age. At Sterling High, football clearly was the most popular sport. Many of the male students played multiple sports, but Butler was always a baseball guy first and chose to focus his efforts on the game he loved.

"I got my love of the game and my talent from my mother," Butler says. "She could talk baseball with anybody, and she was as good a player as any of the boys. She just didn't have the opportunity to play being a girl back in those days."

Butler's mother took her young son to the Black Spinners games where he recalls watching several of the ballplayers who later taught him the game as his coach on his neighborhood little leagues. He also recalls his mother taking him to the Brooklyn Dodgers-Greenville Spinners exhibition game in 1949 when rain spoiled his hopes of getting to see Jackie Robinson play.

Butler was a member of the 1960 Sterling High School baseball team that won the district championship and is considered to be one of the best teams in the school's history. It was rumored that Sterling tried to get a game that year with an outstanding Greenville High team, but the details of such a contest could not be worked out. It would have been a rare event pitting a White and Black high school in competition against each other in a Southern town during segregation.

Butler says his favorite major league player growing up was Willie Mays, and like Mays, Butler was an all-around baseball athlete. He played the game much like his hero. At 6'1" and around 200 pounds, he was a power hitter capable of playing multiple positions and possessing the speed to steal bases.

Butler played a year at SC State before returning home to Greenville, admitting it was the first time he had been away from home, and he had gotten homesick. Back home, he furthered his local baseball legend playing regularly for adult softball teams at Mayberry Park.

The Rev. Jesse Jackson's father, Charles Henry Jackson, played for the Black Spinners in the '40s and '50s and passed along his love of the game to his sons. Jesse was a three-sport athlete at Sterling High from 1956 through 1959. He was a standout quarterback for the football team and a pitcher on the baseball team; those who knew Jackson well agree that football was his best sport. Jackson earned a football scholarship to the University of Illinois but later transferred to North Carolina A&T. Both Whiteside and Butler say that Jackson's younger half-brother Charles "Duke" Jackson was the better baseball player among the two siblings.

Duke Jackson was a hard throwing right-handed pitcher for Sterling during the early '60s. *The Greenville News* reported on a game in 1962 when he struck out 16 of the 21 batters he faced in a win over Lincoln High School. He later moved to California to pursue a musical career and was part of an R&B vocal group called The Independents whose hit single "Leaving Me" sold over one million copies and earned gold record status. The group split up in 1976, and Jackson enjoyed a successful musical producing and writing career, assisting with much of the early work of recording artist Natalie Cole.

Bill Thompson grew up in Greasy Corner and was a 1965 graduate of Sterling where he had a prolific football career and was also a standout baseball player. He played defensive back at Maryland State College (later renamed University of Maryland Eastern Shore) and was a third-round pick of the Denver Broncos in 1969. Thompson played 13 years for the Broncos and was a three-time Pro Bowl selection, and his success as a professional athlete was a source of pride for the residents of Greasy Corner.

Whiteside says of the man known around the neighborhood as June: "June was one of the hardest working young men around. He earned everything he got through hard work and dedication."

As an NFL rookie, Thompson became the only NFL player to lead the league in both kickoff and punt returns. He is re-

Bill Thompson graduated Sterling High School in 1965. He played football and baseball at the University of Maryland Eastern Shore and 13 years with the NFL's Denver Broncos.
(Courtesy of The Hawk, 1968 University of Maryland Eastern Shore Yearbook)

garded by many as the best defensive back in Broncos history and was inducted into their Ring of Fame in 1987. He continued to work for the Broncos after his retirement as a player in 1979.

Thomas Hallums was always one of the biggest kids and best athletes in his class. His exploits on the youth baseball fields were legendary, and he became known throughout the community simply as "Big Thomas." In 1960, he was an 11-year-old pitcher and hitter on an undefeated youth team sponsored by Webb Funeral Home. At Sterling High School, he continued to excel on the diamond as a power-hitting first baseman. By high school graduation in 1966, Hallums was a sturdy 6'3" and 220 pounds. He played collegiate baseball at

Thomas Hallums played first base for the Sterling Tigers and spent four years in the minor leagues in the New York Mets organization.
(Courtesy of The Torch, Sterling High School 1966 Yearbook)

South Carolina State and earned all-conference honors in 1969. He played a year for the Greenville Black Spinners before being tapped in the ninth round of the MLB draft by the New York Mets in 1970.

In his first minor league season with Marion, Hallums led the Appalachian League in total bases, home runs and RBIs. Three years later, he batted .305 for the AA Memphis Blues. His hopes of making it to the majors ended with his fourth minor league season at AAA Tidewater where he batted .249. Hallums died in 2012 at age 63.

When Whiteside and his cousin Marion Butler get together to share baseball memories, the list of names of former neighborhood legends is long, and the stories are endless. They speak of Herbert "Big Hank" Roberts hitting towering home runs beyond the walls of Meadowbrook. They talk about the pitching exploits of Furman "June" Johnson who played for the Black Spinners and briefly with the Indianapolis Clowns in 1954. Johnson and Roberts were two of the baseball legends of Greasy Corner who also taught the fundamentals of the game to the next generation of players like Whiteside and Butler. They are saddened to recall the memory of Johnson tragically losing an arm in an industrial accident but are quick to note that the loss of a limb did not keep him from continuing to play softball at Mayberry Park.

While the two cousins might debate as to who was the very best baseball player to come out of the neighborhood, they are in complete agreement on the best pure athlete to arise out of Greenville's Black community during their era.

"There is no doubt that the most gifted athlete to grow up around here was Willie Belton," Whiteside says emphatically. "He was just naturally gifted in everything he did. People remember him as a great football player, but he was a really good basketball and baseball player."

Belton grew up in the Piney Mountain area of Greenville off North Pleasantburg Drive between the intersection of Rutherford Road and Poinsett Highway. His accomplishments as a youth league athlete and later as a three-sport star at Washington High School earned him legendary status by the time he was a teenager. He was 5'11" and a solid 195 pounds with a time of 4.5 in the 40-yard dash. Belton was ambidextrous, which made him a natural switch-hitter on the baseball field.

He played on the 1967 Wade Hampton American Legion team for Coach Alva Phillips, becoming one of the first Black athletes to play in the historically White local American Legion circuit. Alva's son Randy said his father believed Belton had the potential to play baseball professionally. "I remember my father asking Willie one day if he would consider pursuing a career in professional baseball," Randy said. "Willie told him 'no sir' and that he wanted to play in the National Football League."

Belton played football for a year at Maryland State College where he led his team in scoring before dropping out to join the Marines. Belton continued to showcase his athletic skills playing for service teams at Marine bases in Quantico, Va., and Okinawa, Japan.

After his discharge from the Marines in 1971, he returned home. That summer, the NFL's Atlanta Falcons began holding their preseason training camp at Furman University. Belton's mother was employed by Charles Levin, the owner of a local drapery cleaning business, and Levin convinced the Falcons to give Belton a tryout.

Belton showed up at the Falcons' camp as an unknown with a slim chance of making the team. More than one hundred players were in camp, and only six spots were open on the Falcons' roster. Belton, who was still in excellent shape from his stint in the Marines, immediately impressed the Falcons with his elusive running style. The night before Falcons Head Coach and General Manager Norm Van Brocklin was to announce his final roster, he confided in Dan Foster of *The Greenville News*.

"Your boy's gonna make it," Van Brocklin told Foster. "He's got a little juke step that you just don't teach. You either have it or you don't, and he has it. He could be a helluva player."

Belton was 22 years old when he joined the 1971 Falcons. It was the beginning of a remarkable but short-lived feel-good story. In his first season, Belton was used primarily as a kickoff and punt returner, returning 28 kicks for 706 yards and 30 punts for 163 yards. He was also used as a backup running back and gained 237 yards on 56 attempts.

Belton earned a first-year salary of $14,500 and purchased a new Cadillac after the season. The Falcons increased his salary the following year to $18,500. Belton reported to camp in the summer of 1972 15 pounds overweight, and his performance suffered. He fell from grace with Van Brocklin who put

Willie Belton (above) played professional football for the Atlanta Falcons and St. Louis Cardinals from 1971 to 1974.
(Courtesy of the Atlanta Falcons)

him on waivers at the end of the season. Belton was picked up by the St. Louis Cardinals and played two seasons with them where he was used primarily as a return specialist.

In 1971, Belton's teammate from Washington High School, Roy Kirksey, was drafted in the eighth round by the New York Jets. Kirksey was an outstanding football, basketball and baseball player in high school and played football in college at Maryland Eastern Shore. He participated in many of the neighborhood baseball games at Meadowbrook in the '70s and earned a reputation as a prodigious long ball hitter. Kirksey was 6'1" and 235 pounds and spent four years as an offensive guard in the NFL with the Jets and the Philadelphia Eagles.

While in the Marines, Belton began smoking marijuana. He told Ernie Kastner of *The Greenville News* in 1986: "I had never even smoked a cigarette until I went to Vietnam as a Marine." Belton said he found himself in a war where "both sides were getting high." Marijuana led to a cocaine addiction, which took control of Belton's life. He told Dan Foster that he would even use cocaine during halftime of NFL games "just to get myself together."

After his four years in the NFL, Belton's career came to an end. In 1975, Belton was back in Greenville addicted to a powerful drug and without the money to support his habit, which led him to a path of crime. In November of 1976, he was arrested and charged with committing a series of nine armed robberies. The money taken in the robberies ranged from $18 to $600. Belton plead guilty, and Judge John Gentry sentenced him to 21 years in prison at the Central Correctional Facility in Columbia.

Rick Aldridge was playing baseball for the Free at Last team when he said he ran into Belton in a game at the Columbia prison. Belton was the starting shortstop on the prison team, and Aldridge said he continued to demonstrate tremendous skill on the baseball field as an inmate.

Belton was released from prison in 1984 after serving nine years. He returned to Greenville and said the drug scene had exploded in his hometown. "Everywhere I went, there was cocaine," he told Kastner of *The Greenville News*. Nine months after his release, Belton was arrested for armed robbery and cocaine possession and returned to jail, this time at Greenville County's Perry Correctional Institute.

During his time at Perry, Belton served as the prison's recreational director and became a spokesperson for Nancy Reagan's "Just Say No" campaign to fight drug abuse. Belton was temporarily released on a few occasions to give educational talks about the dangers of drug use.

Accompanied by two armed guards, Belton spoke to an audience of over 200 people at The Greenville Touchdown Club in the Fall of 1986. He openly discussed his personal battle with drugs saying, "Cocaine came out the winner. I lost everything including my freedom. I missed the best years of my children growing up, and society has passed me by."

Belton returned to Greenville after his release from Perry, and his life ended tragically on the evening of December 5, 1992. Police found Belton in his car on Echols Street with the lights on and the motor running. He had been shot four times through the driver's side window. Belton was 43 years old.

———————

John Whiteside knows his life could easily have ended like Belton's. Whiteside said he learned at a young age how to "hustle," a term he defines as "learning how to make money one way or another." His first exposure to hustling came when he was 10 racking billiard balls at the Five Spot pool hall on Birnie Street. Whiteside was paid 10 percent of the 10-cent cost of a game of pool. "If I racked 10 games, I earned a dime. That was big money for me back then," he said.

Growing up around the pool hall, Whiteside eventually became one of Greasy Corner's most accomplished pool sharks. This advanced his ability to "hustle" and brought him into relationship with some of Greasy Corner's shadier characters.

When Whiteside was 19, he left Greasy Corner and went to New York, he said "to take my hustle to the big city." In New York, he continued to run with the wrong crowd, which ultimately led his life into the dark world of drugs and crime. He was arrested for possession on the New Jersey Turnpike in 1969 and sentenced to five years in prison. He was released after serving two years and returned to Greenville.

Back home, he said he lived a life dependent on drugs, ultimately becoming addicted to heroin. "I was in and out jail and unable to function without a regular fix of heroin," he said of that period in his life. At age 31, Whiteside was serving time at Dutchman Correctional Facility in Spartanburg when he suffered a massive stroke. He survived a difficult surgery and rehabilitation and said the stroke was part of a spiritual journey that led to a dramatic change in the direction of his life.

Whiteside credits his upbringing at Greasy Corner's Pilgrim Rest Baptist Church and the love, support and prayers of his mother and grandmother for helping him return to his spiritual roots. Speaking of his time in prison, Whiteside said, "I completely surrendered my life to Jesus Christ, and I finally realized that God was more powerful than the evil forces in my life."

Today, Whiteside is passionate about helping other men who have walked a similar path as his. He volunteers regularly with Soteria Community Development Corporation, a local ministry where he provides friendship, encouragement and biblical teaching to men who are facing the challenges of transitioning back into society after a period of incarceration.

In recent years, Whiteside has been instrumental in helping organize Greasy Corner reunions where former and current residents gather and reminisce about the joys of growing up in the close-knit community. Amidst the food and fellowship of these gatherings, conversations will invariably turn to baseball, and the memories of the great Black ballplayers who roamed Mayberry and Meadowbrook Park are brought back to life.

12
Super Scout

Paul Snyder is the MVP of the good people on the Earth.

—John Schuerholz

Late one evening in May of 1963, Paul Snyder sat in a restaurant in Fort Worth, Texas, listening to his manager, Jack Tighe, deliver the words that no aspiring baseball player wants to hear. Snyder was in his seventh season of minor league ball and had battled a chronic back ailment throughout his career. He was a first baseman for the AAA Denver Bears, and at the time, his batting average was slightly above the .200 mark. Tighe became the courier of a difficult message from Denver's parent club, the Milwaukee Braves.

The Braves offered Snyder a chance to become the player-manager for their Class A team in Greenville, S.C., believing the best contribution that Snyder could make to the organization would be off the field. It was difficult for Snyder to accept that his hopes of making the big leagues as a player were nearing an end. Reluctantly, he accepted the offer and asked for three days to make the cross-country journey to Greenville. Snyder's wife, Petie, was expecting their first child and wanted to stop in and visit her family, as well as his family, on the way to their new assignment.

"We left Denver and drove 1,100 miles to get to my wife's home in Clinton, Michigan, to see her family. Then we drove another 500 miles to see my family in Pennsylvania," Snyder recalled. "Then we take off to Greenville, and the only Greenville I had heard of was

Greenville, North Carolina, which is where we ended up. When we finally got to our hotel in Greenville, South Carolina, my wife is crying her eyes out and thinking she had lost her baby, which thankfully she had not."

Despite Snyder's travel woes, he experienced immediate success as a manager in Greenville, a prelude to a prolific 50-year career in which he became one of the most respected and knowledgeable baseball professionals of the modern era.

Paul Luther Snyder was born in 1935 in the small eastern Pennsylvania town of Dallastown, a few miles south of York. His father was a plumber, and he expected at some point in his life to follow his footsteps into the trade. Sports were the passion of his youth, and he lettered in football, basketball, baseball and track at Dallastown High School. He turned down a baseball scholarship to Penn State and signed to play football at Lebanon Valley College, which was about an hour from his home. Neither of Snyder's parents had attended college, and they were insistent upon his going to college.[1]

In his first year at Lebanon Valley, Snyder injured his back in a football game against Gettysburg College. "It was a dive play, and I ended up landing on my head, and my back went out." The injury ended his football career, and he dropped out of college after his freshman year and returned home. He worked in his father's plumbing business and continued playing baseball in a highly competitive semi-pro league.

Snyder batted .512 in the 1957 York County Twilight League and took part in a series of local tryout games sponsored by major league teams. Milwaukee Braves scout John Ogden signed Snyder to a

$2,500 contract, which was contingent upon Snyder earning a roster spot on a minor league team. In his first season of professional baseball in 1958, Snyder played for the Class D Midland (Texas) Braves where he hit .350 with 15 home runs and 106 RBIs.

Snyder began working his way through the Braves farm system while his back continued to cause him problems. He missed most of the 1960 season after undergoing spinal fusion surgery at Milwaukee General Hospital. While recovering from the surgery, Snyder met his wife, Petie, who was working part-time in the hospital. "What seemed like a bummer [the operation] turned out to be a blessing. That rainbow was clouded when I went in the hospital, but when I came out, all the colors were vivid," Snyder said in 1983 in an interview with *The Atlanta Constitution.*

Snyder returned from back surgery in 1961, but he said he never really came all the way back. He once described himself as a "one-tool player," saying the one thing he could do was hit. In 1961, he batted .310 for Cedar Rapids in the Class B Illinois-Iowa-Indiana League, and in 1962, he batted .312 with a .495 slugging percentage for the Austin Senators in the AA Texas League. In 1963, he was promoted to the Triple A Denver Bears and found himself one step from fulfilling his dream of becoming a major league player.

Early in his season at Denver, his chronic back ailment flared up again. "It was on a day off, and my wife was with me playing soft toss in a cage when my back went out," Snyder said. It was this reoccurrence that led to the late-night meeting with his manager, Jack Tighe, after a game in Fort Worth and his assignment to Greenville.

"I have thanked Jack many, many times for being honest and upright with me," Snyder said. "It taught me a valuable lesson in working with the players I worked with. They knew I wouldn't lie to them. I'll be as honest as I can possibly be."[2]

———————

After the Dodgers organization abruptly left Greenville in the fall of 1962, the city was again without a professional baseball team. Late in 1962, the Milwaukee Braves began to express interest in establishing a Class A team in Greenville. The Braves made World Series appearances in 1957 and 1958, beating the New York Yankees for the championship in '57 but losing to them in '58. Their performance began to decline in the early '60s as did attendance at Milwaukee's County Stadium, and rumors were beginning to mount about a possible relocation to a Southern city. Ultimately, the Braves moved to Atlanta in 1966.

Greenville City Council members had concerns about pursuing affiliation with another big league team after the Dodgers had departed only two years into a five-year lease for Meadowbrook Park. Councilwoman Alden Simpson was the most vocal detractor and told *The Greenville News* after a December 20, 1963 council meeting: "I am very timid in negotiating with anybody else on that park. I rather like it better without having organized baseball." She also said conflicts with televised major league games should be considered and that "the sport is obviously on decline," noting the drop in attendance in the two years that the Dodgers operated a team in Greenville.

Despite the concerns from city council, discussions continued between Braves Farm Director John Mullen, Greenville Mayor David Traxler and Western Carolinas League President John Moss. Mullen visited Greenville to gauge whether there was any local interest in owning the club but quickly determined there was none.

On January 8, 1963, the Braves organization announced it would own and operate a Class A team in Greenville to compete in the WCL. It would be one of two teams in their seven-team farm system that they would own outright. With full ownership, the Braves were required to bear the costs of the club's operations and sponsor the team's spring training at their minor league training facility in Waycross, Ga.

Two weeks after the announcement, the Braves assigned Danny O'Brien as the general manager of the Greenville team. O'Brien had previously served as GM for AAA Louisville in 1960 and '61. He was also the GM of the Braves minor league teams in Jacksonville, Fla., and Boise, Idaho. At the time of his appointment to Greenville, O'Brien was business manager of the Braves major league training camp in West Palm Beach, Fla.

Mullen, the Braves' farm director at the time of O'Brien's appointment, said, "We thought that Greenville was important enough to us, so we changed Danny from the West Palm Beach operation."

A contest in *The Greenville News* asked the community to vote for either "Spinners" or "Braves" as the team mascot, and Greenvillians selected "Braves" by an overwhelming margin. Shortly after Greenville and the Braves worked out their deal, Spartanburg reached an agreement with the Philadelphia Phillies to join the WCL, thus allowing Greenville to renew its professional baseball rivalry with a neighboring city.

––––––––

Snyder had earned the respect of the Braves front office, which led to their offer to become a player-manager in Greenville. He replaced Jim Fanning as Greenville's manager after Fanning was promoted to a position with the major league club. Fanning had a lengthy career in baseball that included a stint as manager of the Montreal Expos in the early '80s.

The 27-year-old Snyder had no managerial experience, and the Braves assigned their lone minor league pitching coach, Walter "Boom Boom" Beck, to work for a short period with Snyder during his transition in Greenville. Beck received his nickname as a pitcher for the Philadelphia Phillies with a propensity to give up line drives that ricocheted loudly off the tin right field wall at Philadelphia's Baker Bowl.

Recalling his first memories of Meadowbrook Park, Snyder laughed when he said, "I remember that the groundskeeper and his family lived at the ballpark, underneath the grandstand. They used to hang their wash out to dry over the outfield fence."

The Braves were 20-17 and a game out of first place when Snyder took over. He won his first game as manager, a 6-0 road win over the Lexington (N.C.) Giants. Greenville won 14 of its next 22 games and clinched first place in the first half of the season, which guaranteed a playoff berth and a chance to compete for the league title at the end of the year. Snyder also frequently inserted himself in the lineup and provided several clutch hits during the Braves run to the first-half championship.

After the successful first half, Snyder found his roster depleted by a handful of midseason promotions. The departures, along with some key injuries, caused the Braves to struggle in the second half as they finished 25-39 and in next-to-last place in the eight-team league.

"That team busted their butts for me, and we won the first half," Snyder said. "Then we sent about four or five guys to Boise in the Pioneer League, and I got four or five guys right out of college and one out of high school to replace them."

Greenville faced the Salisbury Dodgers, winners of the second half, in a best-of-three series for the 1963 WCL pennant. The opening game was on Sunday afternoon at Meadowbrook Park. Approximately 750 fans watched as Snyder, the player, was the hero of the game. With two outs and two runners on base in the bottom of the ninth and the Braves trailing by a run, Snyder ripped a single to center field off the Dodgers' Jack Billingham and scored teammate Bill Eiselstein. When Salisbury's center fielder fumbled the ball momentarily, Levi Brown scored the game-winning run. Billingham, who was the losing pitcher, played 12 years in the majors and was a key contributor for the Cincinnati Reds during the '70s when they won six division titles and two World Series championships.

The following day, Greenville swept the championship with a come-from-behind 5-4 win at Salisbury. Salisbury was managed by George Scherger, who spent 13 years as a bench coach with the Cincinnati Reds. Pete Rose once called Scherger, "the smartest baseball mind in the world."[3]

"After the championship game in Salisbury, I went over to their locker room and knocked on the door, and he [Scherger] wouldn't let me in," Snyder remembered. "I just wanted to congratulate him and his team for a good playoff. Later we became good friends. We have had a few laughs about that."

Local communities took pride in the success of their minor league teams during this era. *The Greenville News* Sports Editor Jim Anderson reminded Greenvillians that it was the first professional championship in their town since 1930 and the first by a team that played in Meadowbrook Park. Snyder expressed his satisfaction to Anderson.

"It's been a very rewarding year, a tremendous experience," Snyder said. "As for me being player and manager, I get a double reward."

Snyder batted .316 for the Braves and completed a seven-year minor league career with a .318 average.

Attendance at Braves games was disappointing in the season's second half. They averaged fewer than 700 fans a game, and many of their second-half contests drew fewer than 300. There was at least one vocal fan who was a regular for Sunday afternoon games at Meadowbrook.

"This guy always came to our Sunday afternoon games, and he sat along the third base line near where I stood in the coach's box," Snyder said. "If we were losing, he would really let me have it."

That third base heckler turned out to be Dr. Clarence "Hots" Easley, the OB-GYN physician who was caring for Snyder's wife during her pregnancy and ultimately delivered their newborn son.

"I went with my wife on one of her OB visits, and I asked Dr. Easley how much this baby was going to cost us because I wasn't making much money, and I thought maybe he would let me pay him in installments. He told me the more games we win, the less the baby will cost me."

Snyder's son Michael was born in Greenville in August, and the Snyders made a final visit to Dr. Easley's office at the end of the season.

"When we were leaving town, we stopped by to settle up our unpaid bill with his office," Snyder recalled. "The girl said there was a note on my bill that said, 'hold all bills.' Dr. Easley had taken care of everything on our behalf, so Michael didn't cost us a penny."

Coaching in the WCL in 1963 and traveling through the segregated South was not without its challenges. Snyder recalled that to stay in certain hotels on the road, his two minority players, Robert Alexander and Raul Calderon, had to stay in his room.

"I'd get a room with two double beds, and they would bring in a cot. I slept in one bed, one player in the other and the other player in the cot," Snyder said. "It was the only way we were allowed to stay in the hotel."

The Braves returned to Greenville in 1964 and finished 63-63, 13 games behind Salisbury. Future major league player and manager Cito Gaston appeared in 49 games for Greenville in 1964. Gaston became the first Black manager to win the World Series when he guided the Toronto Blue Jays to back-to-back championships in 1992 and '93.

At the conclusion of the season, the Braves announced they would not return to Greenville. They finished last in attendance in the WCL, drawing only 24,947 fans, approximately 400 per game. As the Braves left town, Greenville once again found itself without professional baseball.

After his time in Greenville, Snyder continued to manage in the Braves farm system until 1966 when they moved from Milwaukee to Atlanta. Snyder was asked to spend a year as the director of stadium operations at the new Atlanta Fulton County Stadium. He said it was a high-stress job that caused him at times to "sleep in the first aid room" at the stadium.[4]

At the end of 1966, Snyder heard that Tighe, his former manager at Denver, was leaving his position as a Braves scout. Snyder asked Braves General Manager Paul Richards if he could take Tighe's job, and Richards agreed. Snyder was responsible for scouting Michigan, Ohio and Indiana. This marked the beginning of Snyder's lengthy career as a scout and front office executive for the Braves. For a brief time in the early '70s, Snyder also shouldered the responsibility of managing in the minors, including a return to the WCL as manager of the Greenwood Braves in 1972.

After the '72 season, Bill Lucas was named scouting director for the Braves. Lucas was a teammate of Snyder's in Austin in 1962, and the two had developed a mutual respect and close friendship. Lucas tabbed Snyder as his assistant scouting director, and the two began to lay the foundation for a highly successful Braves baseball farm system.

Snyder spent his entire 50-year career in baseball with the Braves, most of that time as the leader of their scouting operations. He was known as a tireless worker who would do whatever it took to help his organization secure the best talent possible. One legendary story about Snyder relates to when he first went to see 15-year-old Javy Lopez catch. Snyder watched from under the stands at a ball field in Urb La Ramble, Puerta Rico, not wanting to be spotted, for fear that another organization might hear that there was a player on the field worth watching.

When asked to share a memorable story about signing a player, he recalled the time when he was trying to sign Jim Acker, a right-handed pitcher who spent nine years in the majors. On that occasion, Acker had completed a workout at Atlanta Stadium. "I asked the scout assigned to him if he signed him. He told me he had not, and so I asked, 'Where is he?' He said he went back to his hotel to go to bed. So, I went to his room and knocked on the door, and his mother answered. She said, 'Jim's sleeping.' I asked her if I could come in, and she said 'sure.' I took my shoes off and crawled in bed with him and said, 'Now let's get this thing done,' and for $5,000 more, we had us a player."

Snyder is credited with building a world-class farm system that propelled the Braves to their historic run of 14 consecutive division titles from 1991 to 2005. He played a significant role in the signing of Braves stars Dale Murphy, Bob Horner, Tom Glavine, Andruw Jones, Javy Lopez, David Justice and Chipper Jones. Snyder stayed committed to his belief that the younger he could sign a player, the better.

Paul Snyder (left) enjoys a laugh with Hall of Famers
Hank Aaron (center) and Bobby Cox (right).
(Courtesy of Paul Snyder)

"We were a high school-oriented organization," Snyder said. "The habits you develop by the time you are 20 or 21 are difficult to change, but if we get you at 17 or 18, we still have a chance. All our teaching was based on an elementary program that we believed in. The 'Braves' Way' was our way of developing the high school player."

Snyder's contributions were widely recognized by those most knowledgeable in the game. At the height of his career, *Baseball America* named him one of the most influential people of the past 25 years. That list included such notables as Cal Ripken Jr., Bud Selig and Barry

Bonds. In 2005, the Braves inducted him into their Hall of Fame, and in 2013, he was also elected to the Professional Scouts Hall of Fame. Thomas Stinson wrote the following about Snyder in *The Atlanta Constitution* in 1995:

> *Since 1985, the (Atlanta) farm system has developed 14 players who have gone on to make 34 All Star appearances. Since 1990, the minors have yielded two rookies of the year (David Justice and Rafael Furcal), a couple of Cy Young Awards (both by Tom Glavine) and an MVP (Chipper Jones). Baseball America, the minor league bible, was inclined in 2001 to name the Braves the Organization of the Past 20 years. The common thread throughout: (Paul) Snyder.*

John Schuerholz served as general manager of the Braves from 1990 to 2007 and president from 2007 to 2016. He summarized the contributions Sndyer made to the Braves organization in Stinson's 2005 article saying, "There is no overstating what he's done, based on what we all know about the players he's signed, his dedication and love for scouting, his work with young scouts and development of scouts. That is trumped by the magnificent sense of friendship and loyalty and character and decency. Those are all qualities that really make what Paul is, beyond what he's done as a professional." When Snyder was inducted into the Braves Hall of Fame, Schuerholz said, "Paul Snyder is the MVP of the good people on the earth."

Ron Morris was a sports writer for *The Durham Herald-Sun* in the early '80s assigned to cover the hometown Durham Bulls, a Class A farm club of the Braves, when he first met Snyder. "He would sit with me at the games and take time to explain the intricacies of the game,"

Morris said. "I learned more about baseball from him than anybody I ever encountered. He was always so generous to me with his time and his knowledge."

After retirement, Snyder continued to attend spring training and be a voice of wisdom to the leaders of the only baseball organization he had ever worked for. He and his wife of 62 years faithfully follow the Braves from their home in the mountains of North Carolina.

Snyder was once asked what he planned to do after baseball. "Be buried," he replied.

13
Kooz and Ryan

In a big game, I was just not going to lose. I was afraid to lose.

—Jerry Koosman

We ended a few of Nolan's [Ryan] games on nine fastballs that the hitters never saw.

—Cliff McWilliams

The New York Mets were three outs away from winning the 1969 World Series. Holding to a 5-3 lead, their fate rested on the left arm of 26-year-old Jerry Koosman. Due up in the top of the ninth for the Orioles was the heart of their batting order. As Koosman took his warmup pitches, Shea Stadium's 57,397 fans were on the brink of pandemonium.

"I go out there for the ninth inning, and the crowed is just going crazy," Koosman recalled. "I mean, they're standing up and hollering, and the guards were already coming down to the front gates along the box seats. It was so noisy, so loud, you couldn't hear yourself think. . . . I was too nervous and excited to be able to control anything, so the only thing I could rely on was velocity. I was just trying to throw my best fastball someplace over the plate."[1]

Koosman opened the inning by walking Frank Robinson but got power-hitting Boog Powell to hit into a force play. Brooks Robinson flied out to right field, and second baseman Davey Johnson stepped up to the plate with the Orioles' last hope. With the count 2-1, Koosman threw a fastball up in the strike zone that Johnson drove deep toward left field. Cleon Jones caught it on the warning track for the final out of the Mets' miracle season and quickly dropped to one knee for a moment of grateful prayer. The miracle was complete.

Koosman immediately ran toward his catcher Jerry Grote and leapt into his arms as thousands of fans raced onto the field. Koosman and Grote's celebratory embrace was splashed across nearly every sports page in America the next day and remains as one of baseball's most famous hugs.

The Mets' victory in Game 5 was the culmination of one of the most improbable championships in the history of sports. Since joining the National League in 1962, they had never finished higher than ninth in the 10-team National League. The Mets were 100-62 and swept the Atlanta Braves in the NLCS, but oddsmakers gave them a 100 to 1 chance of defeating the Baltimore Orioles in the Series.

Koosman was the pitching hero of the '69 Series, throwing 17 2/3 innings and earning two wins, including a complete game victory in Game 5. Greenville sports writer Dan Foster was in the champagne-drenched Mets locker room after the game. Four years earlier, Foster had watched Koosman pitch for the Class A Greenville Mets. Amidst the locker room bedlam, Foster caught Koosman's attention, and the hero of the game looked at him and said, "Meadowbrook was never like this, was it?"

––––––––––

Jerome Martin Koosman was born on December 23, 1942, and grew up on a farm in the small town of Morris, Minn.

"I had a good arm because I threw a lot of rocks, corncobs and whatever I could throw on the farm," Koosman said. After he and his brothers completed their daily chores, they found time for ice fishing, hunting and playing baseball.

By the time he was 13, Koosman joined his older brother on a local semi-pro team where an unfortunate accident led to his path to the pitcher's mound. "I was playing left field, and my brother was playing center field that day. A line drive was hit toward us, and I got down on one knee to catch it, but my brother ran into me and broke his leg," Koosman said. "He was one of our pitchers, so now we needed another pitcher. I had to drive four miles every day to do the chores at his house while he was in a cast for four months, and I became the pitcher that took my brother's place."

Koosman continued to play baseball in high school and area American Legion teams. In 1962, he was drafted into the Army and stationed at Pere Marquette State Park in Grafton, Ill., a base that did not have any baseball facilities. Koosman reached out to his hometown dentist, who was a commanding major general in the Minnesota National Guard, and asked for help in getting transferred to a base where he could play baseball.

While he waited for a transfer that he thought might never come, he enrolled in Officer Candidate School to pursue becoming a helicopter pilot. His transfer eventually came through, and he was sent to Fort Bliss in El Paso, Texas, where he immediately joined their baseball team. Koosman said if not for his dentist, he might have been a helicopter pilot in Vietnam. "Most of those guys didn't come back," he said. "I was two weeks from having my destiny changed."[2]

At Fort Bliss, his catcher was John Luchese from Queens, N.Y. Luchese's father worked as an usher at Shea Stadium, and he suggested that his father reach out to the Mets' front office to send a scout to look at Koosman.

As the perennial cellar dwellers in the National League, the Mets were desperate for talent, so they took a chance on the tip from a stadium usher and sent Red Murff to observe the 6'2" 200-lb. lefty. With Murff watching, Koosman struck out 12 batters in a game, and Murff signed him for $1,200. Koosman said he turned down a larger offer from the Minnesota Twins because he figured the Mets needed immediate help, and it would be a faster path to the big leagues.

Koosman attended the spring training in Homestead, Fla., in 1965, and he remembered getting severely sunburned on his forearms, ears and nose. The Mets assigned their sunburned 22-year-old pitching prospect to Greenville in the Class A Western Carolinas League.

After the Milwaukee Braves ended their two-year stint in Greenville, Mayor David Traxler appealed to his friend and local businessman Tom Hartness to rally a group of citizens to provide the capital and leadership needed for local ownership of a minor league team. Hartness also received encouragement to get involved in professional baseball from another friend, R.E. Littlejohn Jr., who owned the Spartanburg Phillies franchise.

Hartness owned and operated a successful Pepsi-Cola bottling company and was described by *The Greenville News* as a man "whose civic interests are as broad as his business abilities." Hartness' biographer Francis Bonner wrote, "Hartness never intended to be president of a baseball team but accepted Traxler's request because of his strong community spirit and belief that a baseball team was a good thing for the community and would impress anyone considering locating a business in Greenviile."[3]

A steering committee was formed that included Hartness, along with local businessmen T.J. Mims, Jack Foster, Roscoe Powers, William Greer, James Mann and Frank Cope. They organized under the name of Metropolitan Enterprises, Inc. Verner Ross, the owner of a local tire and battery business, also joined the committee and took an active hands-on role in the oversight of the baseball club, relieving Hartness of most of the day-to-day operational responsibilities. Eventually Ross became president of Metropolitan Enterprises, Inc. and was the driving force behind Greenville's professional baseball team for the next several years.

The Mets named Rube Walker as Greenville's manager, but Walker was subsequently released to take a job as pitching coach of the Washington Senators. Walker later became the New York Mets pitching coach in 1968, a job he held until 1981. Ken Deal, a native of Gastonia, N.C., was named manager of the Greenville team. Deal had spent nearly 20 years in the minor leagues as a player or manager and was coach of the Mets' rookie team in Cocoa, Fla., the year before coming to Greenville.

The ownership group hired Arthur Perkins, a 10-year veteran of minor league front office operations, to serve as the team's general manager. About the same time, the Spartanburg Phillies hired Pat Williams, an energetic 24-year-old former minor league player, as its general manager. Williams was a master promoter, and overnight, he made the Phillies the hottest ticket in town.

"I was 24 . . . and I was aggressive. I believed very strongly in promotion and getting people to the ballpark," Williams said of his time in Spartanburg. "Bill Veeck the great baseball marketing genius was an idol of mine and became a mentor . . . anytime there was a ballgame at beautiful Duncan Park in Spartanburg we wanted it to be a marvelous experience, a night of great fun, and good baseball."[4]

Williams served as GM of the team for three years, and during that time, Spartanburg led the WCL in attendance, drawing over 100,000 fans in each of those three seasons. Williams was named Minor League Executive of the Year in 1967, and the following year, he joined the Chicago Bulls front office as business manager, marking the beginning of a distinguished 50-year career as an NBA executive.

To further stimulate the rivalry between Greenville and Spartanburg, a live goat was purchased with the agreement that the loser of each Greenville-Spartanburg game must care for the goat until the next game. Hartness named the goat "Greenburg," a combination of the names of the two rival cities.

Williams, the consummate promoter, intensified the rivalry by writing an open letter to *The Greenville News*, stating, "The goat should expect to spend its summer at Greenville's Meadowbrook Park." He chided the Greenville fans with an added incentive for the first two Phillies-Mets games. "Mayor Bob Stoddard (Spartanburg) and I feel so confident that we have informed general manager Art Perkins that should we happen to drop one of the two openers, Mr. Stoddard and I will serve as ushers at the Greenville Park on our next trip to town on Saturday, May 8," Williams boasted.

Williams never donned an usher's uniform as Spartanburg won the first two rivalry matchups. Shortly after the first game at Meadowbrook, the caretaker for Greenburg left the goat unattended near the third base line, and the goat was stolen. It was one of three goats taken from Meadowbrook during the '65 season.

Koosman admitted that his stint in Greenville was probably the first time he took baseball seriously, saying he enjoyed the game, but also liked to have a good time. "One night, I was goofing around in the dugout, and I remember our manager Ken Deal hollered at me, 'Koosman, if you don't take this game serious, you are going to laugh your way right out of it.' From that point forward, I started to take the game more serious."

The performance of the '65 Greenville Mets was consistent with that of their parent club at the time. The Mets first began play in the National League in 1962 as an expansion team and proceeded to set the record for the worst record in modern day baseball history at 40-120. Rather than build their new team with youth, the Mets elected to sign a series of veterans who were in the twilight of their careers. Drawing on the allegiances of former Brooklyn Dodger and New York Giant fans, the Mets built a faithful following and a reputation as "lovable losers."

Greenville finished the '65 season 44-80 and in last place in the WCL. Throughout the season, the Mets shifted players within their farm system, and Koosman was one of only six players who made it through the entire season with Greenville.

1965 Greenville Mets: Jerry Koosman, first row, second from left; Cliff McWilliams, second row, second from left.

(Courtesy of Cliff McWilliams)

Koosman went 5-11 with an ERA of 4.71. His best performance was a 1-0 shutout win over Thomasville on June 14 in which he struck out 11 and gave up only three hits.

"I always had a good arm, but I had a lot to learn about pitching," Koosman said of his status as a pitcher in 1965. Koosman recorded 128 strikeouts in 107 innings, but also hit eight batters and threw 11 wild pitches, the most of any of his seasons in professional baseball. "Most likely I was having trouble controlling my curveball," he said.

Cliff McWilliams caught most of Koosman's appearances in Greenville in 1965 and may have played a part in keeping Koosman's baseball career alive at the end of their season in Greenville.

"We were packing up our stuff, and our manager was on the phone with Eddie Stankey, who was the director of player personnel for the Mets," McWilliams said. "He held his hand over the phone and told me they were thinking about letting Koosman go. I told him, 'No don't let them do that. He has great stuff. That would be a mistake.'"

Koosman managed to make it back to spring training the following year where he learned to throw a new pitch that altered the trajectory of his career.

"The following year I met Frank Lary, and he taught me how to throw a slider. I caught on really quick, and I could throw it and smile because nobody could hit it," Koosman said.

Lary was acquired by the Mets during the offseason and was known as "the Yankee killer." Between 1955 and 1961, the Yankees won six AL pennants, but during that time, Lary had an impressive 27-10 record against the Bronx Bombers.

Koosman had a solid year at Auburn in the New York-Penn League in 1966, going 12-7 with a league leading 1.38 ERA. He began the 1967 season in New York. Recently married, Koosman said his wife had to drive with the other players' wives to New York after spring training while he traveled with the team.

"She had all of our wedding presents with her when she drove to New York in 1967," Koosman said. "They put her up in a hotel near LaGuardia Airport for her first night, and she parked her car across the street from the hotel. That night, someone broke into her car and stole all our wedding presents. Welcome to New York."

Koosman's first stay in New York was brief as he was sent to AAA Jacksonville for most of the '67 season where he was 14-12 with a 2.24 ERA. The Mets called him back up in September, and he pitched 22 1/3 innings with an 0-2 record and a 6.04 ERA.

Gil Hodges replaced Wes Westrum as the Mets' manager in 1968, and Koosman earned a spot in the starting rotation coming out of spring training. His first start was scheduled against San Francisco, but the assassination of Dr. Martin Luther King forced the cancellation of the game. His first outing of the year was in Dodger Sta-

Jerry Koosman pitched for the New York Mets from 1967 to 1978 and is the winningest left-handed pitcher in Mets history. He played with the Greenville Mets in 1965. In 2021, the Mets retired Koosman's jersey number 36.

(Courtesy of National Baseball Hall of Fame Library)

dium on April 11, and he pitched a four-hit shutout. Six days later, he made his first start in Shea Stadium against the Giants in front of a standing room only crowd of 53,500. "I gave up a hit to the first batter, Tito Fuentes. Jim Davenport reached on an error, and then I walked Willie McCovey. The bases were loaded, and Willie Mays comes to the plate. I'm thinking, 'What in the hell is this farm boy from Minnesota doing here?'" Koosman recalled.

Koosman proceeded to strike out Mays, got left fielder Jim Ray Hart to foul out and struck out catcher Jack Hiatt. He went on to pitch a seven-hit 3-0 shutout. The back-to-back shutouts entrenched Koosman as the number two starter behind future Hall of Famer Tom Seaver. He appeared in his first of two All-Star games in 1968 and struck out Boston's Carl Yastrzemski for the final out of a 1-0 National League victory. Koosman finished the 1968 season 19-12 with a 2.08 ERA, and the Mets ended up 73-89 in next-to-last place.

The following season, Koosman battled a series of injuries but went 17-9 with a 2.28 ERA and made his second All-Star appearance. In the World Series, he won Game 2 after the Orioles had beaten Tom Seaver in Game 1. He had a no-hitter going through six innings and went 8 1/3, allowing only one run on two hits. In the clinching Game 5, Koosman once again baffled the Oriole hitters throwing a five- hit complete game and solidifying himself among the Mets faithful as one of the greatest clutch pitchers in Mets history.

"What made me good in the clutch? I guess I just hated to lose," Koosman reflected. "In a big game, I was just not going to lose. I was afraid to lose. I guess that was my biggest motivating factor."

On August 28, 2021, the New York Mets honored Koosman as the winningest left-handed pitcher in the franchise history by retiring his jersey number 36.

The Mets returned to Greenville in 1966 with a much-improved roster. Anchoring the pitching staff was a hard-throwing 19-year-old right-hander—Nolan Ryan. When he reported to Greenville, Ryan was 6'2" and weighed 162 pounds and had one of the most powerful young arms in the game.

Ryan grew up in Alvin, Texas, the youngest of six children of Lynn and Martha Lee Ryan. In his autobiography, he described his childhood: "It was uncomplicated and without pressures . . . We were all raised to respect other people, to do the right thing, to stand up for our rights, to value the family. . . . My parents' work ethic and dedication shaped my work ethic and dedication, both to my family and to pitching."[5]

Ryan's father took a second job delivering the *Houston Post* to Alvin's 1,500 residents. Ryan recalled helping his father between 1 a.m. and 4 a.m. each morning. "I rolled those papers from the time I was in second grade until I was 14 and old enough to drive a car and have my own route," he said.[6]

Ryan said he was a kid who was always throwing something, whether it was rocks hurled at turtles and snakes or newspapers on his morning route. He began playing baseball on a field that was built by his father and other parents who helped start Alvin's youth baseball program. Pitching for Alvin High School, he was 20-4 with a pair of no-hitters. New York Mets scout Red Murff first saw Ryan pitch during his junior year.

"The skinny handsome righthander threw two fastball strikes— and I was thunderstruck. You could hear that ball explode," Murff said of that initial observation.[7]

Murff convinced the Mets' General Manager Bing Devine to select Ryan in the 12th round of the 1965 baseball draft. Ryan reported to the Mets rookie league team in Marion, Va., in mid-July. It was the first time he had been on an airplane. Ryan appeared in 13 games for Marion and finished with a 3-6 record, struck out 115, walked 56 and hit eight batters. He was a raw, unpolished talent, but his manager Pete Pavlick sent positive reports to the Mets front office.

After his time at Marion, Ryan pitched for St. Petersburg in a winter instructional league. It was here that Ryan changed his pitching motion from a three-quarter delivery to more of an overhead motion while also adding a curve and a change-up to his pitching arsenal.

At the end of spring training, the Mets assigned Ryan to Greenville where he was reunited with Pavlick, who had replaced Ken Deal as Greenville's manager. Pavlick was a journeyman minor league player, spending 13 years as an infielder in the New York Giants farm

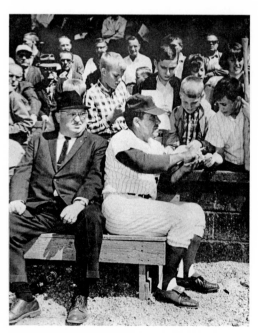

system before embarking on a 14-year minor league managing career with the Giants and the Mets from 1955 through 1969.

New York Mets Coach and former New York Yankee catcher Yogi Berra signs autographs at Meadowbrook Park prior to the Mets-Orioles exhibition game in April 1966. Seated beside Berra is Verner Ross, president of the Greenville Mets.
(Courtesy of Doug Ross)

The 1966 baseball season at Meadowbrook opened with an exhibition contest between the Baltimore Orioles and the New York Mets, a game that featured the best and worst of professional baseball. The Orioles swept the Los Angeles Dodgers in the 1966 World Series while the Mets finished next-to-last in the National League. Despite their poor performance on the field, the Mets continued to build a strong fan base and drew nearly two million fans. Only the Dodgers drew more fans in the National League in 1966.

The Orioles roster featured four future Hall of Famers in Frank Robinson, Brooks Robinson, Jim Palmer and Luis Aparicio. The Mets televised the game back to New York with legendary sportscaster Lindsey Nelson handling the play-by-play duties and Hall of Famer Ralph Kiner doing color commentary. Oriole third baseman Brooks Robinson went three for three and drove in Aparicio for the winning run in a 2-1 Orioles win before a crowd of 3,707 on a cool April Saturday afternoon.

Ryan made his first start for Greenville against rival Spartanburg on April 19. His performance was typical for his year in Greenville. He walked a batter and gave up a pair of singles and one run in a shaky first inning. In the second inning, Ryan struck out the first batter, but the pitch was wild, and the runner reached first base, stole second and scored on consecutive wild pitches by Ryan. Eventually Ryan settled down and overpowered the Spartanburg team that included future Philadelphia Phillies star and five-time All-Star Larry Bowa. Ryan held Bowa hitless in five at-bats and struck out 14 in a six-hit complete game.

Bowa was 20 years old and in his initial season of professional baseball when he faced Ryan for the first time. He recalled his emotional state after going hitless against the hard-throwing Texan. "I was sitting on my stool in the locker room with my head down when Bob Wellman [Phillies Manager] asked me, 'Are you all right?'" Bowa said. "I said, 'Yeah, I'm all right, but if pitching is going to be like this every night, then maybe I need to go back home to Sacramento.' He said, 'Trust me, this kid [Ryan] is going to be something special.' At that time, I was thinking the manager was just trying to give me confidence. As it turned out, it was Nolan Ryan, so everything he told me came true."

Bowa did get some level of revenge in the decisive game five of the 1980 NLCS between the Phillies and the Houston Astros.

"He [Ryan] had us beat 5-2 going into the eighth inning, and I got the hit to lead off the inning . . . they ended up taking him out, and we went on to win that game and win the World Series that year," Bowa said.

Ryan faced Gastonia on the road in his third start and outdueled future Pittsburgh Pirate hurler Bob Moose, throwing a 1-0 shutout. Ryan struck out 15 and gave up only one hit in recording his third consecutive win. It was a typical Ryan performance in which he struggled in the early innings but seemed to get stronger as the game progressed. Seven of his strikeouts came in the last three innings, and he struck out the side in the seventh.

Teammate Cliff McWilliams remembers catching Ryan in several games in Greenville in 1966. "He pretty much had one pitch—the fastball. He hadn't really learned to throw a curveball yet. They wanted Nolan to throw a certain number of fastballs, curveballs and change-ups, but there were times when we wanted to get the game over, and I remember Pete Pavlick holding up one finger. We ended a few of Nolan's games on nine fastballs that the hitters never saw."

Ryan led the WCL in wins (17), strikeouts (272) and walks (127).

He had a 2.51 ERA and was second in the league with wild pitches with 20.

Ryan remembered an unfortunate incident caused by his wildness in Greenville. "In one game a pitch got away from me and hit a woman who was leaning up against the screen behind home plate. Unfortunately, that wild pitch broke her arm. The woman was a season-ticket holder with a good seat up close to the action. Realizing she had a wild-armed kid like me to contend with, she didn't want to take any chances, so she switched her seat to one farther from home plate."[8]

Nearly all of Ryan's outings were night games, and the dimly lit ballparks in the WCL made it even more difficult for hitters to see his blazing fastball.

"Looking back at the lights that we had in those stadiums at that time, it was a pretty tough task," Bowa said. "Ryan was an intimidating figure on the mound, and he had just enough wildness in him that when you came up to the plate, he had you thinking about that. I am pretty sure that if they had one of today's radar guns on him back then, he would have been clocked close to a 100 with every pitch."

Ryan battled blisters on the second finger of his pitching hand while in Greenville but confided in a local reporter that he soaked his fingers in pickle juice to help toughen them up.

On one occasion, his parents and his high school sweetheart and future wife, Ruth, visited Greenville to see him pitch. Ryan struck out a season high 19 with his family in attendance. "I was real excited about pitching for them again and maybe I put a little extra on the ball," Ryan said of his performance.[9]

Ryan's only two losses were to Spartanburg, which finished the season with a 91-35 record and five games ahead of the second place

Mets who were 86-40. Spartanburg hit a stretch during the season, winning 25 games in a row.

"Greenville was our big-time rival and it just so happened that we were the two best teams in the league that year," Bowa said. "I remember we had a few brushbacks and screaming and yelling type things with them that year." Bowa hit .312 and stole 24 bases in his first season of professional baseball.

Attendance at Meadowbrook was 59,078, nearly double the prior year total. When Ryan pitched, or the opponent was Spartanburg, larger crowds than normal usually showed up.

Tom Seaver (left), Nolan Ryan (middle) and Jerry Koosman (right) were teammates with the New York Mets. Ryan pitched for the Greenville Mets in 1966 and went 17-2 and struck out 272 batters.
(From the author's collection)

Ryan recalled his time in Greenville: "Greenville was a sleepy town of about sixty thousand people, and we drew only about seven hundred or so fans to a game. There wasn't much to do in Greenville, and I was bored most of the time. I missed Ruth and my family a lot. The dressing rooms in Greenville were under the stands. They were dirty and cramped and you had to wait your turn to dress and undress—that's how small and cluttered it was. I had gotten used to the conditions—two showers and no hot water."

Despite the miserable and typical minor league living conditions and small-town boredom, Ryan remembers his days in Greenville fondly: "All in all, I consider my year at Greenville as one of the most pleasant I've ever had in baseball. It was, overall, a very successful season for me. Pete Pavlick was my manager again, and that was a plus."[10]

Mary Sue Ross Key, daughter of the team's president, Verner Ross, was in high school in 1966 and remembers her father introducing her to Ryan. "Daddy introduced me and a friend to Nolan that year, and Nolan asked us if we would go play putt-putt with him on some of his nights off, and so we did that," Key said. "He was such a nice young man and so enjoyable to be around. My father was so proud of him and all that he accomplished."

Sports writer Dan Foster spent many nights in the small press box atop the roof of Meadowbrook Park watching Ryan and the Mets in 1966. In a column in 1979, Foster described one of those nights:

> One evening in 1966 at Meadowbrook Park, the Greenville Mets baseball team was in a routine early inning of a Western Carolina League game. About the time one batter stepped down from the plate and another was stepping

up, there was rap on the press box door. We used to keep it locked back then as a precaution against possible invasions of aroused fans who did not understand the finer points of official scoring. But when it was opened there was no hostility standing outside. Instead, there was a lean, clear-eyed, clean-cut youth of 19 years. "Would it be all right," he asked, "if I sat up here and watched part of the game? I'm one of the Greenville pitchers. That would eventually become perhaps the greatest bit of understatement ever made in Meadowbrook Park. The young man was Nolan Ryan. He was "one of the Greenville pitchers" as Babe Ruth was one of the Yankee outfielders or Muhammad Ali was one of the boys in the gym.

Foster noted that Ryan returned to the press box on several occasions to scout opposing batters from atop the grandstand and then sat in the stands for another angle on the hitters. Foster's column was written 13 years after Ryan's time at Meadowbrook, and by this time, Ryan was well on his way to a Hall of Fame career in which he collected 324 wins with 5,714 strikeouts and set the record for the most no-hitters with seven.

Ryan married his high school sweetheart Ruth Holdorff in 1967, but it was while he was in Greenville that he purchased her engagement ring. "Nolan went to Daddy and asked him if he were to buy a ring for Ruth if Daddy would store it for him in the safe, and of course, Daddy said he would," Mary Sue Key said. "So, Nolan bought the ring in Greenville, and Daddy kept it for him until it was time to give it to Ruth."

While playing in Greenville, Ryan lived in a rented home near

Cleveland Park with three of his White teammates. Greenville was still a very segregated community in 1966, and Ryan's Black and Hispanic teammates had to find alternative housing arrangements. Club President Verner Ross relied on the help of local Black citizens to open their homes to some of the minority ballplayers. Willie T. Smith was 10 years old, as he recalls, when his grandparents Albert and Lillie Mae Clark rented a room in their home on Jenkins Street near Sterling High School to Black and Hispanic baseball players. Smith said his grandmother shouldered most of the landlord responsibilities, and he remembered getting to know two of her tenants in 1966: utility player Arsenio "Chico" Diaz and pitcher Ed Figueroa.

Smith said Ryan frequently provided his teammates with a ride to his grandmother's house after ballgames, but one night when Diaz didn't catch a ride with Ryan, Smith said, "He was walking through Greasy Corner following a game, and he witnessed someone get shot, and he ran all the way to my grandmother's house."

Smith used a Polaroid camera to snap photographs of his grandmother's tenants and his new baseball friends and said Diaz gave him one of his bats. "It was a fun time in a kid's life," Smith said.

Ed Figueroa stands outside the home of Albert and Lillie Mae Clark where he lived during his time with the Greenville Mets in 1966.
(Courtesy of Mrs. Anna C. Smith)

Figueroa arrived in Greenville near the end of the season from Marion (N.C.). He is shown in the team's picture still wearing his Marion cap. He appeared in only two games for Greenville, and Smith recalled that Figueroa didn't speak any English and relied on Diaz to come to the mound to translate for the catcher or the manager. Figueroa went on to play nine years in the majors, including four with the New York Yankees from 1976 to 1979. The Yankees won three consecutive AL pennants (1976-1978), and Figueroa won more games (55) than any Yankee pitcher during that era.

Cliff McWilliams remembers one of his early days in Greenville when he went to a department store to buy some shirts, and he held the door open for a Black female who was entering. He said he was immediately cornered by two White men who saw what he had done. "They asked me, 'You aren't from around here, are you?'" McWilliams said. "They said, 'We don't do that for those people here.'" McWilliams also said a neighbor in Greenville invited him to join the Ku Klux Klan.

Larry Bowa's memories of Meadowbrook Park relate to an unfortunate incident involving Spartanburg first baseman Ronnie Allen, the younger brother of Phillies standout Dick Allen. "I remember in Greenville that Ronnie was the target of some racial slurs, and I remember everybody going over to the first base line and telling the usher to get that guy out of the ballpark," Bowa said. "Unfortunately, that kind of thing was common back then, but we made sure we always had our teammates' backs."

One Black player who played in Greenville during the early '60s declined to be interviewed in connection with this book saying, "My time spent in Meadowbrook Park brings back only bad memories. Every day and night I played there, I was called the 'N' word and many other derogatory words. I could not wait to get out of there, and to this day, I will not go to the Carolinas. That is how bad it was being a Black person there."

1966 Greenville Mets: Front row: Doug Ross, Pete Pavlick, Curt Brown, Joe Cahill, Duffy Dyer, Tom Garrett, Mike Mitchell; Second row: Bobby Heise, Nolan Ryan, Fred Reahm, Barry Raziano, Mike Kenyon, Paul Alspach, Ron Taylor, Chris Putnam, Chico Diaz; Third row: Don Shaw, Nyal Leslie, Dave Smith, Ed Figueroa, Steve Wright, Ron Paul, Hal Roberson, Gary Puttmann, Glenn Ezell, Joe Campbell
(Courtesy of Doug Ross)

Joining Figueroa and Ryan as future major leaguers from the 1966 Greenville squad were catcher Duffy Dyer, infielder Bob Heise and pitchers Don Shaw and Dick Selma. Spartanburg's Bowa and second baseman Denny Doyle were called up to the Philadelphia Phillies in 1970.

Another notable member of the '66 team was Mike Martin Sr.,

who joined the team after completing his senior season at Florida State. Martin was an outfielder who appeared in only 32 games in Greenville and had a brief three-year minor league career. In 1980, he became the head baseball coach at Florida State, a position he held until his retirement in 2019. Martin collected 2,029 victories at FSU and is the all-time winningest coach in NCAA history.

Perhaps the most unusual incident of the 1966 season occurred in the second game of a July 4 doubleheader against archrival Spartanburg. The first game was played in the afternoon in Spartanburg before a crowd of 3,977 and the nightcap in Greenville in front of another large crowed of over 3,500. In the bottom of the ninth inning, Greenville's Ken Ezell drove a ball deep to center field that was dropped by Spartanburg's Gil Torres. Ezell reached third on a three base error and later scored the tying run. The Mets went on to win the game, giving them a sweep of the twinbill.

Spartanburg third baseman Tony Silicato claimed Ezell had missed second base and began screaming in the face of base umpire Devoil Butcher. After the game, Silicato continued to voice his displeasure with Butcher's call and Butcher punched Silicato in the face, knocking him to the ground.

"We had a few run-ins earlier in the season. He was a troublemaker ballplayer," Butcher said of Silicato in an interview with *The Gaston Gazette* in 1971. "He didn't like a decision I had made on a play, and he wouldn't let me leave the ballpark, plus he spit in my face. I just decided that it was time for a change in my life. I had been pushed around all my life, and I just decided I wasn't going to be insulted any longer."

WCL Commissioner John Moss had no choice but to fire Butcher for his actions, ending his seven-year career as a minor league umpire. Moss, who, at the time, was also the Mayor of Kings Mountain, N.C., helped Butcher secure a job at the Kings Mountain Water Plant, and Butcher continued to umpire high school, American Legion and college baseball games.

———————

Ryan's and Koosman's less favorable memories of their days in Greenville relate to travel. "Some of our road trips on those old broken-down buses lasted almost eight hours," Ryan said. "We played every other day at home, so our road trips were one day, every other day. This put us on the road a lot more than we should have been."[11]

Koosman remembers an eventful bus ride that summer. "We had an old bus without air conditioning," he said. "One night a back tire blew out and came up through the floorboard of the bus. There was dust everywhere."

McWilliams was a light-hitting catcher who spent the '65 and '66 seasons in Greenville. His childhood dream of becoming a major leaguer was curtailed by a shoulder injury during the 1966 season. His claim to fame was that he got to catch three of baseball's best pitchers in spring training—Tom Seaver, Nolan Ryan and Jerry Koosman, but McWilliams did not have the big league memories to overshadow the misery of the minor leagues. His take on the travel in the Western Carolinas League, however, contrasted with that of his teammates Ryan and Koosman.

"I loved those long bus rides with my teammates," McWilliams said. "Those are great memories."

14
Kat

We like to believe that countries having a common interest and a great sport would rather fight it out on the diamond than on the battlefield.
—*Sporting News*, January 3, 1935

No player drew more attention at the 2021 Major League All-Star baseball game than the Los Angeles Angels' Shohei Ohtani. The 27-year-old Japanese superstar became the first player in All-Star history to compete in the Home Run Derby and also pitch in the Midsummer Classic.

A capacity crowd at Denver's Coors Field cheered wildly as Ohtani launched a series of tape-measure blasts during the home run competition, including six that carried over 500 feet. The following night, Ohtani pitched a scoreless first inning in which his fastball topped out at over 100.2 mph and was credited with the win for the American League.

Young women swoon over Ohtani's heartthrob good looks, baseball purists marvel at his unprecedented two-way skills and the media is smitten by his humility and self-deprecating personality. Even his fellow All-Stars were seen snapping selfies with Ohtani.

The value of Ohtani's memorabilia has skyrocketed with some of his most highly sought-after rookie cards fetching more than $25,000 each from collectors. In his fourth season with the Angels, he has emerged as baseball's biggest international star and the most legitimate two-way player since Babe Ruth. Single-handedly, he has made baseball cool again.

Ohtani grew up in Oshu, Iwate, a city of approximately 120,000 in northern Japan. His father introduced him to baseball, and from a young age, he demonstrated extraordinary talent that drew the attention of scouts from all parts of the world. He played five seasons professionally in Japan before bringing his game to the United States in 2018.

He signed with the Angels with the understanding they would use him as a pitcher and designated hitter. Ohtani was the American League Rookie of the Year in his initial season but was slowed by elbow and knee injuries throughout his first three years. He was healthy as the 2021 season began and finished the year with 46 home runs, 100 RBIs and 26 stolen bases to go along with a 9-2 record on the mound. Ohtani was the unanimous selection for the 2021 American League Most Valuable Player Award.

Eighty years before baseball fans fell in love with Ohtani, America was at war with Japan. The Japanese attack on Pearl Harbor on December 7, 1941, cast a dark shadow of suspicion over anyone of Japanese ancestry living on American soil. Japanese-Americans were feared, discriminated against and generally treated with disdain by most Americans.

A second Japanese attack on the U.S. mainland was anticipated, which led to precautionary wartime measures, such as moving the 1942 Rose Bowl to Durham, N.C. The most far-reaching of these measures was President Franklin Roosevelt's issuance of Executive Order 9066 in February of 1942, which led to the mass eviction and incarceration of over 110,000 Japanese-Americans.

Even though America was also at war with Germany and Italy,

immigrants from those European countries remained free. One leading U.S. military officer made a plea that German and Italian aliens should also be locked up. A San Francisco lawyer debated the issue before a congressional hearing and used Giuseppe and Rosalie DiMaggio, parents of New York Yankee superstar Joe DiMaggio, as an example of a loyal, hardworking immigrant family. He asserted that if they were jailed, it could potentially lower the morale of the country. At the time, there were no Japanese-American baseball stars playing in the United States.[1]

Federal agents began carrying out Executive Order 9066 by detaining Japanese-American community leaders and ransacking their homes in search of evidence of collaboration with Japan. Their searches found no radio transmitters or anything else that could prove espionage.[2] Despite the lack of proof, U.S. officials moved forward with the incarceration of anyone of Japanese descent.

Most of the Japanese immigrants were farmers and fisherman who had settled in Western-Pacific states. Language and religion, along with the hostility from Americans, forced them to become isolated and self-sufficient. They had built self-contained communities that provided for all their needs, not unlike what Black Americans had built during the era of Jim Crow laws. The Japanese were extremely industrious. By 1910, it was estimated that Japanese farmers in California produced nearly 70 percent of the state's strawberries while farming less than 10 percent of the land; this was a source of jealousy and disdain for California's White farmers.[3]

The internees were given 10 days to prepare to leave their homes and instructed that they could bring only two suitcases of belongings with them. The 110,000 Japanese were moved first to massive assembly centers and then to facilities that became known as Japanese

Internment Camps. Seventy percent of the detainees were American citizens, some having lived in the United States for more than four decades. Forty percent were children.[4]

One of the children detained was four-month-old Katsuhiro "Kat" Shitanishi. Kat's father, Yutaka, was a grape farmer near Fresno, Calif. He and his wife, Kimiko, had three sons and a daughter, all under the age of 6 at the time of their relocation.

The Shitanishis were assigned to the internment camp at Jerome, Ark. They endured a torturous four-day journey aboard an overcrowded locomotive where they were forced to sleep upright. During the trip, they were allowed off the train once, only for a few minutes in the middle of the desert.

The internment camp in Jerome was one of 10 facilities built to house the Japanese detainees. Most camps were in the West, but two, Jerome and Rohwer, were built on top of swampland in a desolate section of the Arkansas delta. These two sites had been previously abandoned by landowners and were susceptible to frequent flooding, leaving the camps infested with poisonous snakes.[5]

The camps consisted of a collection of hastily constructed wooden buildings surrounded by barbed wire fencing. Housing quarters were spartan, lacking comfort and privacy. Multiple families were jammed into the communal buildings. Armed guards were stationed atop ominous towers on each corner of the compounds. Residents were allowed to work and earn a token wage of roughly $12 per month.

Pat Morita, who later went on to fame as an American actor best known for his role as Arnold on ABC's long-running comedy *Happy Days*, was detained in a prison camp as an 11-year-old. "Uncle Sam and we Americans like to use euphemistic words or invent words if we think certain other words are too harsh," Morita said. "So they called them 'relocation centers,' but they were America's version of concentration camps."[6]

The world of sports was a popular distraction from the harshness of the confinement, and nearly every camp had organized baseball leagues. The origins of baseball in Japan date to the late 19th century, and its popularity spread quickly among the Japanese. Kerry Yo Nakagawa wrote in *Japanese Baseball in California*:

> . . . *With its beautiful symmetries and mathematical logic and mysteries, the discipline of baseball found a congenial home far from the country of its origin. It also became an important vehicle of cultural exchange across the Pacific. For American-born Japanese, baseball provided a connection to the ancestral country even as it enabled them to become "Americanized."*

Many of baseball's top stars took part in goodwill baseball tours in Japan, including Lou Gehrig, Babe Ruth and Joe DiMaggio. The tours drew hundreds of thousands of fans and advanced the popularity of the sport as well as helped with relations between Japan and the United States. Connie Mack, the manager of the U.S. team that toured Japan in 1931, told the *New York Times* that the baseball tour was, "one of the greatest peace measures in the history of nations." After the 1934 tour that included Ruth, the *Sporting News* wrote:

> *We like to believe that countries having a common interest and a great sport would rather fight it out on the diamond than on the battlefield.*

While thousands of Japanese were being detained in the camps, a group of Japanese men enlisted to fight for the United States in World War II. They formed the 442nd regiment and trained in Shelby, Miss., before fighting bravely in Germany and Africa. They are regarded as one of the most decorated American military units. The 442nd was made up of approximately 18,000 men who earned 4,000 Purple Hearts, 4,000 Bronze Stars, 560 Silver Medals, 21 Medals of Honor and seven Presidential Unit Citations.[7]

Near the end of their detention period, the Shitanishi family was relocated to Tule Lake Internment Camp in northern California. Tule Lake was utilized for Japanese who were considered a higher security risk or those who had refused to sign a controversial loyalty questionnaire that asked among other things if they would be willing to serve in combat for the country that had stripped them of their freedom.

Kat's father was born in the United States but raised in Japan and therefore was most likely considered a higher security risk with a strong loyalty toward Imperial Japan. Approximately 25 percent of the detainees were eventually moved to Tule Lake where it was planned that they would be re-patronized for citizenship to Japan.

At the end of the war, the Shitanishi family, along with the other 110,000 detainees, was released from the camps. Most of them had spent nearly three years imprisoned and had lost their homes, property and savings. Upon release, they were given $25 and a chance to start over.[8]

The Shitanishis returned to California and settled near Madera, about 30 miles north of Fresno. They re-established themselves as growers of Thompson's seedless grapes. A fourth son was born while they were detained at Jerome and a fifth son after their release.

"It's something my parents never talked about," Kat Shitanishi said of his family's internment experience. "I know it had to be a very difficult time, especially for my mother."

Yutaka and Kimiko Shitanishi were supportive of their children's interests and activities while stressing the importance of their education. All six children earned college degrees.

Sports became Kat's outlet, due in part to his lack of interest in farming. He joked, "The more sports I played, the less I had to work on the farm." As a senior at Madera High School, he was a 5'7" 125-pound quarterback in football, a slick fielding infielder in baseball and a hustling defensive specialist in basketball. He quarterbacked his junior varsity football team to an undefeated season and the varsity team to an unblemished conference record his senior year. "I was definitely more suited for baseball, size-wise, but I really enjoyed all sports," Shitanishi said.

Shitanishi also served as vice president of his senior class and was one of three male students selected to attend California Boys State, an annual gathering of the state's brightest and most promising high school seniors.

Kat's 1960 high school yearbook is filled with inscriptions from teachers, coaches and friends attesting to his athletic skills, academic achievements and all-around likeability. An assistant football coach wrote, "To one of the greatest athletes I've ever coached. A terrific future is in store for you."

Kat's only negative memory of his high school days was being dropped off each day by the bus nearly a mile-and-a-half from his home in the dark. "I hated the dark and was scared of dogs. I hit the ground in a full sprint to get home after practice every day," Shitanishi said.

Shitanishi followed professional baseball as a youth and became a fan of the Brooklyn Dodgers. "I remember sitting on my bed with the radio crackling, listening to the Brooklyn Dodgers," he recalled. "I had two favorite players, Duke Snider with the Dodgers and Bobby Richardson, second baseman for the New York Yankees."

After high school, Shitanishi attended UC Santa Barbara for a year on a baseball scholarship but admitted he was "terribly homesick." His parents made him finish the year, and then he returned home and enrolled at nearby Fresno State. He walked onto the baseball team and by his junior year established himself as the starting second baseman for the Bulldogs. Playing alongside Kat at shortstop was Jimy Williams, future major league manager with the Blue Jays, Red Sox and Astros. In 1999, Williams was named the American League Manager of the Year.

Kat Shitanishi (right) kneels beside 1964 Fresno State teammate and future major league manager Jimy Williams.
(Courtesy of The Campus, 1964 Fresno State Yearbook)

Shitanishi was playing in the sandlot leagues around Los Angeles when the Boston Red Sox's veteran scout Glenn Wright offered him the opportunity to play professionally. "I signed for $5,000, and I remember getting $5 for my signature on a Topps bubblegum card contract, which I thought was pretty cool at the time," Shitanishi said.

Wright had been watching Shitanishi since his high school days, and after signing him, he told the *Fresno Bee*: "Kat is a good line-drive hitter, has good hands, good speed and an excellent attitude. I have always liked his actions, especially his hustle."

Shitanishi split his first season of professional baseball between Oneonta (N.Y.) in the New York-Penn League and Waterloo (Iowa) in the Midwest League. After spring training in 1967, the Red Sox assigned him to their new Class A team in Greenville. The New York Mets had ended their two-year relationship with Greenville at the end of the '66 season.

"I had never been in a place that was segregated, and that's the first thing I noticed," Shitanishi said of his arrival in Greenville. "When we started the season, we didn't have a Black player, and the Black fans kind of adopted me as their favorite. The Black fans sat in the bleachers near our dugout, and I think they liked the way I played the game. I stole bases and hustled all the time. They were constantly yelling encouragement at me. For a while, I wasn't sure if I was sup-posed to be White or Black or Japanese, but it all worked out well for me. It seemed to help me that I was different, and people noticed me. I hope I used it to my advantage."

Midway through the season, Jimmy Walker, a Black catcher and outfielder from Southern University, joined the team, and Shitanishi said the support of the Black fans "shifted real quick" to Walker.

Perhaps the biggest challenge facing professional baseball in 1967 was the impact of the Vietnam War. In June of 1967, *Sports Illustrated* reported, "For the first time since World War II both major league pennant races could be determined by military obligations. Before the season ends 40 top ballplayers will have been drafted or will have spent some time training with the armed forces."

The impact of the draft and military obligations was felt the strongest in the minor leagues where teams struggled to complete their rosters. When the Greenville Red Sox arrived in town on April 14, 1967, they brought 20 players, most of whom had no experience beyond the rookie leagues. Over the course of the '67 season, 47 different players would rotate through the Greenville clubhouse.

One player who almost appeared in Greenville was future Hall of Fame catcher Carlton Fisk. After being selected in the first round of the amateur draft in 1967, Fisk was assigned to Greenville for his initial professional season, but Uncle Sam had other plans for the 19-year-old catcher and sent him to Fort Dix (N.J.) for six months of Army Reserve duty.

The youth and inexperience of Greenville's players was readily apparent, and the team found itself deep in the Western Carolinas League cellar by late May. *Greenville Piedmont* Sports Editor Dan Foster wrote of the team's poor start:

> *They were playing so badly that when people asked us why they didn't get more publicity, it was tempting to answer because the owners are good friends of ours. There was a time in April when if a batter got two hits in a game, some thought they should have stopped the game and presented him with the ball. There were nights when the starter got seven good innings, but the relievers came on like drunks . . . they had more ways to get to the basement than the bootlegger.*

Adding to their early season woes was a locker room break-in that resulted in the theft of 13 of the players' gloves. Around the same time, Meadowbrook's scoreboard was deemed inoperable due to damage from neighborhood kids throwing rocks and breaking most of the lights. Eleven of the 13 stolen gloves were returned two weeks later when police caught four young boys who were the culprits.

One early season bright spot was Shitanishi, who was starting at second base and batting in the leadoff spot. Two weeks into the season, he was second in the league in hitting, at .367, behind future Pittsburgh Pirate infielder Dave Cash of Gastonia. Shitanishi said his spacious home field fit his style as a hitter.

"I didn't have the power to hit it over the fence," he said. "I liked the big parks like Meadowbrook that gave me room to hit the ball in between the outfielders and use my speed."

Once colleges completed their spring classes, Greenville added several talented players who improved the team. In addition to Southern University's Walker, the Red Sox signed right-handed pitcher Don Newhauser from Broward College (Fla.) and infielder Kris Krebs from State College of Florida.

At the end of June, the Red Sox moved 19-year-old Billy Conigliaro from their single A team in Winston-Salem to Greenville. Conigliaro was a first-round selection of the Red Sox in the 1965 baseball draft and the fifth overall pick. He brought an instant spark to the Red Sox offense and a competitive spirit to the locker room that helped ignite a dramatic turnaround in the team's performance.

While Conigliaro was playing in Greenville, his older brother Tony was the starting right fielder for the Boston Red Sox. Less than six weeks after appearing as a starter in the 1967 All-Star game, Tony was struck in the face by a pitch thrown by California Angels pitcher Jack Hamilton. He was knocked unconscious and suffered a serious eye injury that ultimately derailed his promising career.

On May 28, Greenville was 14-24 and 15 games out of first place. With a revamped roster, Greenville won 14 of their next 22 games and finished the first half of the season in third place behind the leading Spartanburg Phillies. The Red Sox won seven of their last eight games in the first half, and Shitanishi drew praise for his contributions from manager Matt Sczesny. "Kat's a great fielder, but he's been getting those important hits for us," Sczesny said in an interview with Chip Gray from *The Greenville News*. Shitanishi's performance in the first half earned him a spot in the WCL's All-Star Game.

On July 14, Greenville defeated league-leading Spartanburg 8-3 for its eighth consecutive win of the season over their archrival. Shitanishi turned in one of his best performances, reaching base in all five trips to the plate. He got four singles, drew a walk, stole four bases and scored two runs. He also turned in several sparkling defensive plays at second base.

Walker hit seven home runs in his first month with the club, after hitting only two in his college career. In an interview with the *Greenville Piedmont*, Walker explained the sudden surge in power: "Well you see they didn't have many fences where I played in college. The fences in this league help. They can't go get 'em when they go over the fence. I hit a lot of doubles and triples in college."

The Red Sox finished the second half 31-29, three games behind Spartanburg, which won both halves. Walker led the Red Sox in hitting with a .324 average. Shitanishi finished with a .279 average and led the team in stolen bases with 31 in 39 attempts and walked 60 times to go with only 36 strikeouts in 348 at-bats.

Katsuhiro Shitanishi as a member of the 1967
Greenville Red Sox where he hit .279 and
was selected as an All-Star second baseman
in the Western Carolinas League
(From the author's collection)

During his stay in Greenville, Shitanishi roomed with pitcher Ed Phillips who was the ace of the Greenville staff. Phillips was born in Oklahoma but grew up in Maine. He was a three-sport athlete at Deering High School (Portland, Maine) and went on to play basketball and baseball at Colby College in Waterville, Maine. After a senior season in which he went 5-0 with a 0.50 ERA, the Boston Red Sox signed him to a $9,000 contract.

Phillips went 14-6 in Greenville and was second in the league with a 2.37 ERA. Phillips pitched with a three-quarter delivery and relied on control to get batters out. He appeared in 18 games in relief for the Boston Red Sox in 1970.

Most of the players on the Greenville roster made between $600 and $700 a month and were responsible for their own living expenses and transportation. "Ed [Phillips] and I wound up buying an old beat-up car for three hundred dollars," Shitanishi said. "The people we bought it from told us to put a quart of oil in the gas tank when we filled it up. When we finished the season, we just left it on the side of the road."

The players received meal money for road trips, but while in town, they learned to live frugally. "I recall we ate at a lot of those all-you-can-eat buffets where you could get your money's worth," Shitanishi said. "I also remember back then you would take the biggest suitcase you could get on your first road trip so you could load up on sheets, pillows, soap and towels from your hotel because you couldn't afford to buy that stuff."

While Shitanishi was playing in Greenville, there were no Japanese national or Japanese-American major leaguers. The first Japanese national to play in the big leagues was Masanori Murakami who pitched for the San Francisco Giants in 1964 and 1965. The next Japanese national to appear on a major league roster was Hideo Nomo who joined the Los Angeles Dodgers in 1995. Mike Lum, a Japanese-American who was adopted and raised by Chinese parents in Hawaii, became the first Japanese-American to play in the majors when he joined the Atlanta Braves in 1967.

Shitanishi remembers his minor league experience as generally positive but did recall a single unfavorable incident during his time in the Carolinas.

"We were traveling somewhere in North Carolina and were having a few drinks in a bar when a drunk looked over at me and said, 'We killed your people in the war.' I must have said something back to him, and he came at me with a bottle. We got out of there before anything really happened."

Shitanishi's opportunity to play in the big leagues ended in 1970. He said he started to realize things were coming to an end the year before while he was playing in Pittsfield of the Class AA Eastern League. "We were on a long bus ride back from Binghamton to Pittsfield, and all of a sudden, I started to think for the first time, 'What if I don't make it?'" Shitanishi said. "After that season, I went back to California and started working on my MBA at Long Beach State and began to give some serious thought to life after baseball."

Shitanishi played a final season in 1970 at Boston's AA affiliate in Pawtucket. He ended his five-year minor league career with a .247 batting average.

He said his biggest shortcoming as a ballplayer was his size. At 5'7" he believed he did not have the physical prowess to make it to the next level, but he said he made up for his lack of size with a strong competitive spirit. That spirit carried into his life after baseball where he has achieved significant success in the business world. After working several years in different industries, Shitanishi helped establish Owner American Corporation and currently serves as its President and CEO. The company is a distributor of Owner Fishing Hooks and is one of the most highly respected brands in the fishing industry.

––––––––––––

In 1988, President Ronald Reagan signed the Civil Liberties Act, which recognized that the internment of Japanese-Americans during World War II was "without adequate security reasons" and was motivated "largely by racial prejudice, wartime hysteria, and a failure of political leadership." The law that President Reagan signed, despite significant opposition from members of his own political party, provided a $20,000 payment to any surviving person who had been interned and included a formal public apology.[9]

Angela Duckworth wrote *Grit, The Power of Passion and Perseverance* in 2016, a *New York Times* bestseller in which she attempted to identify the most common predictor of success in a person's life. She stated that "grit" is a combination of passion and perseverance that allows individuals to overcome obstacles without giving up.

Grit is a quality that was clearly demonstrated by many of the

Japanese detainees, who, after their release from internment camps, overcame significant obstacles to lead highly successful and productive lives.

In addition to the actor Pat Morita, the list of former detainees included Michael Makoto "Mike" Honda, who served in Congress from 2001 to 2017; George Takei, an actor best known for his role as Sulu in *Star Trek* and George Tetsuo Aratani, an entrepreneur and philanthropist who founded Mikasa China and owned Kenwood Electronics. Many former detainees made significant contributions across a variety of fields including civil service, art and entertainment, education and business.

Baseball continued to be a beloved sport of the Japanese-Americans during postwar times. It provided an outlet for the reality of the struggles they continued to face as they attempted to restart their lives.

"Even after the war, we were considered terrible traitors," Henry Honda, a detainee from the Manzanar camp in California, said. "Baseball was a way to prove ourselves loyal." Honda had been a promising young pitcher from San Jose who had signed a contract with the Cleveland Indians in 1941 before the bombing of Pearl Harbor ended his hopes of a professional baseball career.[10]

Kat Shitanishi grew up in a home where Japanese was the primary language. When he entered first grade, he did not speak English. He recalled being ridiculed by his classmates and sent to the principal's office by his teacher who didn't know what to do with a student who spoke no English. With the help of his older siblings, Kat learned the language and eventually excelled in the classroom. His natural competitive spirit enabled him to hold his own on the playground and later the athletic field, earning him the respect and friendship of his peers. By the time he was in high school, he said his school experience was "ideal."

Shitanishi is nearly 80 years old and continues to work daily as the CEO of his successful fishing products company. He enjoys playing golf in his spare time and was recently asked a question by one of his golfing buddies that caused him to reflect on his life.

"After I hit a particularly good shot, one of my buddies said, 'Hey Kat, aren't you glad you didn't make it in baseball?' I thought to my-self, 'What an awful thing to say— why would he say that?' After I thought about it, I'm not sure I would have the life I have now if I had stuck with baseball. He was 100 percent right," Shitanishi said.

After a brief pause, he added, "But playing baseball sure was a lot of fun."

15
Verner

My dad may have not had time to toss the baseball with me in the yard, but he bought me a baseball team.

—Doug Ross

Verner Ross pushed back from the table at Charlie's Steak House on E. Coffee Street in downtown Greenville. He had just finished the last bite of Charlie's signature porterhouse T-bone steak. It was a little past midnight on what had been a long, hot August day. Ross had eaten many late-night meals at Charlie's, but none had tasted as good as the one he ate that night.

For Ross, the day began early when he opened the doors of his successful tire and battery business on Westfield Street. He left there midafternoon and made the short trip to Meadowbrook Park where he began his second-shift job as the president of the Greenville Red Sox. His team was scheduled to play a doubleheader against the Greenwood Braves. The outcome of the games would determine the champion of the 1970 Western Carolinas League.

Seated with Ross in the dimly lit restaurant was his field boss, Rac Slider. In between bites of their steaks, the two men rehashed the pitch-by-pitch details of the games against the Braves. Late-night dinners with members of his baseball team were the very best part of his day. It gave him a chance to talk about the game he fell in love with as a young boy growing up in rural South Carolina.

Baseball had now become a business enterprise for Ross, albeit one driven by passion rather than profits. Since taking over as president of Greenville's minor league operations in 1965, Ross had poured his heart and soul into keeping professional baseball alive in his hometown. He fought gallantly against a series of obstacles including a river that often flooded his ballpark, a rising crime rate in Meadowbrook's surrounding neighborhoods and the growth of baseball on television.

Ross had become the face of professional baseball in Greenville and the de facto caretaker of Meadowbrook Park where he spent countless hours tending to the details of his baseball club.

"We knew in the summertime we wouldn't get to see him very much," Ross' daughter Mary Sue Key remembered. "Dad was always at the ballpark, and if we saw him in the summer, it was usually at Meadowbrook."

Doug Ross, the youngest of Verner's three sons, said he practically grew up at Meadowbrook. He filled several roles for his dad's teams including batboy, trainer and all-around gopher for whatever needed to get done. Doug inherited his love of baseball from his dad, and he speaks with a childlike fondness of the time he spent at Meadowbrook. "I loved that old ballpark," Doug Ross said. "I knew every inch of the place. It was a great place for a kid to grow up."

Doug saw the hidden benefit of his father's investment in the fledgling minor league franchise. "My dad may have not had time to toss the ball with me in the yard, but he bought me a baseball team," he said.

Earlier that evening, Greenville had won the first game of the doubleheader against Greenwood, and, combined with a loss by second-place Sumter, it clinched the pennant. Ross bought a case of champagne for the occasion, and between games, he led a celebration in Meadowbrook's cramped home locker room. Ross invited his good friend *The Greenville News* Sports Editor Dan Foster into the Red Sox clubhouse for the festivities. In his column the next day, Foster mentioned that at one point during the celebration, he observed Ross standing alone in a corner shedding a tear.

Ross was 57 years old at the time. He was physically a big man with a demonstrative personality and powerful leadership gifts, but for a moment on that August evening in 1970, he was a tenderhearted little boy who had just experienced his baseball dream come true.

Verner Ross was born the year before World War I began (1913) in Pelzer, S.C. He spent his formative years in Joanna, a small town halfway between Greenville and Columbia, where his father worked at a local textile plant. From a young age, he had a passion for sports and began his college days as a promising lineman on the football

Verner Ross, first row, second from right, was a member of the Wingate Junior College baseball team, circa 1936.
(Courtesy of Mary Sue Ross Key)

team at Furman University. Midway through college, he transferred to Wingate (N.C.) Junior College where he was co-captain of the football team and a member of the baseball team.

Ross married Evelyn McLeod in February 1939, and the two established their home in Greenville. Ross went to work at the Rawlings Tire Company and was promoted to store manager within a year. In 1947, he purchased the tire and battery business from Rawlings and opened Ross Tire and Battery on McBee Avenue. He later opened a second location on Buncombe Street and eventually consolidated the two stores into a new facility on Westfield Street.

While Ross was a big man with a sometimes-gruff demeanor, those who knew him best speak of a compassionate and caring heart beneath his rough exterior. He was civic minded and invested his time, talents and money heavily into the Greenville community. He was a leader in the Greenville Lions Club, the Elks Lodge #858 and the Salvation Army Boys Club. He and his wife were active members of First Presbyterian Church.

Mrs. Ross channeled her energies into her four children, as well as many church and community related activities. Her flower gardens often drew praise in the local papers.

In 1952, the March of Dimes ran a two-week fundraising competition in which citizens paid for the right to vote for "Greenville's Most Beautiful Man." Ross was nominated by the local Elks Lodge and won the "Beautiful Man" title after receiving 218,236 votes.

When Tom Hartness organized a group of community leaders to own and operate the Greenville Mets in 1965, he needed someone that would be "hands-on" in overseeing the day-to-day activities of the team. With his tire and battery business running smoothly, Ross had the margin he needed to assume the role of president of the team. After the franchise switched from the Mets to the Red Sox in 1967, Ross increased his ownership and operating responsibilities with the club.

"There are a thousand things that must be done when you are running a club," Ross told *The Greenville News* in 1968. "You have to look after your concessions, ticket sales, travel, towels, uniforms and numerous other things. You have to keep an eye on the ballplayers and help them out if they need any assistance. But I really don't mind doing all these things because I enjoy it. It's something I like to do and I'm in the business because I love it, and not for financial reasons."

A breakeven year financially for a minor league team during this era would have been considered a windfall. Ross' Greenville franchise faced added pressures as the area surrounding the park was in a rapid state of decline. The women's stockade was adjacent to the gravel parking lot outside the ballpark's main entrance, and often fans were greeted with "cat calls" from the inmates as they peered through the steel bars of the unairconditioned prison. Directly across from the park on Mayberry Street was Goodlett's junkyard with mountains of metal scrap and junk piled up against its chain-link fences. The local dog pound was within earshot on Hudson Street, and with the rising drug culture of the '60s, crime rates surrounding Meadowbrook made it one of Greenville's least desirable after-hours destinations.

Meadowbrook was also beginning to show its age. Primarily constructed out of wood and cinder block, it was always in need of fresh paint. Also, on a moment's notice, it could be submerged in water from dugout to dugout after a rainstorm pushed the Reedy River beyond its banks. None of these factors could dissuade Ross from working diligently to provide Greenvillians with a respectable professional baseball team.

Meadowbrook suffered through many episodes of flooding.
This photo was taken after a heavy rainfall in 1969.
(From the author's collection)

From 1965 to1972, Ross was a fixture at Meadowbrook. Once the game started, he could usually be found perched in his office at the top of the grandstands behind home plate. He struck a familiar pose, leaning against the windowsill of his office observing the game while also keeping a keen eye out for any possible disturbances within the grandstands.

Meadowbrook's concession stand was known for serving delicious hot dogs and hamburgers. The grill was operated by Frank Crick, who prided himself on his hand-patted hamburgers that he smothered in grilled onions. Ross was particularly fond of the hot dogs and was known to finish off a "bag full of them" while he nervously watched his team perform.

Doug Ross recalled the many errands his father had him perform during his days of hanging out at Meadowbrook. "I would run down to a drugstore on Pendleton Street and get pine tar for the pine tar rags. I filled sanitary socks with resin and taped them up with athletic tape for the pitcher's resin bags," he said. "And when we needed bats, I would go to the Greyhound bus station to pick up a new shipment."

Chip Gray was a reporter for *The Greenville News* in August of 1966 and later worked for Ross as the official scorer at Meadowbrook for the 1967, '70 and '71 seasons.

"Verner was at the ballpark every night, and he poured his heart and soul into his teams," Gray recalled. "He took great care of his players. He'd find them a place to stay and help them out with tires for their cars and just made sure they had whatever they needed."

Gray recalled that Ross introduced him to an old baseball superstition. "Verner would put three pennies over the top of the door to his office. He put them on the door sill facing heads up. If the team needed to change its luck, he would turn them over," he said.

Attendance during the eight years Ross operated the club ranged from a high of 59,368 (1968) to a low of 11,481 (1972). While ticket sales may not have reached the levels that Ross would have hoped, the team had a loyal following, and certain fans attended every game. "I remember one rather large, tattooed lady named Ruby who sat close to the field," Doug Ross said. "She was there every night and used to ride the umpires and opposing players. I remember she also baked a cake for each of our players on their birthday."

Ross developed a strong working relationship with the Boston Red Sox organization, especially Neil Mahoney, the director of farm operations and player procurement. Mahoney made many visits to Greenville during Ross' tenure, and the two men became friends and effective partners in the operations of the Greenville team from 1967 to 1971. During this period, Ross also took his family to Boston where they had the opportunity to enjoy the spoils of minor league ownership by watching the Red Sox at Fenway and meeting the Red

Sox executives, including owner Thomas Yawkey.

Both the '67 and '68 teams finished third in the WCL, and their rosters contained several future major leaguers including outfielder Billy Conigliaro, and pitchers Mike Nagy and Don Newhauser. The '69 team dropped to sixth place in the WCL and included three notable future big league players: Cecil Cooper, who batted .297 in 62 games; Ben Oglivie, who led the team in hitting at .317; and left-handed pitcher John Curtis, who went 6-12 during his season in Greenville.

Cooper played 17 years in the majors and was a five-time All-Star with a .298 lifetime batting average. Oglivie played 16 seasons for four American League teams. He had a .273 lifetime batting average and appeared in three All-Star games. Curtis spent 15 years in the major leagues with four teams.

In August of 1969, former Cleveland Indians Hall of Fame pitcher Bob Feller appeared at Meadowbrook and conducted a clinic prior to the Red Sox game. Veteran minor league hitting instructor and Greenville native Randy Phillips was 12 at the time and attended the clinic.

"There were about 12 of us standing around him on the pitcher's mound, and he said, 'OK who wants to catch me?'" Phillips said. "I raised my hand, and he said, 'OK, get behind the plate.' So when people ask me who is the best pitcher I ever caught, they are surprised when I tell them Bob Feller."

After the clinic, Phillips said Feller showered and sat behind home plate where the two of them talked baseball for a long while. "He was as nice as he could possibly be," Phillips said. Feller had also appeared at Meadowbrook in July of 1966.

Hall of Fame pitcher Bob Feller (center) conducted pitching clinics at Meadowbrook in 1966 and 1969. In this photo, taken in 1966, he talks with WCL President John Henry Moss (left), R.E. Littlejohn, president of the Spartanburg Phillies (center) and Verner Ross (right).
(Courtesy of Doug Ross)

Rachel Wayne "Rac" Slider was named Greenville's manager for the 1970 season. Slider grew up on a truck farm in Simms, Texas, and was working in an oil field when he decided to give professional baseball a try. He spent 11 years as a minor league infielder, finally calling it quits in 1964 after a serious ankle injury. Slider began a 21-year career as a minor league manager in the Red Sox organization in Harlan, Ky., in the Appalachian League in 1965.

Slider helped groom several future Red Sox stars, including Dwight Evans, Rick Burleson, Mike Greenwell, Wade Boggs, Ellis Burks and Roger Clemens. Slider came to Greenville after a 76-53 season with Winter Haven in the Class A Florida State League and had built a reputation as an old-school disciplinarian with a passion for winning.

"I was a disciplined coach because as a player I was only 5'7", and

287

I had to work hard to get everything I got," Slider said from his home in DeKalb, Texas. "I wasn't trying to be harsh. I just wanted to get the best out of everyone. I always felt it was a shame to see a player with lots of talent who didn't put their best effort into it."

Slider became one of the most successful and well-respected managers in Meadowbrook's minor league history. He brought a fiery competitiveness to the locker room that drove his players to give their best. Doug Ross said of Slider, "For a little guy, he could really

1970 Western Carolinas League Champion Greenville Red Sox: Front center, batboy Frank Smith; First row—Bill Sandstedt, Fernando Santiago, Mike Neal, Felix Maldonado, Lonnie Keeter, Mike Cummings, Ken McCormick, Ramon Aviles, John Fletcher, John Hamilton, Tom Hanegan, Jim Powers and Manager Rac Slider. Second row—Craig Skok, John Stephen, Jeff Guenther, Jim Jackson, Keith Terry, Ken Watkins, Tom Walsh, Woody Hill, Dwight Evans, Scott Neal, Bill Barry and Paul Sparkman
(Courtesy of Doug Ross)

kick a metal trash can across the locker room floor to get his players' attention."

The strength of the '70 Greenville team was its pitching staff, which was led by hard-throwing righty Paul Sparkman and crafty lefthander Craig Skok. Sparkman (16) and Skok (14) finished first and second respectively in wins in the WCL. Mike Cummings was the team's only .300 hitter. Future Red Sox star Dwight Evans played right field and hit .276.

"I remember the Red Sox asked me one time if I thought Dwight Evans could play right field at Fenway Park," Slider recalled. "I told them he covered a lot of ground in right field for me at Meadowbrook Park in 1971 and told them how big that outfield was. He really sharpened his skills as an outfielder when he was in Greenville."

Evans was a three-time All-Star and won eight Gold Gloves as a right fielder during a 20-year major league career. He is a member of the Red Sox Hall of Fame.

Slider and Ross enjoyed many postgame meals typically at one of Ross' two favorite restaurants, Charlie's Steak House or Capri's Italian Restaurant on Stone Avenue. The two developed a close friendship that lasted beyond Slider's time in Greenville. Doug Ross said, "We still get a Christmas card every year from Rac and his wife."

Slider jokingly admitted that he named a bull on his livestock farm in Texas after Ross. "I named him Verner because I told Verner the bull reminded me of him," Slider said with a laugh. "He was big and stubborn, and he looked like Verner."

The Red Sox got off to a slow start in 1970 and by mid-May, they found themselves in last place with an 11-16 record. They won 26 of their next 34 games and ended in a tie for first place with the Greenwood Braves in the first half of the season. A one-game playoff to crown the first-half champion was scheduled for Saturday, June 22, at Greenwood's Legion Field.

Slider picked Skok to take the mound in the decisive game for the Red Sox. Skok was a graduate of Florida State and in his first professional season. His record stood at 7-4, and he had won his last three starts.

Skok's most recent victory was a 4-1 win over Gastonia on June 23, which drew praise from Dan Foster of *The Greenville News*. ". . . there was a special bit of heroics to his [Skok's] seventh victory of the year. Skok stepped off an airplane from New York only four-and-a-half hours before the game. He had been on military reserve training over the weekend," Foster wrote.

Greenville catcher Sam Fletcher hit a solo third-inning home run to stake the Red Sox to a 1-0 lead. Skok pitched flawlessly for 7 1/3 innings, giving up only four hits and no runs. Sensing that Skok was beginning to tire, Slider called on Sparkman to replace Skok in the bottom of the eighth inning. When Skok left the game, he had thrown 13 1/3 consecutive scoreless innings.

Sparkman shut down the Braves and secured the first-half championship for the Red Sox. It was the first title for a Greenville team since player-manager Paul Snyder led the Greenville Braves to the championship in 1963.

For most of the second half of the season, the Red Sox battled the Sumter Indians for the top spot. On Monday, August 24, Sumter defeated Greenville 3-2 in a rain-delayed game at Meadowbrook that gave it a one-half game lead. To make up several postponed games, the Red Sox had to close out the season by playing doubleheaders on three consecutive nights.

The following evening, Greenville and Sumter split a twinbill, and

Sumter retained its one-half game lead. On Wednesday, Greenville swept a doubleheader at Greenwood, and Sumter lost to Gastonia, giving the Red Sox a one-game lead on the final day of play. The Red Sox hosted Greenwood on Thursday and needed to win only one game of the doubleheader to clinch the second-half title.

Greenville defeated Greenwood 6-2 in game one, making them the outright 1970 WCL champions. Amidst a wild celebration between games, Slider kept trying to remind everyone that they had another game to play, and Ross kept telling him that game didn't matter. Wearing champagne-soaked uniforms, the Red Sox won game two 9-2 behind the complete game pitching of Skok, giving them an overall season record of 77-52.

"We just had a great group of guys that all got along really well and played great baseball," Skok said of his teammates. The Red Sox led

John Henry Moss (left), president of the Western Carolinas League, Red Miller (center), general manager of the Greenville Red Sox and Verner Ross (right) display the 1970 WCL championship banner.
(Courtesy of Doug Ross)

the league in fielding and committed the fewest errors of any WCL team while their pitchers posted a league-leading ERA of 3.60.

Skok remembered Ross as "a very nice man who was always willing to help out his players with whatever they needed." That even included helping Skok rent a TV.

The 1970 championship was the highlight of Verner Ross' career as a minor league executive. It had been a season marked by personal grief for the team owner. Ross relied heavily on a small staff of people led by General Manager Faye Smith and his assistant M.E. "Red" Miller to help him handle the operations of the baseball team. In May, Smith died at the age of 46.

Smith had begun her affiliation with the Greenville baseball club when she moved there in 1961 with the Dodgers organization to assist Spinners General Manager Bill Singer. She stayed on with the Braves in '63 and '64 and was hired by Ross to help him with the Mets in 1965. Smith oversaw the everyday details of processing payroll, passing out meal money, arranging travel, distributing tickets and managing player contracts. She was invaluable to Ross on a day-to-day basis, as he spent time juggling the responsibilities of his tire and battery business and the baseball team.

Ross named Miller as the team's new general manager shortly after Smith's death. Miller's history with the team went back to 1948 when he worked as a batboy for the Greenville Spinners. After graduating from the University of South Carolina, he operated a cabinet design business in Greenville, and he took on the role as assistant to the president for the baseball team in 1965.

Shortly after Smith died, WCL umpire Doc Kanupp was killed in a single-car accident near the Enoree Bridge on Interstate 85. Kanupp was driving to his home in in Hickory, N.C., after calling a game in Greenville. Ross was known to vocally disagree with many of Kanupp's umpiring decisions in games at Meadowbrook, but the two were good friends who often enjoyed a postgame meal together.

Dan Foster wrote of Ross' grief over the loss of Smith and Kanupp, "He is a man with an extraordinary concern for the people around him, so the blows came with great force."

Slider returned to Greenville to manage the '71 Red Sox but was unable to guide his team back to the championship. The Red Sox finished 62-63 and in third place behind the Greenwood Braves, who won both halves of the '71 season. Rick Burleson was one of five of Greenville's players on the '71 team who eventually saw major league action. Burleson played 13 seasons in the majors and appeared in four All-Star games. He is a member of the Boston Red Sox Hall of Fame.

Slider was called up to Boston in 1987 to fill a role as bullpen coach for manager John McNamara. When McNamara was fired in July of 1988, Slider's friend Joe Morgan took over and promoted Slider to third base coach, a position he held until 1990.

In June of Slider's final year with the Red Sox, Morgan was suspended for three games, and Slider filled in for him. In Slider's brief stint as a big-league manager, the Red Sox split a pair of road games against archrival New York and beat the Baltimore Orioles. Slider retired from baseball after the 1990 season.

Along with Ross' passion for baseball, he had a soft spot for youth and in particular those who may have been disadvantaged in some way. For nearly 15 years, he was chairman of the Elks Camp for Underprivileged Children and was responsible for sending thousands of Greenville youth to a two-week summer camp at Cedar Mountain in Brevard, N.C. The camp operated for three two-week sessions; the first and the third weeks included about 100 boys each, and the week in the middle was an all-girls camp.

Ross liked to say the camp was not for underprivileged children but for "deserving children." He used a network of churches, youth clubs and personal contacts to identify deserving youth to attend the camp each year. For many of these youth, it was first time that they had ventured beyond the Greenville city limits.

Ben Gilliard grew up in Greenville's Poe Mill community and was one of the hundreds of local youth who were recipients of the camp experience. Gilliard and his brother attended the camp for several years beginning in 1955.

"We were told to report to the ballroom at the Elks Club on Coffee Street to sign in, and then we were loaded on buses and driven up Highway 276 to Cedar Mountain Camp," Gilliard said. "My parents both worked at Poe Mill and put in 48 hours a week and earned about $40 a week each. Paying for a summer camp would have never been in their budget."

Gilliard said the camp experience consisted of swimming, baseball, horseshoes, and a variety of other sports, along with three good meals a day topped off with ice cream each night. "It was the highlight of my summer," he said.

Ross' daughter recalled her dad's fondness for the camp. "My dad loved that place," Mary Sue Key said. "I can remember him telling us stories about some of the kids he would get from the various children's homes to go up there and how it was such a great experience for them. Daddy was the person who raised all the money for whatever the camp needed. It was a real passion of his."

After a devastating fire at Meadowbrook on Valentine's Day in 1972, Ross somehow managed to keep baseball alive for one additional year as a single-A farm club of the Texas Rangers. The Rangers were credited with drawing only 11,483 fans for their season, and Ross had to fold the organization after the final game in 1972.

Ross liked to boast that in his nine-year tenure as an owner/executive in the Western Carolinas League, they had "more boys make the big leagues during the last nine years than any other club in the league." An estimated 37 Greenville Mets, Red Sox and Rangers players eventually made it to the big leagues.

In 1973, Ross reached out to an old friend, Bing Devine, who was the general manager of the St. Louis Cardinals. Devine had previously held that role for the New York Mets during the time Ross operated the Greenville Mets. The Cardinals granted Ross and a business partner the opportunity to establish a Class A WCL farm club in Orangeburg, S.C., 140 miles from Ross' Greenville home. Former Boston Red Sox outfielder Jimmy Piersall was hired as the team's manager. After a single season in which the team went 50-72 and drew 20,857 fans, the Cardinals pulled the plug on the Orangeburg operations.

Ross continued to operate his tire and battery business in Greenville with hopes that the city would build a new baseball park and he could help bring professional baseball back to his hometown. This would not happen in Ross' lifetime.

Ross suffered a debilitating stroke in 1975. While recuperating in the hospital, he received well wishes from many former players, along with several of baseball's top executives including Peter O'Malley, president of the Los Angeles Dodgers, and Joe McDonald, general manager of the New York Mets. Rac Slider called to check on him nearly every day. The stroke left him partially paralyzed and restricted to a wheelchair.

Ross died in his home on the evening of August 14, 1980. *The Greenville News* featured an editorial piece that spoke of his legacy.

*How many people now contributing to the community owe
part of their success to the work of Verner Ross on behalf of
underprivileged children over the years?*

*The number has to be legion. He spent a good part of his
66 years working as much for the community as for himself . . . The Salvation Army Boys Club, the Elks Camp for
the underprivileged, the Lions Club programs, the March
of Dimes—these were the endeavors which commanded his
most enthusiastic attention and effort.*

*And those endeavors will continue to bear good fruit for
many, many years, in Greenville and the surrounding region, so long as the institution he helped to build remains in
operation to help young people help themselves.*

Of all the players who made their way through Greenville during
Ross' tenure, none was more special to him than future Hall of Famer Nolan Ryan. Ross' daughter and son both attest that "Nolan was
his favorite." One of the first phone calls the 22-year-old Ryan received in the locker room after recording a save in Game 3 of the
1969 World Series was from Ross. Ross made trips to Atlanta to see
Ryan pitch against the Braves and to visit with him in the Mets clubhouse.

Ryan unknowingly provided his former boss and biggest fan with
the perfect memorial baseball tribute. On the evening Ross died,
Ryan took the mound for the Houston Astros at San Diego's Jack
Murphy Stadium. He squared off in a pitcher's duel against John
Curtis, a member of Ross' 1969 Greenville Red Sox. Ryan threw a
three-hit complete game to lead the Astros to a 2-1 win over the Padres. Rest in peace, Verner Ross.

16
The Alamo

If you can play here [Meadowbrook], you can play anywhere.

—Rich Revta

Verner Ross stood silently among the charred remains of Meadowbrook Park. The night before, a massive fire had ravaged the historic ballpark. Ross was awakened in the early morning hours on Valentine's Day 1972 by a phone call from the team's general manager Red Miller letting him know that Meadowbrook was on fire.

Police Sergeant R.D. Cook was riding by the park around 3 a.m. and noticed flames emanating from the center of the grandstand area. By the time firefighters responded, the fire had burst through the stadium's roof and was spreading rapidly throughout the wooden structure. At sunrise, Meadowbrook was a pile of scorched rubble.

The fire destroyed the main grandstand. Twisted structural steel, evidence of the fire's intensity, lay smoldering atop the stadium's concrete foundation. The outer brick and block wall remained standing, but sunlight was shining through two large cracks. Fire Chief J.E. Poole called the fire "very suspicious," noting that firemen answered another call in the same neighborhood at Michaels Grocery Store two hours before Meadowbrook caught fire.

Ross stood near the third base dugout and pointed to three wooden box seats that had miraculously escaped the pervasive devastation of the blaze. He sadly told a fireman standing next to him, "Those seats came from Yankee Stadium."

Ross looked down and saw a baseball partially covered by ashes. He picked it up and held it gently between the thumb and forefinger of his right hand. Three box seats and a discolored soggy baseball symbolized the bare remains of Ross' minor league baseball operations.

The 59-year-old minor league club president had made countless personal sacrifices to keep professional baseball afloat in Greenville over the previous six years. He had withstood the challenges of multiple floods from the Reedy River, thefts of baseball equipment by neighborhood juveniles, declining attendance and the impact of the Vietnam War on his ability to complete a roster. Even before the fire, Ross had been disheartened by the city's imminent plans to sell Meadowbrook and the surrounding land to make way for a planned freeway loop around downtown.

At the end of the 1971 season, the Boston Red Sox notified Ross that they would not renew their agreement for their Class A team in Greenville—but only weeks before the fire, Ross brokered a deal with the Texas Rangers to provide one final season of professional baseball at Meadowbrook. Ross dreaded the call he would need to make later that day to inform the Rangers front office about the fire.

Meadowbrook was insured by the city for only $42,500, and officials quickly diverted the majority of the insurance proceeds to a general fund with no intent of rebuilding or salvaging the 34-year-old ballpark. It appeared that professional baseball in Greenville would once again cease to exist.

Amidst the hopeless days following the fire, Ross somehow caught a vision to salvage the upcoming season. He still had a working agreement with the Rangers, and he knew it would be nearly impossible for them to find an alternative city with opening day less than two months away. The six-team Western Carolinas League was counting on an entry from Greenville. Ross felt a sense of responsibility to both the Rangers and the WCL that fueled his unwillingness to give up hope.

The city eventually offered a meager $2,000 from the insurance proceeds to help clean up the park. Their insufficient gesture seemed to all but seal the fate of the historic park. Ross said to his friend Dan Foster of *The Greenville News*, "It looks dark . . . very dark."

Ross persisted with his efforts, and in early March, city officials agreed to absorb the full cost of the labor to remove the charred debris from Meadowbrook. He was still in need of funds to make needed plumbing and electrical repairs and to construct restrooms and locker rooms.

The outer wall to the stadium was severely damaged, but Ross believed he could put temporary seating inside the wall and create a

The remains of the outside wall of Meadowbrook Park after the February 14, 1972 fire that destroyed the main grandstand

(Courtesy of the city of Greenville)

299

suitable stadium for play. He ultimately convinced city council to chip in another $8,400 to make the bare minimum repairs that were needed.

When it opened in 1938, Meadowbrook was proclaimed as one of the finest minor league ballparks around. For the 1972 season, it would be difficult to find a minor league park in worse condition than Meadowbrook. Despite the conditions of their home field, the 1972 Greenville Rangers wrote a memorable final chapter to Meadowbrook's story.

———————

In the summer of 1971, Rich Donnelly was a 24-year-old catcher for the Denver Bears, the AAA affiliate of the Washington Senators. Midway through the season, Donnelly learned that the Senators were on the verge of calling up a catcher. Donnelly was hitting a respectable .270 at the time and demonstrating outstanding defensive skills behind the plate. He could sense that he was one small step away from fulfilling his baseball dream, but Donnelly's hopes were dashed when teammate Rick Stelmaszek got the nod from the Senators' manager Ted Williams.

Later that season, the Senators played an exhibition game in Denver. Donnelly, still irate and disappointed about being overlooked by Williams, decided to use his play in the exhibition to vent his lingering anger.

In the early innings of the game, Donnelly gunned down three different Senators attempting to steal second base, including speedsters Dave Nelson and Lenny Randle. After the third caught stealing play, Donnelly said he turned to Williams in the Senators dugout and yelled, "Keep running. I'll throw every guy you got out." Donnelly added, "When I got home that night, I told my wife I think my time in baseball is over. I just trashed Ted Williams."

Donnelly finished the season with a .267 batting average and was first in the American Association in assists. He exhibited strong leadership skills and had an advanced baseball IQ. The following season, he was not invited to the major league spring training by the Senators who had now become the Texas Rangers. Entering his fifth season of minor league ball, the Steubenville, Ohio native reported to the Rangers minor league camp in Plant City, Fla., where he was told he was being sent back to Denver to be used as a backup catcher.

A combination of a minor league career headed in the wrong direction and the hot Florida sun brought Donnelly to his breaking point. One afternoon after completing one too many bullpen sessions, he walked off the practice field and kept walking nearly three miles to a Holiday Inn where he was staying. He called his wife and told her he was quitting.

When the Senators heard of Donnelly's plans, the club's farm director Hal Keller reached out to him. "He said, 'Don't leave yet. We want to keep you in the organization, and Ted Williams suggests that you'd be a good manager because you have some fire in you,'" Donnelly said. Buoyed by Williams' recommendation, the Senators offered the 25-year-old Donnelly the managerial position in Greenville.

"I thought about it. My wife was pregnant with our first son, and they were going to double my salary. I wouldn't be bouncing around. I'd be in one place. So, I accepted," Donnelly recalled.

The Rangers' Keller waited until Donnelly accepted the position to share with him the details about the St. Valentine's Day fire at Meadowbrook. "He said, 'There's nothing there. No clubhouse. No backstop. All that's there is a wall.' I said, 'It can't be that bad,'" Donnelly said.

Donnelly recalled pulling into the gravel parking lot outside Meadowbrook a few days before the start of the season. "I almost broke down and cried. It was between a jail and a house of prostitution, and it looked like a bomb hit it. All there was, was ashes," he said.

By opening day, the remains of the wooden grandstand, along with the twisted steel, had been removed from Meadowbrook. Structural damage to the 30-foot outside wall required that it be reduced to approximately nine feet. The sunken concrete dugouts were intact, and there was a small stand of portable metal bleachers down the right field line. The concrete foundation remained, and Ross encouraged fans to bring folding lawn chairs to games for seating.

While arson was suspected, no one was ever charged with setting the fire. Ross' son Doug, who later became a Greenville police officer and arson investigator, said a fellow officer had an informant who claimed that he had set Meadowbrook on fire. Several years after the fire, he told Ross that he did it, "just for the heck of it." No formal charges were filed against the informant.

Eventually Donnelly chose to look on the bright side of his new assignment. He told *The Greenville News*: "The way I look at it is that the fans will be closer to the players than ever before. To me every game will be one big get-together, and I like that."

Donnelly promised Greenville's fans an exciting brand of baseball. "I told Red [Miller] that we were going to break at least two WCL records this year," Donnelly said. "I told him that we would lead the league in stolen bases and that we would lead the league in players getting thrown out of the game. We've got a bunch of competitors."

Donnelly is credited with tagging Meadowbrook "the Alamo" for its final season. "Some fans used to put up ladders against the wall and peek in or sit on top of the wall," Donnelly said. "It looked like the Mexicans were climbing the wall at the Alamo." A handful of promotional bumper stickers were printed that read "Meet Me at the Alamo."

Greenville's pitching coach for the season was Ed Nottle, a 33-year-old journeyman minor leaguer. Born in Philadelphia, Nottle had a hardscrabble childhood that included a severe bout with rheumatic fever at age 9. He said he spent a year and a half in bed, and during that time his father, a coal yard laborer, moved their family to Riverton, N.J.

"I left home when I was 13," Nottle said. "I was a troubled kid. I was a punk. I was sleeping in stolen cars when I got picked up by the police and sent to Bordentown (N.J.) Reformatory."

When he turned 17, Nottle was released and enlisted for service in the U.S. Army. "That was the best thing that ever happened to me. I joined the 101st Airborne unit and was the benefactor of General [William] Westmorland's desire for the 101st to field a baseball team."

Nottle became a standout pitcher for the military team and drew the attention of professional scouts. When he left the Army in 1960, Branch Rickey Jr. extended an invitation to attend Pirates spring training.

"I hung around for a couple weeks before the Pirates cut me," Nottle recalled. "I started hitchhiking around Florida trying to get a second chance with another team." Unable to catch a break, Nottle found himself homeless and with zero prospects for the future.

"One night, I walked down to the beach and took off my clothes and just started swimming out into the ocean. I was going to end it all right there," Nottle said. "I got scared and eventually made it back to shore about two miles from where I started."

Nottle kept knocking on doors and eventually convinced the Pensacola Angels of the Class D Alabama-Florida League to give him a tryout. He pitched three innings in an exhibition game at a nearby Air Force base and said, "I struck out 11 of the 12 batters I faced, and they signed me for $185 a month."

Nottle spent the 1960 season at Pensacola, which was the first of his 18 seasons as a minor league player. He was a player-coach for the Anderson (S.C.) Senators in 1971, and the following year, he assumed that same role with Greenville. Nottle got his first managerial position in 1978, and for the next 29 years, he managed in the Athletics and Red Sox farm systems. He spent one season in the major leagues (1983) as a bullpen coach for the Oakland A's.

While in Pensacola, Nottle needed to find additional work to supplement his modest minor league salary. One night, he was in a piano bar when he said he heard one of the worst singers he had ever heard. He ended up singing a couple of Sinatra tunes for the owner and was hired on the spot. The owner agreed to provide Nottle with free beer and food in return for his nightly singing. Nottle said, "Singing became a tool to eat," and he spent many of his off-seasons singing in nightclubs.

Nottle showcased his singing talents when he released an album, *To Baseball With Love*, in 1983 under his private label, Nott's Landing Records. The album cover featured a baseball card of Nottle in his Oakland A's uniform set against the backdrop of Oakland-Alameda Coliseum. Nottle was known throughout baseball circles as "Singing Ed."

Nottle was a happy-go-lucky free spirit who provided much comic relief during the G'Rangers season. He once walked on his hands onto the playing field at Meadowbrook before a practice session wearing nothing more than upside down catcher's gear. On another occasion, Donnelly was informed that a Rangers game had been rained out, and he used the off day to attend to some personal business. Later that evening, Donnelly received a call from Nottle.

"He said 'I've got good news and bad news for you,'" Donnelly recalled. "He told me the bad news was that they went ahead and played the game today. He said the good news was that he pitched seven and two-thirds innings, and we won the game."

Nottle was 32 years old at the time, and his pitching arm had seen its better days. Donnelly later learned that Nottle had gone around town that day taking bets that he could pitch seven innings in a game. Donnelly said he thinks Nottle won about $200 off that pitching performance.

Throughout Nottle's career in baseball, he was known for his ability to keep his teams loose. While managing for Tacoma in 1981, he was thrown out of a game against Edmonton. On his way to the clubhouse, he convinced his team's mascot to let him borrow his costume. Nottle proceeded to come back on the field dressed as a Tiger where he continued to harass the umpire. When the mascot/manager huddled with Tacoma's third base coach for a brief strategy session, the umpires began to move toward him to question his identity. Nottle made a quick exit before they could remove his mask.

Both Donnelly and Nottle shared a passion for professional wrestling. On Monday nights, the two frequently joined the packed crowds at Greenville Memorial Auditorium to watch their favorite Mid-Atlantic Wrestling stars.

Donnelly confessed he and Nottle on occasion had gone to Meadowbrook on Monday mornings and "put a hose to the field." He said they would then call their scheduled opponent and tell them the field was in bad shape and the game had been cancelled. "We did that so we could make it to the Monday night wrestling matches at the auditorium," he said.

While on the road throughout the Carolinas, the team frequently ended up in the same hotel as many of the wrestlers. Donnelly said they got to know several of them well including Ric Flair, Wahoo McDaniel and Dusty Rhodes.

The Rangers opened the season April 14 against rival Spartanburg. The Phillies had a talented club that included Jerry Martin, a former standout baseball and basketball player at Furman University. Martin played nine seasons in the major leagues for five teams.

Donnelly tabbed left-hander Dexter Baker as his opening game starter. Baker was a gifted three-sport athlete from Racine, Wis., and a second-round pick by the Senators in the 1967 draft. He played three seasons in the minors before he served a two-year stint in Vietnam in the Marines. The 23-year-old Baker was attempting to salvage his baseball career.

Baker pitched well through nine innings, giving up six hits and no earned runs. The Rangers committed seven errors and were trailing 3-2 in the ninth inning when Baker committed a base-running blunder that ended the Rangers' hopes of an opening-night victory.

With two outs and the bases loaded, Greenville's Mark Munoz was at the plate with a 3-1 count. On the next pitch, Baker mistook the umpire's grunt for called ball four, and he began to walk home. The umpire, however, had called a strike, and before Baker could retreat to third, he was tagged out by the Spartanburg catcher to end the

306

game. In his next start, Baker redeemed himself by pitching a no-hitter against Charlotte.

Opening night was the start of a disappointing first half of the season. The Rangers finished with a 28-34 record and 21½ games behind league-leading Spartanburg, which won 51 of 65 games. Greenville began the second half of the split season with a 5-4 win over Gastonia as catcher Rich Revta drove in the winning run in the top of the 10th inning. The victory marked the beginning of a dramatic second-half turnaround by the Rangers.

Revta graduated in 1971 from Lehigh University where he played linebacker on the football team and catcher on the baseball team. He was selected by the Senators in the 26th round of the draft. Revta's play behind the plate and clutch hitting were not his only contributions to Greenville's improved second-half play.

"We didn't have a locker room at Meadowbrook. Our players were dressing at home and then coming to the ballpark. It made them feel like an American Legion team," Donnelly said. "Our catcher, Rich Revta, was a carpenter on the side, so I had him build us a makeshift clubhouse. Boy was it makeshift . . . four pieces of plywood with hooks on the wall and one shower that was always three feet deep in water because it didn't have a drain—but I wanted our guys to dress in a clubhouse so they could feel like a team. Once we built that locker room, we really became a close-knit bunch."

Revta told Dan Foster of *The Greenville News* that at some point during the season, he and his teammates refused to use the deplorable condition of their home ballpark and sparse attendance as an excuse for their play. He said they rallied around a belief: "If you can play here [Meadowbrook], you can play anywhere."

Donnelly added, "We got to the point where I told them we need to stop feeling sorry for ourselves." The turning point for the Rangers fortune was a July 4 road game against Spartanburg. Greenville trounced its archrival 11-5 behind a five-RBI performance by power-hitting first baseman Buddy Caldwell.

"We went over there and beat them good, and from then on, we had the confidence we needed," Donnelly said.

Caldwell had played at the collegiate level at the University of South Carolina for former New York Yankee second baseman Bobby Richardson, whom he referred to in an interview with *The Greenville News* as "the most fantastic man I ever met in my life." The free-swinging 6'1" 195-pound Caldwell ended up leading the WCL in 1972 in both home runs (19) and strikeouts (103). He finished second in RBIs with 107 behind the Phillies' Martin. Caldwell had not hit for a high average in the past, but in Greenville, he finished the season at .337. He attributed his improvement to having spent long hours in front of a pitching machine in spring training sharpening his ability to hit a breaking ball.

Along with their freshly constructed clubhouse, the team also acquired a new shortstop in New Orleans native Charlie Bordes. He was a recent graduate of Southwest Louisiana and joined the team in late May. He quickly became a catalyst for the team's turnaround.

After hitting .377 as a sophomore in college, Bordes was drafted by the San Francisco Giants but opted to complete his education before turning pro. He hit .378 in his senior year, and when he turned 21, he was eligible for the draft again. Bordes was the first selection of the Texas Rangers in the winter draft of 1971. He signed for $6,000 and was assigned to Greenville. He recalled his initial impressions of Meadowbrook:

"I remember pulling into the ballpark in my lily blue Pontiac Bonneville Rocket 88," Bordes said. "The prison across the lot was full of females who were looking out the windows at me. When I got out of my car, they started yelling at me 'When you gonna come and pay us a visit?' I looked around the park and said to myself, 'What have I gotten myself into?'"

Bordes had an immediate impact on the Rangers with his consistent bat, solid defensive skills and an all-out hustling style of play. He quickly established himself as the best shortstop in the Western Carolinas League.

Bordes credited Donnelly for much of the team's success. "Rich was an unbelievable guy to play for. He was always willing to do anything he could to help you out," Bordes said. "There wasn't much separation between us in age . . . I was 22, and he was 25, but when he said something, you made sure you listened."

Indicative of the turnaround of the team's fortunes was an odd play involving Bordes in a game against Charlotte in late July. The Hornets had the bases loaded when Greenville left fielder Gary Boyce snagged a deep fly and quickly turned and threw the ball toward third base. Bordes cut the throw off and casually walked toward second base with the ball in his glove. As he dragged his foot over the bag, the umpire threw up his hand with an out signal. He called the Charlotte runner out for leaving the base too early, and that ended the inning.

"When Charlie came into the dugout, I asked him if he had appealed, and he said he hadn't even thought about it, but we were out of the inning," Donnelly told *The Greenville News*. "It's funny. We make 99 appeals during the year and get nothing. Then a guy accidentally kicks second base, and we get a double play."

Gary Boyce was second on the team behind Caldwell in RBIs. The clutch-hitting 5'7" left-hander told *The Greenville News* he "liked to spray the ball around the field" and "hit for average." Boyce played baseball at Michigan State, helping lead the Spartans to the Big Ten championship in 1971. He was also a placekicker on the Spartans football team for three years.

Caldwell, Bordes and Boyce battled throughout the year for the league batting crown, which Bordes eventually won with a .352 average. Caldwell and Boyce finished second and third, respectively.

As predicted by Donnelly, the Rangers led the WCL in stolen bases with 174. Speedy second baseman Dave Daniels was the league leader with 57, twice as many as his nearest competitor. Daniels' steal total is even more remarkable given that he hit .210 that year.

Ed Layman emerged as one of the Rangers' most reliable pitchers. Layman was nearly 25 years old and had just come off eight months of military duty in Vietnam. He had pitched for nearby Belmont Abbey College and was selected by the Senators in the 39th round of the 1969 amateur draft.

Layman had played two years of minor league ball, including the 1970 season with the Anderson Senators, before responding to his draft notice. He struggled early in his professional career with arm trouble, and a hidden blessing in his military service was that it provided him with a much-needed rest.

"When I came out of the Army, I hadn't thrown a ball in two years, and I think my arm must have healed up," Layman recalled. "When I got home from Vietnam, I took a week at home, and spring training was just about over, so I called the Rangers, and they told me to report straight to Greenville."

Layman had pitched in Greenville while playing for Anderson in 1970 and remembered Meadowbrook as "a nice old wooden ballpark." He said because of its predominately wooden structure, "It had that unique sound that echoed throughout the park when the ball came off the bat." Upon his return to the burnt-out Meadowbrook in 1972, he described it simply as an "ugly place to play baseball."

Layman was a slender right-hander who relied on a fastball and curveball to get hitters out but admitted that his failure to develop other pitches resulted in his not advancing beyond AA ball. Layman was used exclusively in Greenville in relief and finished with a 13-3 record and a 1.27 ERA. He recalls Greenville fondly as it was where he met his future wife, a local schoolteacher who lived in the apartment complex where he was staying.

By the end of the first week of August, the Rangers were 29-13 and held a four-and-a-half game lead over Spartanburg. The players had formed a strong team chemistry on and off the field.

"Several of us lived in an apartment complex that was next to a drive-in movie theater [the Skyland Drive-In]," Bordes recalled. "We'd take our wives and climb through a hole in the fence in the back of the of the drive-in and throw blankets on the ground. We'd turn the volume on the speakers way up and watch whatever movie was playing. Those were some good times."

Drive-ins usually picked up movies a year or two after their initial release and included among the Skyland Drive-In's features that summer were *Billy Jack, Patton* and *Kelly's Heroes.*

Also near the apartment complex was a local pub that became the team's regular hangout. It was small stone building adjacent to a driving range and within walking distance to their residence off Poinsett Highway. "We'd gather there, have a few beers, hit some golf balls and tell stories," Bordes recalled.

Donnelly felt the need to keep some degree of separation between himself and the players, and he said he typically didn't join them at the stone house pub, but one night, near the end of the season, he said they asked him to stop in for a visit. Unbeknownst to Donnelly, the team had planned an impromptu tribute that evening for their field boss.

"When I walked in, the jukebox started playing Bill Withers' "Lean on Me," and they all started singing along. They told me the song was in honor of me. I got choked up," Donnelly said. "Lean on Me" was the team's theme song and rallying cry that summer.

With its battered outer shell, Meadowbrook became an easy target for thieves during its final season. By mid-July, it had experienced nine break-ins, seven in the concession stand and two in the locker room. Verner Ross told *The Greenville News*, "The thieves even stole the phone book, and those things are free."

The Valentine's Day fire also damaged some of Meadowbrook's light poles, and Donnelly remembered a league official requesting to test the lighting one evening. "He goes out to center field after a game to take a reading, and he asks if any of us have a flashlight he could borrow to read his meter."

On August 9, a severe thunderstorm with tornado like winds ripped through Greenville and delivered Meadowbrook with a final gut punch. The heavy rains flooded the ballpark, and the high winds toppled over a significant portion of Meadowbrook's left field wall.

"They had to bring in tractors to haul off all the debris, which left about a 60-foot gap in the outfield wall," Donnelly recalled. "We had two batboys, and I told them to go out there and hold a rope up between that gap. A ball hit over the rope was a home run and under it is a double. I told the kids I'd give them five bucks to lower that rope when we came up to bat. I think we hit six or seven home runs into that opening."

Buddy Caldwell (left), Ted Savia (center) and Charlie Bordes (right) tread water in the home dugout at Meadowbrook after heavy rains flooded the ballpark during the 1972 season.
(Courtesy of Charlie Bordes)

It was Ross' most difficult year as president of the club, and his Herculean efforts were appreciated by Donnelly. "I loved that man. He was like a dad to me and Ed [Nottle]," Donnelly said of Ross. "He truly loved the game of baseball. He never did understand though how we ended up winning in that old burnt-out ballpark."

Despite the third-world conditions of Meadowbrook, the team emerged as a pennant contender. They made believers out of the handful of fans who attended the games as well as the local media. With the Rangers holding the first place position in late August, sports columnist Dan Foster quipped that if Greenville won, "ole Meadowbrook could finish dying with a smile on her face."

On the evening of August 25, the Rangers hosted the Anderson

Giants with a chance to clinch the second-half pennant, in what would turn out to be the final professional game played in Meadowbrook. Caldwell hit a two-run home run in the bottom of the eighth inning to give Greenville a 6-3 win. Layman pitched the final two innings in relief and was credited with his 13th win of the season. The Rangers' victory, coupled with a loss by Spartanburg, secured the second-half pennant and provided one final lasting memory for Meadowbrook Park.

"I just can't believe it," Donnelly told *The Greenville News* after the win. "I have been in professional ball for five years and have been on a pennant winner every time, but I never have been associated with anything like this. These kids just never quit."

The Rangers and the Spartanburg Phillies were scheduled to play a best-of-three series to determine the overall league champion. The opening game was scheduled for Greenville, but Verner Ross concluded that Meadowbrook was not suitable for playoff baseball and agreed to play all three games at Spartanburg's Duncan Park.

"Our park is just no longer adequate," Ross told *The Greenville News*. "The lighting is too poor, and we cannot rebuild the gap in the left field wall for only one game."

Greenville opened the series with an 8-1 win behind the bat of Caldwell, who went 2-4 including a towering fourth-inning home run over the center field wall. The following night, the Phillies evened the series with an 8-1 win. Jerry Martin hit a two-run home run to key the Phillies' victory.

The deciding game was set for Friday evening September 2 at Duncan Park. A smaller than anticipated crowd of around 1,000 showed up as the date conflicted with the opening of high school football season. Greenville took a 1-0 lead in the first inning after

Dave Daniels doubled, stole third and scored on a passed ball—but Spartanburg erupted for six runs in the bottom of the third inning and defeated Greenville 8-2.

1972 Greenville Rangers—First row: (left) Doug Ross (trainer), Rich Revta, Mike Miller, Charlie Waymire, Dave Moharter, Dave Daniels, Gary Boyce, Danny Baker, Charlie Bordes, unidentified batboy. Back row: (left) Rich Donnelly (manager), Scott Goodwin, Bob Ormond, Buddy Caldwell, Rich Bechtel, Bob Spinner, Ron Noe, Wade Frye, Jim Redmon, Dave Harper, Ed Layman, John Brown, Jack Crable, Larry Brooks, Chip Maxwell, Jim Owen, Bruce Sydnor, Ed Nottle (coach)
(Courtesy of Doug Ross)

After the game, Donnelly was emotional in praising his team. "I am proud as hell of our players. I feel they had more to overcome than any other team in minor league ball," he said.

Donnelly was selected WCL Manager of the Year. Caldwell was named by his fellow players as the league MVP while the league's media representatives gave the MVP award to the Phillies' Martin. Four Rangers: Caldwell, Bordes, Boyce and center fielder Bob Skinner made the WCL All-Star team.

The recorded home attendance for the Rangers' final season was 11,481, an average of a little more than 160 per game, a figure Donnelly believes was overstated. "At most, we drew 300 people for the year. There were no seats. None," Donnelly said. "I do remember one particular lady named Ruby who brought her lawn chair every night. She was a Greenville legend. She was there with about four other people every night."

Only one member of the Rangers, Jeff Terpko, eventually played in the major leagues. Terpko, a right-handed pitcher, appeared in one game for Greenville in 1972 and made brief appearances in the major leagues for the Texas Rangers in 1972 and '74 and with the Montreal Expos in 1976.

———————————

After his time in Greenville, Rich Donnelly became the manager of the Gastonia Rangers where he served for the next two years and then managed a final year in the WCL at Anderson in 1975. He led Gastonia to the WCL championship in 1974 and was once again named the league's manager of the year. In 1983, Donnelly became a coach with the Texas Rangers, and for the next 24 years, he coached in the major leagues with the Rangers, Pirates, Marlins, Rockies, Brewers and Dodgers.

Donnelly was the third base coach for the 1997 World Series champion Florida Marlins. Over a career in professional baseball that spanned five decades, he earned a reputation as one of the most well-respected baseball minds in the game.

Donnelly's daughter Amy died in 1993 of brain cancer at age 17. She once wondered what her dad said to the players as they got to the base where he was coaching. She asked him, "Are you saying to them the chicken runs at midnight or something like that?" That phrase became a rallying cry as Amy battled her illness.

Four years after his daughter's death, Donnelly was coaching third base for the Marlins. Craig Counsell, whose nickname was "Chicken," was a member of the team. Counsell earned his nickname because of the way his left arm flapped when he ran.

In the 11th inning of Game 7 of the 1997 World Series, Edgar Renteria drove in Counsell for the game's winning run. Donnelly's 10-year-old son Tim was working as a batboy for the Marlins and ran to his dad during the post-game celebration and said, "Dad, look at the clock. It's midnight. The chicken runs at midnight." Donnelly believes it was a message from his daughter from heaven.

Amy's life was the inspiration for Donnelly's best-selling book *The Chicken Runs at Midnight*. Tragically, in 2018, Donnelly also lost a son, Michael, who was killed in an accident while acting as a good Samaritan to a stranded motorist. Donnelly has used these tragedies, along with his life experiences and renewed faith, as a platform for delivering motivational speeches to various groups.

Pitching coach Ed Nottle followed Donnelly to Gastonia and Anderson before beginning his own 29-year career as a minor league manager. Nottle was named Minor League Manager of the Year after leading the 1981 Tacoma Tigers to a first place finish in the northern division of the Pacific Coast League. While he was with the Pawtucket Red Sox in 1987, he was selected as the International League Manager of the Year.

In retirement, Nottle is active in the Highland Challenge League in Evansville, Ind. The organization is part of The Little League Challenger® Program, which provides a safe and fun baseball environment for children with physical and intellectual challenges.

"I always had a heart for kids. I am a hugger because I didn't get many hugs as a kid," Nottle reflected.

Over his 50-year baseball career, Nottle is quick to point out his greatest thrill in the game. "Back in 2018, our challenge league got a $15,000 grant to take 15 of our kids to Williamsport to play an exhibition game prior to the Little League World Series," Nottle said. "We had about 145 kids in our league at the time, and I asked our board, 'Who is going to tell the other 130 kids that they can't go?'"

"I told them I would raise $75,000 to get the rest of the kids to the game, which was kind of funny because I've never had more than $2,000 in my own account," Nottle laughed. "We ended up raising $175,000, and I got a private jet to fly all the kids and their parents to Williamsport for the game. It was my greatest thrill in baseball, no doubt."

In 1972, 28-year-old Warner Fusselle got his first sports broadcasting job when he became the play-by-play announcer for the Spartanburg Phillies. Fusselle had a lengthy and successful career in broadcasting that included working alongside Hall of Fame announcer Mel Allen on MLB's television series, *This Week in Baseball*.

Fusselle took several home movies of the burnt-out Meadowbrook Park in 1972 and later used them to produce a feature segment about Meadowbrook's final season that appeared on *This Week in Baseball*. Fusselle narrated the feature and closed it with the following words:

> *The Alamo (Meadowbrook) did not stand the test of time as did the original Alamo in San Antonio . . . but, for those who were there in 1972, we will always remember the Alamo.*

Afterward

The planned freeway loop around downtown Greenville that was to dissect Meadowbrook Park never materialized. The decaying remains of the park lingered along Mayberry Street as an ugly epitaph to the former home of baseball royalty. Eventually, and mercifully, the park's outer walls and concrete foundation were cleared away, leaving behind only the playing field, a few light poles and the right field scoreboard.

The field continued to be used by local softball and baseball teams as well as some area high schools. The scoreboard slowly disappeared behind overgrown trees and shrubbery. The entire area was eventually utilized as a hub for the city's maintenance vehicles, which permanently removed any evidence of the site's baseball history.

Meadowbrook Park, circa 1978
(From the author's collection)

After the Rangers left town in 1972, professional baseball was absent from Greenville until 1984 when local business leader Sam Phillips spearheaded a successful effort to convince the Atlanta Braves to move their AA affiliate from Savannah, Ga., to Greenville. A new 7,000-seat stadium was built in the suburb of Mauldin, and it became home for the Greenville Braves for the next 20 years. The park, known as Municipal Stadium, was a nondescript concrete structure that featured a large, uncovered horseshoe-shaped seating area.

The Braves competed in the Southern League, and several of the key contributors to Atlanta's 14 consecutive divisional championships from 1991 to 2005 passed through Greenville, including Chipper Jones, Tom Glavine, Javy Lopez and David Justice. The 1992 Greenville Braves were considered one of the top 100 teams in minor league baseball history. They were 100-43 and won both halves of the Sally League season. Twenty players from that team made it to the big leagues.

In 2004, Greenville and the Braves parted ways when a deal to construct a new baseball park could not be reached. The Braves relocated their AA franchise to Pearl, Miss., leaving Greenville on the verge of once again going without professional baseball.

The city entertained three different proposals for teams to replace the Braves, the most intriguing of which came from the Capital City (Columbia, S.C.) Bombers, a Single A affiliate of the Boston Red Sox. Included in the pitch was a promise by its owners to fund the construction of a 6,000-seat downtown baseball stadium. After much debate, discussion and wrangling of local politics, the city accepted the Bombers' offer, and plans were initiated to build the new ballpark in the city's historic West End district.

The team's owner, Craig Brown, is quoted in *Reimagining Green-*

ville, Building the Best Downtown in America, as saying "We were the only ones who were aggressive enough or crazy enough or probably a little bit of both to approach the city with the plan for us to build the stadium."

The Bombers played their 2005 season at Municipal Stadium and finished with a 72-66 record, Greenville's first winning season since 1997. The following year, the Bombers were renamed the Greenville Drive and moved to Fluor Field, its new picturesque downtown ballpark.

Fluor Field became the centerpiece of the rebirth of Greenville's West End. It is a miniature replica of Boston's Fenway Park, complete with a 37-foot green monster wall in left field and "Pesky's Pole" down the right field line. Its outfield dimensions are identical to Fenway. The distinctive exterior of the park includes reclaimed bricks from area textile mills and the Shoeless Joe Jackson Museum located just outside the stadium gates.

Since its opening, Fluor Field has been a catalyst in Greenville's rise to becoming one of the top destination cities in the country. On the Greenville Drive website, team owner Craig Brown states: "It [Fluor Field] has become a place where the community comes together. It really is Greenville's front porch. In the South, the front porch is where you celebrate success, and if you have adversity, you come together. To have Fluor Field viewed as integral to the community is the journey we set out on 15 years ago."

The Greenville Drive has consistently ranked near the top of their league in attendance and was selected by *Baseball America* as the best single A minor league franchise in the nation in 2020. Several of the Boston Red Sox's best prospects have spent time in Greenville on their way to the big leagues, including Xander Bogaerts, Clay Buchholz, Anthony Rizzo and 2018 American League MVP Mookie Betts.

Fluor Field is located less than a half a mile from old Meadowbrook Park. It is different from Meadowbrook in so many ways. It is built on high ground, safe from any potential flooding from the Reedy River. It is part of a neighborhood where families can walk freely without fear after dark. Instead of a junkyard and a prison as its neighbors, Fluor Field is surrounded by modern residential living spaces, offices, restaurants and retail outlets.

However, the two parks are bonded by their similarities. Between the lines, the game was and is the same. The bases are 90 feet apart, and the pitcher's mound is 60 feet 6 inches from home plate. Both parks have been incubators for baseball dreams, and both are a part of Greenville's rich baseball history.

In spring of 2022, thousands of visitors will begin enjoying Greenville's new Unity Park. The 60-acre complex will encompass the land where Meadowbrook Park once stood, and plans for the park include playgrounds, walking trails, pedestrian bridges, a baseball field and an 80-foot observation tower that will give visitors a panoramic view of Greenville and its surrounding area.

Washington Post sports columnist Thomas Boswell once said, "Every baseball park has its best place to perch." For Meadowbrook Park, that spot was likely in its wooden rooftop press box. On a clear day, a press box visitor could look out beyond the baseball field below and observe the beauty of the Blue Ridge Mountains. The northwest view from Unity Park's observation tower will be similar, minus the ballpark.

While the physical structure of Meadowbrook can no longer be viewed, one can only hope that the Voices from Meadowbrook Park will never be silenced.

Rendering of Greenville's new 60-acre Unity Park that will include a refurbished Mayberry Park, along with walking trails, playgrounds, pedestrian bridges and an 80-foot observation tower.
It is scheduled to open in the spring of 2022.
(Courtesy of MKSK Studio Architects)

Author's Reflections

So why write a book about an old ballpark? To answer that question, I must go back to my childhood because it was as a child that I fell in love with baseball.

I became a devoted Braves fan when they moved from Milwaukee to Atlanta in 1966. I like to think that my bedtime prayers were responsible for a few of Hank Aaron's 755 home runs. I went to sleep most nights with my transistor radio pressed against my ear listening to Milo Hamilton and Ernie Johnson call the Braves games. I am convinced that it was Milo and Ernie's description of the friendly confines of Wrigley Field that ignited my passion for old ballparks.

Baseball cards were my childhood obsession. I spent every nickel of my allowance on them. I got in trouble once for using the mercury dimes and buffalo nickels from my coin collection to purchase "Topps Bubble Gum" packs.

I wasn't much of a baseball player—all field and no hit, as the story goes, but that never stopped me from dreaming about hitting a walk-off grand slam in Atlanta-Fulton County Stadium or imagining myself being carried on the shoulders of my teammates after hurling a no-hitter in Game 7 of the World Series.

My lifelong fascination with the subject of this book began around the time I was 7 when I first visited Meadowbrook Park to attend my older brother's youth football game. I used that opportunity to explore every aspect of the empty ballpark. That day, my mother snapped a couple of photos that show three young boys in the distance standing near the first base dugout. I am confident one of those youngsters is me.

Meadowbrook Park in September of 1966, prior to a youth football game
between Civitan and St. Mary's
(From the author's collection)

I remember attending a handful of minor league games at Meadowbrook between 1967 and 1972. A few memories from those visits include:

- Driving into the parking lot and being a little fearful as I saw inmates staring at me through the bars of the neighboring prison.
- Walking through the portal and smelling the freshly cut infield grass.
- Watching the groundskeeper soak the infield dirt with gasoline and then lighting a match to dry it quickly. It sure seemed cool at the time, but looking back, it probably wasn't the wisest thing to do in an old wooden ballpark.
- Seeing the "No Pepper" sign on the concrete wall behind home plate and having no idea what that meant.
- Attending bat night and watching two young boys wailing away

at each other with their new bats.
- The night a sharply hit foul ball off the end of the bat of a Gastonia Pirate nearly took out my younger brother—I still have that ball.
- Cheering for my favorite player, Paul Campbell, a home-run-hitting first baseman for the 1968 and 1969 Greenville Red Sox; his nickname was "Gomer" because of his likeness to Jim Nabors (TV's Gomer Pyle). I regret that I could not interview him for the book before he died in early 2020.

I often drove by what was left of Meadowbrook Park during the late '70s and early '80s. Sometimes I parked along Mayberry Street and walked out among the crabgrass that covered the once immaculately manicured playing field. It was there that I first heard the faint *Voices From Meadowbrook Park*. Those voices called me to write this book.

Appendix 1
Professional Teams at
Meadowbrook Park

Year	Team	League	Record	Finish	Affiliation
1938	Spinners	South Atlantic	53-83	8th	Washington Senators
1939	Spinners	South Atlantic	64-76	5th	Washington Senators
1940	Spinners	South Atlantic	77-72	4th	Washington Senators
1941	Spinners	South Atlantic	60-77	7th	Washington Senators
1942	Spinners	South Atlantic	61-74	6th	None
1943	No team				
1944	No team				
1945	No team				
1946	Spinners	South Atlantic	76-62	3rd	Chicago White Sox
1947	Spinners	South Atlantic	77-77	5th	Brooklyn Dodgers
1948	Spinners	South Atlantic	84-69	3rd	Brooklyn Dodgers
1949	Spinners	South Atlantic	82-72	3rd	Brooklyn Dodgers
1950	Spinners	South Atlantic	68-85	6th	Brooklyn Dodgers
1951	Spinners	Tri-State	38-98	8th	None
1952	Spinners	Tri-State	63-76	6th	None
1953	No team				
1954	Spinners	Tri-State	68-72	3rd	None
1955	Spinners	Tri-State	60-55	2nd	Milwaukee Braves
1956	No team				
1957	No team				
1958	No team				
1959	No team				
1960	No team				
1961	Spinners	South Atlantic	72-66	3rd	Los Angeles Dodgers
1962	Spinners	South Atlantic	65-75	5th	Los Angeles Dodgers
1963	Braves	Western Carolinas	59-65	6th	Milwaukee Braves
1964	Braves	Western Carolinas	63-63	4th	Milwaukee Braves
1965	Mets	Western Carolinas	44-80	8th	New York Mets
1966	Mets	Western Carolinas	86-40	2nd	New York Mets
1967	Red Sox	Western Carolinas	59-61	3rd	Boston Red Sox
1968	Red Sox	Western Carolinas	68-54	3rd	Boston Red Sox
1969	Red Sox	Western Carolinas	56-68	6th	Boston Red Sox
1970	Red Sox	Western Carolinas	77-52	1st	Boston Red Sox
1971	Red Sox	Western Carolinas	62-63	3rd	Boston Red Sox
1972	Rangers	Western Carolinas	71-57	2nd	Texas Rangers

Source: Statscrew.com

Appendix 2
From Meadowbrook to the Hall of Fame

Note: The following table lists players and coaches who appeared in Meadowbrook Park and have been inducted into the Baseball Hall of Fame in Cooperstown, N.Y.

Year	Player	Team/Game
1938	Al Simmons	Washington Senators—Exhibition vs. Greenville Spinners
1938	Goose Goslin	Washington Senators—Exhibition vs. Greenville
1938, '40, '41	Bucky Harris, Mgr.	Washington Senators—Exhibition vs. Greenville
1939	Joe DiMaggio	New York Yankees—Exhibition vs. Brooklyn Dodgers
1939	Lou Gehrig	New York Yankees—Exhibition vs. Brooklyn Dodgers
1939	Bill Dickey	New York Yankees—Exhibition vs. Brooklyn Dodgers
1939	Lefty Gomez	New York Yankees—Exhibition vs. Brooklyn Dodgers
1939	Joe Gordon	New York Yankees—Exhibition vs. Brooklyn Dodgers
1939	Red Ruffing	New York Yankees—Exhibition vs. Brooklyn Dodgers
1939	Joe McCarthy, Mgr.	New York Yankees—Exhibition vs. Brooklyn Dodgers
1939	Leo Durocher	Brooklyn Dodgers—Exhibition vs. New York Yankees
1939	Tony Lazzeri	Brooklyn Dodgers—Exhibition vs. New York Yankees
1940	Rick Ferrell	Washington Senators—Exhibition vs. Boston Bees
1940 1958	Casey Stengel, Mgr.	Boston Bees—Exhibition vs. Washington Senators New York Yankees—Exhibition vs. Philadelphia Phillies
1941	Hank Greenberg	Detroit Tigers—Exhibition vs. Washington Senators
1941	Charlie Gehringer	Detroit Tigers—Exhibition vs. Washington Senators
1941	Hal Newhouser	Detroit Tigers—Exhibition vs. Washington Senators
1949	Tommy Lasorda	Greenville Spinners
1949 1959	Hoyt Wilhelm	Jacksonville Tars Tom Brewer's All-Stars vs. Billy O'Dell's All-Stars

Voices from Meadowbrook Park

Year	Player	Team/Game
1956, '57	Ted Williams	Boston Red Sox—Exhibition vs. Philadelphia Phillies
1955, '56, '57	Robin Roberts	Philadelphia Phillies—Exhibition vs. Boston Red Sox
1956	Jocko Conlan	Umpire for Phillies—Red Sox Exhibition
1957	Richie Ashburn	Philadelphia Phillies—Exhibition vs. Boston Red Sox
1958	Mickey Mantle	New York Yankees—Exhibition vs. Philadelphia Phillies
1958 1966	Yogi Berra	New York Yankees—Exhibition vs. Philadelphia Phillies Coach—New York Mets
1958	Enos Slaughter	New York Yankees—Exhibition vs. Philadelphia Phillies
1958	Whitey Ford	New York Yankees—Exhibition vs. Philadelphia Phillies
1958	Richie Ashburn	Philadelphia Phillies—Exhibition vs. New York Yankees
1958	Robin Roberts	Philadelphia Phillies—Exhibition vs. New York Yankees
1960	Hank Aaron	Negro Major League All-Star Exhibition Game
1961	Willie Stargell	Asheville Tourists
1962	Tony Oliva	Charlotte Hornets
1962	Satchel Paige	Goose Tatum Harlem Stars—Exhibition vs. Kansas City Monarchs
1964	Steve Carlton	Rock Hill Cardinals
1964	Dizzy Dean	Promotional visit
1965	Sparky Anderson	Rock Hill Cardinals (Mgr.)
1966	Nolan Ryan	Greenville Mets
1966	Whitey Herzog (Coach)	New York Mets
1966	Brooks Robinson	Baltimore Orioles—Exhibition vs. New York Mets
1966	Frank Robinson	Baltimore Orioles—Exhibition vs. New York Mets
1966	Luis Aparicio	Baltimore Orioles—Exhibition vs. New York Mets
1966	Jim Palmer	Baltimore Orioles—Exhibition vs. New York Mets
1966, '69	Bob Feller	Pitching clinic
1971	Jim Rice	T.L. Hanna vs. Greenville High

Acknowledgements

This book would not have made it to print without the contributions, sacrifices and many acts of kindness that were extended me during the researching and writing process.

To my wife and best friend, Cindy—Thank you for the patience and support you continue to show your "worst-selling" author/husband—and special thanks for 35 years of putting up with me stopping along the road of life to satisfy my endless appetite to see old ballparks, stadiums and arenas.

Ron Morris—I remain deeply indebted to you for once again red-lining those very ugly initial drafts. I remain humbled by your continued willingness to use your time and skill to guide and encourage me through the writing process.

To Bette Ann and Steve Phillips—I am deeply grateful to you for allowing me to peer into the soul of your late husband and father, Bill Phillips. Coach deserves an entire book dedicated solely to his life and legacy. I was blessed to have several conversations with him about Meadowbrook.

To Randy Phillips—your love for the game of baseball and your affection for old Meadowbrook motivated me to tell this story. I will always treasure your late-night phone calls on your way home from the "cage" as you shared with me another priceless memory from your encyclopedia of baseball knowledge. I am grateful that you had the wisdom to remove the grandstand sign from Meadowbrook's façade prior to the park's final destruction.

Randy Phillips holds the grandstand sign from Meadowbrook Park.

To Doug Ross—Thank you for your trust and cooperation and your willingness to share your memories of "growing up at Meadowbrook." The first time we met for lunch, I realized I had found someone who loved Meadowbrook even more than I do. I truly hope this book honors your father's legacy and his love of that that old park by the river.

To Mary Sue Ross Key—Thank you for digging through the family pictures and sharing your memories of your dad and especially for helping me understand his passion for helping children in need. You are the only person I know who can say they got to play putt-putt with Hall of Famer Nolan Ryan.

To Dan Wallach—As curator of the Shoeless Joe Jackson Museum in Greenville, you have helped to create a world-class baseball museum,

Doug Ross, son of Verner Ross, wearing the Western Carolinas League Championship ring he earned while serving as a trainer for the 1970 Greenville Red Sox

for which our city owes you much. Thanks for your guidance and support and for all you do to accurately preserve the great history of baseball in our community.

To John Whiteside—You were the answer to a prayer as you unlocked for me the many lesser-known stories of the outstanding Black athletes who played at Meadowbrook and Mayberry parks. I know your mother and grandmother are grateful for all you do to keep the legacy of "Greasy Corner" alive. The true hidden blessing of writing this book is now having the great honor of calling you friend.

John Whiteside stands on the baseball field at Mayberry Park in the approximate location where he played shortstop for Sterling High School.

To Doug Williams—Thanks for contributing your masterful copy-editing skills to the book, but more importantly I appreciate your genuine interest in the project and your friendship throughout.

In memoriam, I offer my thanks and appreciation to Joseph Cambria, J. Kenneth Cass, Jimmy Gaston, Steve Kelly, Jack Foster, Tom Hartness, Verner Ross and the many other community leaders who made significant sacrifices to field professional baseball teams in Greenville during the life of Meadowbrook Park.

I am deeply indebted to all those who were kind enough to grant interviews, provide photos and share their memories of Meadowbrook:

Rick Aldridge, Archie Black, Charlie Bordes, Larry Bowa, Diana Brissie, Rob Brissie, Marion Butler, Rich Donnelly, Roberto Gonzalez Echevarria, Lester Erwin, Camilo Estevis, Ben Gaillard, George Gaston, Hugh Glymph, Jimmy Grantham, Chip Gray, Rudy Jones, Jerry Koosman, Tom Latham, Ed Layman, Mike Lum, Mike McCall, Cliff McWilliams, Jerry Moore, Ronnie Moore, Donnie Moore, Ed Nottle, Hortensia Otero, Steve Phillips, Randy Phillips, Bette Ann Phillips, Al Phillips, Rich Revta, Bobby Richardson, Doug Ross, Mary Sue Ross Key, Paul Scimonelli, Butch Scott, Kat Shitanishi, Craig Skok, Rac Slider, Paul Snyder, Anna C. Smith, Willie T. Smith III and John Whiteside.

Bibliography

Books

Barthel, Thomas, *Baseball Barnstorming and Exhibition Games 1901-1962: A History of Off-Season Major League Play*. McFarland & Co., Inc. 2007.

Berkow, Ira and Brokaw, Tom, *The Corporal Was a Pitcher: The Courage of Lou Brissie*. Triumph Books. 2009.

Bjarkman, Peter C., *A History of Cuban Baseball, 1864-2006*. McFarland & Co., Inc., 2007.

Bjarkman, Peter C. and Nowlin, Bill, *Baseball's Alternative Universe: Cuban Baseball Legends*. Society for American Baseball Research, 2016.

Bjarkman, Peter C., *Fidel Castro and Baseball*. Rowman & Littlefield, 2019.

Bonner, Francis, *Tom Hartness*. Furman University. 1985.

Boswell, Thomas, *Why Time Begins on Opening Day*. Penguin Books, 1984.

Boyanoski, John and White, Knox, *Reimagining Greenville: Building the Best Downtown in America*. History Press, 2013.

Cramer, Richard Ben, *Joe DiMaggio: The Hero's Life*. Simon & Schuster, 2000.

Echevarría, Roberto González, *The Pride of Havana: A History of Cuban Baseball*. Oxford University Press, 1999.

Engelberg, Morris and Schneider, Marv, *DiMaggio, Setting the Record Straight*. MBI Publishing Company, 2003.

Gay, Timothy M., *Satch, Dizzy & Rapid Robert: The Wild Saga of Interracial Baseball Before Jackie Robinson*. Simon and Schuster, 2010.

Gunderson, Colin, *Tommy Lasorda: My Way*. Triumph Books, 2015.

Henninger, Thom, *Tony Oliva: The Life and Times of a Minnesota Twins Legend*. University of Minnesota Press, 2015.

Kennedy, Kostya, *56: Joe DiMaggio and the Last Magic Number in Sports*. Sports Illustrated Books, 2011.

Leavy, Jane, *The Last Boy: Mickey Mantle and the End of America's Childhood*. Harper Collins Publishers, 2010.

Nestor, Bob, *Baseball in Greenville and Spartanburg.* Arcadia Publishing, 2003.

Paige, Leroy (Satchel) as told to David Lipman, *Maybe I'll Pitch Forever.* University of Nebraska Press. 1993.

Perry, Thomas K., *Textile League Baseball.* McFarland & Company, Inc., 1993.

Ribowsky, Mark, *Don't Look Back: Satchel Paige in the Shadows of Baseball.* Simon and Schuster, 1994.

Rogosin, Donn, *Invisible Men: Life in Baseball's Negro Leagues.* Kodansha America, Inc, 1993.

Ryan, Nolan and Frommer, Harvey, *Throwing Heat: The Autobiography of Nolan Ryan.* Doubleday, 1988.

Shamsky, Art and Sherman, Erik, *After the Miracle: The Lasting Brotherhood of the '69 Mets.* Simon and Schuster, 2019.

Smith, Red, *Out of the Red.* Alfred A. Knopf, Inc., 1950.

Thompson, Joe, McCloskey, Mary, and Thompson, Jack, *Growing Up With "Shoeless Joe," The Greatest Natural Player in Baseball History.* JTI Publishing, 1998.

Tye, Larry, *Satchel: The Life and Times of an American Legend.* Random House, 2009.

Williams, Ted and Underwood, John, *My Turn at Bat: The Story of My Life.* Simon and Schuster, Inc. 1969.

Articles

Blakemore, Erin, *The Grisly Story of America's Largest Lynching*, (2018, Sept.). https://www.history.com/news/the-grisly-story-of-americas-largest-lynching

Bloodgard, Clifford, When a .400 Batting Average Wasn't Good Enough, *1940 Baseball Magazine* (Online). https://www.shoelessjoejackson.org/media/1940-baseball-magazine.

Considine, Bob, Ivory from Cuba, *Colliers, The National Weekly*, August 3, 1940.

Hoekstra, Dave, Finding Belonging in Cuban Baseball. *Dave Hoekstra's Route 66.* December 31, 2014.

Regalado, Samuel G., Latin Players on the Cheap. Professional Baseball Recruitment in Latin America and the Neocolonialist Tradition. *Indiana Journal of Global Studies.* Fall 2000.

Newspapers

Asheville Citizen-Times

Baltimore Sun

Charlotte Observer

Greenville Piedmont

Greenwood Index Journal

Kings Mountain Herald

Miami Herald

New York Times

Spartanburg Herald-Journal

Sumter Item

The Atlanta Journal-Constitution

The Boston Globe

The Boston Herald

The Chattanooga Times

The Fresno Bee

The Gaston Gazette

The Greenville News

The State

Valley Morning Sun

York Daily Record

Magazines

Colliers, The National Weekly

Sporting News

Sports Illustrated

Websites

Ancestry.com

Italian Sons and Daughters of America.org

Newspapers.com

Sfmuseum.net

SABR.org

Thehistorybox.com

Unityparkgreenville.com

Other

The United States Navy Memorial Interview Archive

Notes

Throughout the book, I attempted in many cases to provide direct accreditation to the sources within the text of the book. However, it would have been difficult to create a reasonable flow of the narrative if I included reference to every source document. Therefore, the following notes relate to certain sections of the book that relied heavily upon these sources that were not accredited within the text.

I depended primarily on newspaper archives, especially *The Greenville News* and *Greenville Piedmont* throughout my research and have omitted specific note references for newspapers, however, a complete list of newspapers used is included in the Bibliography section. Also, a complete list of interviews conducted is included in the Bibliography section.

Chapter 1—Beginnings

1   *Baseball Americana*, Library of Congress, (Online). https://www.loc.gov/exhibitions/baseball-americana/about-this-exhibition/origins-and-early-days/baseballs-roots/earliest-mention-of-baseball/ (2018, June).
2   Perry, Thomas K., *Textile League Baseball*: McFarland & Company, Inc., 1993.
3   Clifford Bloodgard (1940). *When a .400 Batting Average Wasn't Good Enough*. https://www.shoelessjoejackson.org/media/1940-baseball-magazine.

Chapter 2—Papa Joe

1   Ancestory.com
2   Medina, Merriam, *The Italian American Experience*, Historybox.com.
3   Blakemore, Erin, *The Grisly Story of America's Largest Lynching*, (Online). https://www.history.com/news/the-grisly-story-of-americas-largest-lynching (2018, Sept.).

4   Ibid.

5   Ibid.

6   McKenna, Brian, *Joe Cambria*, Society for American Baseball Research, (Online). https://sabr.org/bioproj/person/joe-cambria/.

7   Ibid.

8   Bjarkman, Peter C., *A History of Cuban Baseball, 1864-2006*: McFarland & Co., Inc., 2007.

9   Henninger, Thom. *Tony Oliva: The Life and Times of a Minnesota Twins Legend.* University of Minnesota Press, 2015.

10   Ibid.

11   Considine, Bob, Ivory from Cuba, *Colliers, The National Weekly*, August 3, 1940.

Chapter 3—90 Days

1   *Preparing for the Transformation*, Greenville Online, (Online). https://unityparkgreenville.com/news.

2   Thompson, Joe, *Growing Up With "Shoeless Joe," The Greatest Natural Player in Baseball History*: JTI Publishing, 1998.

Chapter 4—Yankee Clipper

1   *Joe DiMaggio, The Yankee Clipper*, The San Francisco Museum, (online). http://www.sfmuseum.net/hist10/dimaggio1.html

2   Engelberg, Morris and Schneider, Marv, *DiMaggio, Setting the Record Straight*. MBI Publishing Company, 2003.

3   Ibid.

4   Cramer, Richard Ben, *Joe DiMaggio, The Hero's Life*. Simon & Schuster, 2000.

Chapter 5—Mike and Reggie

1   Echevarría, Roberto González, *The Pride of Havana, A History of Cuban Baseball*: Oxford University Press, 1999.

2   Wolf, Gregory, Society for American Baseball Research, (Online). https://sabr.org/bioproj/person/pat-crawford/

Chapter 6—War Years

1   Berkow, Ira, *The Corporal Was a Pitcher, The Courage of Lou Brissie*, Triumph Books. 2009.
2   Ibid.
3   Ibid.
4   Ibid.
5   Ibid.
6   Ibid.
7   *The United States Navy Memorial Interview Archive*; Personal interview with Lou Brissie, (Online). https://www.youtube.com/watch?v=AbWdEOrlWtY

Chapter 7—Jimmy

1   Trexler, Phil and Strasen, Marty, *Ballparks Yesterday & Today*, Publications International Limited. 2011.
2   Singer, Bill, *All-American Girls Professional Baseball League*, (Online). https://www.aagpbl.org/profiles/elizabeth-mahon-lib/57
3   Jaffe, Jay, *Rocky Bridges (1927-2005)*, (Online). http://www.futilityinfielder.com/wordpress/2015/02/rocky-bridges-1927-2015.shtml. 2015.
4   Ibid
5   Ringolsby, Tracy, *From Humor to Knowledge, Bridges a Vintage Baseball Guy.* (Online). https://www.mlb.com/news/tracy-ringolsby-rocky-bridges-vintage-baseball-guy/c-107939788. January 30, 2015.

Chapter 8—Coach

1   Markusen, Bruce, *The Blackballing of Dick Dietz*, The Hardball Times, October 25, 2003. https://tht.fangraphs.com/the-blackballing-of-dick-dietz/

Chapter 9—Ted and Mickey

1   How They Play, Ten Things You Didn't Know About Ted Williams, April 7, 2020 (Online). https://howtheyplay.com/team-sports/ten-things-you-didnt-know-about-ted-williams

2   Ted Williams: *A Perfectionist Ballplayer With Many Demons*, WBUR Boston Public Radio, December 3, 2013. (Online) https://www.wbur.org/npr/248246844/ted-williams-a-perfectionist- ballplayer-with-many-demons.

3   Nowlin, Bill, *Ted Williams*, Society for American Baseball Research, (Online). https://sabr.org/bioproj/person/ted-williams/.

4   Posnanski, Joe, *The Boudreau Shift*, JoeBlogs, (Online). https://joeposnanski.substack.com/p/the-boudreau-shift

5   Williams, Ted and Underwood, John, *My Turn at Bat, The Story of My Life*. Simon and Schuster, 1969.

6   Leavy, Jane, *The Last Boy, Mickey Mantle*, Harper Collins Publishers. 2010.

7   The Mick—The Greatest Power and Switch Hitter in Baseball History, MickeyMantle.com.

8   Mickey Mantle, National Baseball Hall of Fame. (Online). https://baseballhall.org/hall-of-famers/mantle-mickey

Chapter 10—Big Chief

1   Fox Sports MLB Nicknames. (Online). https://www.foxsports.com/mlb/gallery/mlb-baseball-best-nicknames-creative-monikers-041912

Chapter 12—Super Scout

1   Lowenfish, Lee, *Paul Snyder*, Society for American Baseball Research, (Online). https://sabr.org/bioproj/person/paul-snyder/.

2   Paul Snyder as a Baseball Scout, July 26, 2001. YouTube Snyder interview. (Online). https://www.youtube.com/watch?v=Lma5bPA3T2s

3   Loomis, Tom (August 17, 1984). "Rose at Center Stage With Candor, Charm". Toledo Blade.

4   Lowenfish, Lee, *Paul Snyder*, Society for American Baseball Research, (Online). https://sabr.org/bioproj/person/paul-snyder/.

Chapter 13—Kooz and Ryan

1   Shamsky, Art and Sherman, Ed, *After the Miracle, The Lasting Brotherhood of the '69 Mets*. Simon and Schuster, 2019.

2   Goldfarb, Irv, *Jerry Koosman*, Society for American Baseball Research. (Online). https://sabr.org/bioproj/person/jerry-koosman/

3   Bonner, Francis, *Tom Hartness*. Furman University, 1985.

4   Caravelis, Dean, *Outrageously Remarkable*, The Blog of Dean Caravelis, September 19, 2018. (Online) https://deancaravelis.com/pat-williams/

5   Ryan, Nolan and Frommer, Harvey, *Throwing Heat, The Autobiography of Nolan Ryan*. Doubleday, 1998.

6   Ibid.

7   Ibid.

8   Ibid.

9   Ibid.

10   Ibid.

11   Ibid.

Chapter 14—Kat

1   Nakagawa, Kerry Yo, *Japanese American Baseball in California, A History*. History Press, 2014.

2   *Time of Fear*, Directed by Sue Williams, PBS Home Video. 2005.

3   Pearson, Bradford, *The Eagles of Heart Mountain, The True Story of Football, Incarceration and Resistance in World War II America*. Atria Books. 2021.

4   *Time of Fear*, Directed by Sue Williams, PBS Home Video. 2005.

5   Pearson, Bradford, *The Eagles of Heart Mountain, A True Story of Football, Incarceration and Resistance in World War II America*, Atria Books. 2021.

6   Chang, Rachel, *George Takei and Pat Morita's Harrowing Childhood Experiences in Japanese American Internment Camps*. Biography.com, May 4, 2021. (Online) https://www.biography.com/news/george-takei-pat-morita- japanese-american-internment-camps.

7   *Going for Broke, The 442 Regimental Combat Team*, The World War II National History Museum, New Orleans, La. September 24, 2020. (Online) https://www.nationalww2museum.org/war/articles/442nd-regimental-combat-team

8   Nakagawa, Kerry Yo, *Japanese American Baseball in California, A History*. History Press, 2014.

9   *Mike Honda: What My Time in a Japanese Internment Camp Taught Me About Hate*, Time Magazine. December 16, 2015. (Online) https://time.com/4152095/rep-mike-honda-japanese-internment-camp/

10   Nakagawa, Kerry Yo, *Japanese American Baseball in California, A History*. History Press, 2014.

About the Author

Mike Chibbaro is a native of Greenville, South Carolina, and a graduate of the University of South Carolina. He spent 31 years with a national accounting and consulting firm and for the past 10 years has worked as a leadership consultant and executive coach. Mike is a passionate storyteller with a strong interest in preserving stories that relate to faith, sports and history. He lives in Greenville with his wife Cindy, and they have three sons and five grandchildren.

Mike can be contacted at mike@thirtysevenpublishing.com.

OTHER BOOKS BY
MIKE CHIBBARO

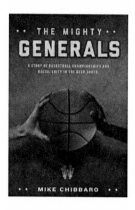

THE MIGHTY GENERALS

On the morning of February 17, 1970, 300 black students were added to the enrollment of Wade Hampton High School in Greenville, South Carolina. Five of these students joined the all-white boys basketball team and were instrumental in leading the team to the state championship. *The Mighty Generals* tells the inspirational story of a group of student athletes who overcame differences, bonded together as a unified team and became champions.

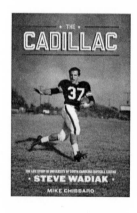

THE CADILLAC

Steve Wadiak emerged from the sandlots of the south side of Chicago to become a college football legend at the University of South Carolina. He dreamed of playing football in the National Football League and moved ever so close to fulfilling his dream before his life intersected with tragedy. *The Cadillac* is a must read for football fans of all ages and a historical treasure for University of South Carolina faithful.

Purchase any of Mike Chibbaro's books at:
www.ThirtySevenPublishing.com